# RENOVATIONS
## AN INSPIRATIONAL DESIGN PRIMER

# RENOVATIONS

## AN INSPIRATIONAL DESIGN PRIMER

### RICHARD WILCOCK

RIBA Publishing

© Richard Wilcock, 2016

Published by RIBA Publishing, 66 Portland Place, London W1B 1AD

ISBN 978 1 85946 502 8

Stock code 80473

The right of Richard Wilcock to be identified as the Author of this Work has been asserted in accordance with the Copyright, Designs and Patents Act 1988.

British Library Cataloguing in Publications Data
A catalogue record for this book is available from the British Library.

Commissioning Editors: James Thompson and Sharla Plant
Designed and typeset by Phil Handley
Printed and bound by W&G Baird Ltd, Great Britain
Cover image: Whistler Street, London by Coffey Architects (pages 119–24) © Timothy Soar
Frontispiece: Hampstead Beach House by Hayhurst and Co (pages 139–41) © Kilian O'Sullivan / www.kilianosullivan.com

RIBA Publishing is part of RIBA Enterprises Ltd, www.ribaenterprises.com

# Foreword

As a child in Britain in the 1950s, I accompanied my parents on trips to some of the first country houses to be open to the public after the Second World War. This began my interest in the design and layout of houses, from castles and mansions to suburban villas and humble cottages, from advanced modern houses to Iron Age settlements. I taught myself the history of architecture as part of an A level in Art, poring over the copious drawings and photographs in Banister Fletcher's *A History of Architecture* and Doreen Yarwood's *The Architecture of England* with its evocative line drawings.

There were few plans, however, in these books and the plans of houses fascinated me. I spent many hours drawing the plans of imaginary houses and visualising the activities and furnishings of each individual room. Town houses were particularly ingeniously planned; in a very tight space, a wide range of room types could be accommodated, each with their own traditions, rituals and formalities. Grander town houses had a rigid hierarchy with spaces for high-status family members, lesser members of the family such as aunts and children, rooms to impress for entertaining and for parties, and suites of rooms set aside for visitors. Behind the baize doors were service rooms and living space for servants, squeezed in around the family rooms. Discreet service access was provided via back stairs and hidden doors.

Amazingly, these intricately planned houses have survived centuries of social change. Having been knocked about, sometimes divided and threatened with demolition or suffering complete destruction by fire or bombing or slum clearance, the most robust urban houses have survived to be adapted for a new generation. I have selected the best examples of urban houses which have been refurbished and extended to suit a contemporary lifestyle.

Richard Wilcock

# SIBERIAN LARCH

## THE MOST NATURALLY DURABLE TIMBER ON THE PLANET

At Mumford & Wood we use engineered Siberian larch in our core window and door specification. Because of the location, growth is very slow producing timber with exceptionally tight growth rings. It is their closeness that results in an especially dense material which is naturally durable and able to withstand testing climatic conditions.

The Siberian larch used by Mumford & Wood has a density of more than 600 kg/m$^3$ and needs no further treatment to resist fungal or insect decay. The European redwood used by our competitors has a lower density of 510 kg/m$^3$ which is classified as nondurable and must be treated with a preservative to give it longevity.

# ACKNOWLEDGMENTS

My architectural journey began in the Yorkshire Dales where I grew up amongst the craggy fells, tumbling waterfalls and verdant valleys. In the 1950s and 1960s there were some attempts to introduce modern architecture to this landscape of ancient stone barns, farmhouses and medieval churches. My very first job as an architectural assistant was during a summer break from studies at the Liverpool University School of Architecture. Mary Wales occupied an office right next door to the impressive gateway to Skipton Castle. I saw how she produced sensitively designed modern buildings which respected and drew on the rich local vernacular architecture.

Liverpool is one of the best places in the UK to appreciate the power, innovation and delight of 18th- and 19th-century urban architecture so, with an early copy of Pevsner in hand, I embarked on an architectural journey, exploring Art Nouveau pub interiors and the Hollywood drama of the interior of Scott's Liverpool Cathedral, still then under construction, in stark contrast to the spiky, leaking, ephemeral Roman Catholic Cathedral perched on Lutyens's massive crypt, an abandoned dream of Catholicism in England. There were streets of once grand, now decaying Georgian townhouses, the majestic Albert Dock buildings, the Victorian mansions around Sefton Park, and the richness, grandeur and technological inventiveness of the buildings in the Liverpool Maritime Mercantile City, now a UNESCO designated World Heritage Site.

Although there were some attempts at a contextual modern architecture in Lancashire at the time, in the post-war period it was felt that a new age was dawning, one of huge concrete industrialised architecture and this philosophy ruled at Liverpool School of Architecture. In a dusty room, amongst his manuscripts, sat Dr 'Bunny' Morgan, a survivor of the purge against the teaching of the history of architecture in schools of architecture. In America, the Post-Modern Movement was gathering pace and a new generation of architects was rediscovering ancient building skills, methods, proportions, delight, the symbolism and spirituality of architecture. We rediscovered Dr Morgan and taught ourselves how to design in context.

After leaving Liverpool for London, my first architectural job was at Green, Lloyd and Adams. The offices were in Pickering Place, a perfectly preserved Georgian courtyard behind Berry Bros wine merchants in St James's Street. The senior partner was Sam Lloyd. His father had married the daughter of the founder of the firm, Curtis Green, one of the best exponents of the design of major commercial buildings along the streets of the City of London and the West End as well as a noted draughtsman. Here I learned how historic buildings were constructed, the best methods of repair and restoration and how to adapt them for new uses and to introduce contemporary elements.

However, my real aim had always been to write about architecture, so, one day, I crossed St James's Park for another firm housed in a splendid Georgian interior: the Architectural Press, still then under the control of the Hastings family. As a member of the team on the *Architects' Journal*, I could not have had better guidance and support; Simon Esterson, one of the leading graphic designers in the UK, was the art editor, and Helen Buttery was the chief subeditor. I took these skills to the *RIBA Journal* which I edited for several years at a time when the City was booming. Modern buildings were transforming the face of London and buildings such as Covent Garden Market were in peril. But the conservation movement, led by John Betjeman, was growing in strength.

All the skills I have learned in the art of architecture, in contextual design, in analysing architecture in print, in graphic design have been brought to bear on the creation of this book. I would like to thank all the staff at RIBA Publishing who have been involved in the book's production: Steven Cross, Philip Handley, James Hutchinson, Sharla Plant and James Thompson. Credit is also due to the clients who commissioned the case study projects, to their architects and to the dedicated engineers, other building professionals, building contractors, subcontractors and craftsmen. I would also like to draw attention to the quality of the hundreds of images in this publication and thank all the photographers involved for allowing their work to be reproduced. Also to be thanked are Mumford & Wood who have generously sponsored the book, supporting the production costs.

Last but not least, I would like to thank my wife, Paulene, for coping with the peaks and troughs of the inception and production of this book. Our historic 1930s' home on the Yorkshire coast is our refuge from the vicissitudes of life. Apologies for maybe one too many clichés, but home really is where the heart is: a concept at the very centre of the contents below.

Richard Wilcock, June 2016

# Contents

*continued*

# Introduction

## Long life, loose fit

The Energy Savings Trust estimates that 80% of the houses that will be occupied in the UK in 2050 have already been built, with one in five of these houses built before 1919. The UK's historic housing stock has proved to be durable, adaptable and sustainable; it is a valuable resource which needs to be maintained and enhanced. As living standards have risen and lifestyles have evolved, the need to improve and adapt existing dwellings has become more pressing. The upgrading of existing buildings has become even more urgent with the need to conserve the planet's energy sources and material deposits. Saving energy and cutting carbon emissions are not just essential from an environmental standpoint but are an economic necessity, as energy costs spiral ever upwards.

This book sets out to examine the challenges of adapting traditional house types; how to retain historic features whilst introducing modern interventions – extensions and internal remodelling of the highest design quality – and the practicalities of incorporating high levels of insulation and new energy-saving technologies in a traditionally constructed home. Advances in technology over the past few decades, including new glazing techniques, improvements in flat roof construction and structural innovations in steel and timber, have influenced the nature of the small house extension and increased the palette of forms and materials available to the architect. Computer-aided design has also revolutionised building design and construction methods, liberating the architect's imagination.

## Selection criteria

The 32 projects featured here are my own personal selection following more than two decades of research into the adaptation and extension of this building type. The majority of the featured houses have been completed in the past decade, a period which has seen a marked improvement in design quality in this particular sector. As a northerner, I hoped that there would be a good regional spread, but the economic dominance of the capital with the resultant rise in property prices has meant that many of the best schemes are in London. With a number of notable exceptions, the most innovative and ambitious architects will gravitate to the area of best opportunity, the part of the country where their talents can be better fulfilled.

The two projects in the Midlands and the north of England – Kit Knowles' house in Manchester (pages 29-35) and John Christophers' house in Birmingham (pages 43-7) – are developments by architect owner/occupiers who are using their own homes to trial new low-energy and sustainable techniques, systems and materials; they have no short-term need to realise the financial investment in the property. House prices in central London continue to rise and with the typical family home in

▲ **Blytheman House, Inverleith Gardens, Edinburgh, 1991 by Richard Murphy Architects.** Windows slide away so that the enclosed room becomes an open veranda with far-reaching views over the city. The barrier between exterior and interior dissolves and the occupant can sit, literally, suspended in space.
*Photo: Richard Murphy Architects*

▲ **Francis House, Gilmour Road, Edinburgh, 1994 by Richard Murphy Architects.** Glazed doors and windows slide away to expose the corner with its cantilevered exterior window seat, opening up views from the kitchen towards Arthur's Seat. *Photo: Allan Forbes.*

the most desirable areas costing well into seven figures, significant further investment in a property can be justified. This sometimes extraordinary increase in house values has had a huge effect on the advances in the quality of house refurbishment projects in the South East.

Upgrading the building fabric and installing technology to improve energy efficiency whilst retaining the historic character of a building is another key factor examined in this book. It is possible to turn a Georgian or Victorian terraced house into an energy-efficient home but there are many challenges, particularly when it comes to maintaining the character of the street façade in a conservation area. If few historic features remain on the interior, it is possible to achieve Passivhaus standards by means of completely gutting a house and, in effect, constructing a new 'eco' home within the fabric of the retained shell. This can be an extremely expensive process and much historic fabric, even though it may not be considered worthy of saving under current planning legislation, is lost. This is unfortunate both from a conservation viewpoint and in terms of sustainability; building materials go to landfill and new materials have to be transported to site, increasing the construction carbon footprint.

Pioneering architects such as Justin Bere have devoted their working life to promoting sustainable design and clients will approach dedicated firms such as this one specifically for a low-energy solution. In most other domestic refurbishment projects there is a variable requirement for the incorporation of energy-efficient features. The client is invariably the driving force, as they will have a set budget and a comprehensive house refurbishment following Passivhaus principles can be significantly more expensive than simply remodelling a home and building an extension. Extensions in themselves can transform an existing building's performance. They are built to present-day Building Regulations with the enhanced statutory levels of insulation. They can be designed to harvest solar gain and passively heat the total house volume. Retaining and reusing as much of the existing building fabric is, in itself, a sustainable approach to domestic refurbishment.

## House types

The featured projects have been limited to those in urban or suburban areas. There are some excellent examples of projects in rural areas where a traditional building has been transformed into a modern, energy-efficient home – if the planning system allows this to happen. But this is a subject for another publication. Where there is more space and fewer constraints from nearby buildings, the extension and remodelling of an existing structure can be more extensive. There is also more opportunity for the incorporation of energy-saving features such as wind turbines, solar panels and ground-source heat pumps.

The houses included here are the most common traditional building types: terraced or semi-detached houses from the Georgian or Victorian eras and from the early 20th century. Modern additions to historic buildings are a particular personal interest. Buildings can be revitalised – their life greatly extended – by a 21st-century intervention, and the juxtaposition of old and new creates an exciting tension which is, in itself, a modernist condition.

In the search for a structure for the book, to make the content more accessible, the featured projects could have been grouped according to age, but a Georgian terraced house is very much like one built in the Victorian era; the advance of technology was much slower several centuries ago. Instead the revitalised houses have been separated into eight sections which reflect different lifestyle choices and physical constraints, more closely reflecting the client's brief and the restrictions of adding innovative structures to a mature built environment:

- *Low-energy retrofits includes* four projects which are the best examples of sustainable retrofits which also meet the criteria of high design standards and sensitive remodelling of a period building;

- *Space for family living* features four schemes, either end of terrace or semi-detached properties with larger gardens, where there is plenty of space for the addition of a new kitchen/dining/living space and plenty of room for the designer's imagination to run free;

- *Reinventing the closet wing* covers four additions to houses either listed or in conservation areas where a traditional solution of incorporating service rooms in a single or multi-storey rear wing is given a non-traditional makeover;

- *Sustainable timber framing* examines four interventions where this form of construction is more practical and economic as well as more sustainable;

- *Illuminating the basement* looks at four ways of extending the lower ground floor of terraced houses, extending the space, improving the connection between the house and the garden, and admitting light into previously dark interiors;

- *Two-storey additions* includes four extensions where planning issues have been overcome successfully and existing interior space improved on a number of levels;

- *Room on the side* features five excellent examples of a typical project brief: how to infill the narrow courtyard formed between the party wall, the back of the main house and the wall of the existing rear wing of a terraced house to create an open-plan kitchen/dining/living space opening on to the garden;

▲ **Palmer House, Abbotsford Park, Edinburgh, 1996 by Richard Murphy Architects.** In this extension, the steelwork is more massive and expressive; the remaining 'ruinous' stonework has become a minor element. Sliding glazed doors open up the corner of the structure so that the kitchen/dining space flows out into the garden.
*Photo: Allan Forbes*

• *Three Scottish projects* illustrates three of the best domestic refurbishment projects in Scotland which have a particular regional character, enhancing the penetration of natural light, opening up views and responding to the demands of the country's climate and culture.

## Energy performance

Although in recent decades there have been a succession of government campaigns, backed up by public funding, to improve the energy performance of existing houses, particularly the installation of loft and cavity wall insulation and the installation of more energy-efficient central heating boilers, the main focus of energy conservation in domestic properties has been on new-build housing. However, it is almost 30 years since the international EnergyWorld exhibition, held in Milton Keynes in 1986, which featured 51 demonstration homes exploring a wide range of developments in the design and construction of low-energy houses and a host of methods for evaluating domestic energy efficiency. Although the exhibition received a great deal of publicity and had some impact on the raising of building regulation standards, the UK government has been slower than many European countries in legislating for higher insulation standards and the reduction in carbon emissions from the construction and heating of dwellings.

It is only in this century that research into the methods for improving the energy performance of existing houses has been undertaken in the UK. In 2006, the Building Research Establishment (BRE) opened the Innovation Park in Watford, which aims to promote a sustainable and low-carbon built environment and to demonstrate and evaluate modern methods of construction. Over the past decade a number of low-energy houses have been built in the park, including the world's first certified zero-carbon home, the Kingspan Lighthouse, completed in 2007, and the Barratt Green House designed by architects Gaunt Francis, completed in 2008, the first house to be built by a national housebuilder which achieves Level 6 of the Code for Sustainable Homes.

Retro-fitted projects have not been overlooked in the Innovation Park. Supported by The Prince's Foundation, the Victorian stable block adjacent to the BRE's headquarters has been converted into three terraced houses in order to demonstrate how older buildings with solid walls, no insulation, single-glazed windows and inadequate heating can be refurbished to provide energy-efficient accommodation. Completed in 2011, the Victorian Terrace is just one of around 300 refurbishment projects, covering a wide range of house types all over the UK, which BRE is monitoring.

Also in 2006, the results of the BRE Trust's research into the effectiveness of renovation schemes for Victorian and Edwardian houses were published in a book, *Sustainable Refurbishment of Victorian*

*Housing* by Tim Yates. The publication outlines a method of assessing the refurbishment of traditional houses dating from 1840 to 1919, similar to that used in BREEAM (the Building Research Establishment Environmental Assessment Method) EcoHomes. Issues covered include how to achieve the latest energy and acoustic standards in an existing building and the durability, reliability and future maintenance of the retained fabric. The economic, environmental and social benefits of conserving and improving the traditional housing stock are also examined. Three projects are covered in more detail: the Nelson Housing Market regeneration scheme; the Flagship project, Beaufort Gardens, London; and the Nottingham Ecohome.

In 2012 BREEAM replaced the EcoHomes method of assessment with the Domestic Refurbishment scheme in recognition of the importance of the refurbishment sector in the government's aim to meet carbon emission reduction targets. EcoHomes was originally introduced in 2000 to assess and improve the environmental performance of housing and was applied primarily to new-build housing although it was also used to certify refurbishment projects. In 2007, BREEAM's Code for Sustainable Homes replaced EcoHomes for new-build properties. The Domestic Refurbishment scheme aims to improve the sustainability and environmental performance of existing dwellings, in the process helping building owners and occupiers to save operating costs and reduce the environmental impact of refurbishment projects. Construction projects are inspected by an assessor and a rating is awarded from 'pass' to 'outstanding'.

## Judging design excellence

There is no set standard, however, for building design excellence. Award schemes organised by the RIBA and the Civic Trust recognise a wide range of projects, from small domestic refurbishment schemes to large public and commercial developments. In recent years, the quality of domestic renovation work has increased significantly with several of the leading architects in the UK undertaking this type of work, but the limitations of the planning system make innovation in this sector difficult. Some planning officers and planning committee members prefer a 'pastiche' approach when it comes to adding new structures to a historic building. But, as many of the designers featured in this book emphasise, aping the style of a previous age only dilutes the quality of the original architecture; new additions need to reflect 21st-century lifestyles and utilise the best materials and technology of today.

In the decade of research for this volume, it has been rewarding to discover dozens of innovative architects producing high-quality domestic renovations and extensions. The highest level of design standards can only be achieved with the positive contributions of architect/designer, client,

▲ **Lambert House, Wooler, Northumberland, 2001, by Richard Murphy Architects.** In a rural location with far-reaching views, an old smithy has been converted to create an elegant modern home. The new extension is very much to the fore with the older structure merging into the background.
*Photo: Peter Guthrie*

**▲ Morrison/Gait House, Dirleton, East Lothian, 1998, by Richard Murphy Architects.** Timber-framed windows along the back of the curving kitchen 'console' can be winched upwards into a horizontal postion below the eaves so that, in summer, the large, free-flowing kitchen can be opened right out into the garden. *Photo: Simon Morrison*

contractor and specialist subcontractors working closely together towards a unified goal. In this Introduction I would like to highlight the work of one pioneer in the domestic extension sector, Richard Murphy, and also the work of Alison Brooks, one of the most innovative architects currently practising in the UK.

Richard Murphy set a new standard for the design of domestic extensions at a time when this building type was overlooked. He responded to the constraints of introducing modern interventions into the historic architectural fabric of Edinburgh and worked sensitively with the typology of the Scottish urban home to produce a series of award-winning projects. Some of these earlier projects are described below. They set a benchmark for younger architects to follow. Alison Brooks is a more recent example of an architect who uses domestic projects as a laboratory for developing radical design concepts, in partnership with enlightened clients and skilled contractors. Some of her earlier projects are discussed below and two more recent projects are included in the case studies. Both architects acknowledge the importance of these small projects in the development of their own design skills. This expertise feeds through into larger public and commercial projects. They seek to bring the benefits of good design enjoyed by the more privileged to a wider public.

## Edinburgh pioneer

In 2001, Richard Murphy Architects celebrated a decade of practice in an exhibition at the Fruitmarket Gallery in Edinburgh. Four key projects were selected from his recent domestic work and, in explaining his approach, Richard highlighted the 'dissonance between a Victorian/Edwardian lifestyle and its equivalent today. Then, there was a maid in a scullery at the back, the rear garden was for drying clothes and the major rooms were placed at the front. Now family life revolves around the kitchen and in the pleasures of the back garden.' His carefully crafted and thoughtful reinterpretation of domestic spaces in Scotland introduces technologically advanced elements which enhance the existing historic structure.

The four projects all draw on a common architectural language. Murphy views the retained parts of previous rear extensions – 'build-outs' as they are known in Scotland – as 'ruins', on top of which he constructs his modern additions using an architectural language which he has developed over a number of years. The main elements are expressed steel framework, 'disappearing' corner windows – a modernist spatial concept pioneered by Gerrit Rietveld, and the use of top lighting from concealed sources to brighten the interior.

An extension to a terraced house in Inverleith Gardens, Edinburgh, 1991, comprises a garden room which sits on top of the kitchen. Steelwork attached to the exterior wall supports an oversailing lead roof with the thinnest of edge details. The timberwork of the balustrade cantilevers out and incorporates a window seat – built-in furniture is another theme of the work of Rietveld. Windows slide away on two walls so that the enclosed room becomes an open veranda with far-reaching views over Edinburgh. The barrier between exterior and interior dissolves and the occupant can sit, literally, suspended in space. Packing even more interest into the limited volume, the interface between the new first-floor addition and the existing house is intriguingly complex.

In a later first-floor extension to a semi-detached Victorian villa in Gilmour Road, 1994, Murphy continues the architectural themes of Inverleith Gardens. The rear 'build-out' has been partly demolished, leaving the massive stonework as a base for the new construction. 'Expressed external flying' steelwork supports the tapering lead roof and incorporates a cantilevered exterior window seat and staircase to the garden. Glazed doors and windows slide away to expose the corner and open up views from the kitchen towards Arthur's Seat.

In two single-storey extensions to semi-detached houses with larger gardens, Murphy had the confidence and the space to become even bolder. At Abbotsford Park, Edinburgh, 1996, the steelwork is bigger and more expressive; the remaining 'ruinous' stonework has become a minor element and sliding glazed doors open up the corner of the structure so that the kitchen/dining space flows out into the garden. In an acknowledgment of the Scottish climate, there are internal insulated timber shutters and insulated ceiling panels can be moved into place to seal off the clerestory window and the rooflight to the kitchen.

At a 19th-century house in Dirleton, East Lothian, 1998, existing rear service buildings have been remodelled to create a large, free-flowing kitchen which can be opened right out into the garden. An Aga, storage units and appliances are all housed in the rear wall. On the garden side is a curving kitchen 'console' incorporating a continuous worktop. Above this, timber-framed windows on counterweights can be winched upwards into a horizontal position below the eaves, so that in summer it is like cooking in the open. At the far end of the 'build-out' is a nursery with window seat and sliding windows which open the space into the garden.

Crossing the border into England, RMA designed a large extension to a former smithy in northern Northumberland. Completed in 2001, the house sits in a rural location with far-reaching views. The original smithy has been converted into three bedrooms and bathrooms, retaining its layout of small cellular rooms, and a new open-plan extension facing south/south-west has been built to accommodate a living/dining/kitchen space. Richard Murphy's familiar vocabulary of elegant steel

▲ **Fold House, 2001, by Alison Brooks Architects.** The geometric extension is like a piece of structural origami; a single skin of brass is 'cut and folded' to form the roof, columns, walls, light reflectors and benches.
*Photo: Dennis Gilbert/VIEW*

framework, thin flat metal roof – in this case, aluminium – wall panels of Douglas fir cladding, sliding glass doors and rooflights, together with insulated shutters and ceiling panels which can be moved into place at night is even more refined. Here the new extension is very much to the fore with the older structure merging into the background.

Planning restrictions in the Borders are just as strict as in the historic heart of Edinburgh and this latter project is the successful outcome of a battle with planning officers. The brilliance and sophistication of RMA's designs do not always win through however; for example, proposals for an ambitious new round house in the Borders were recently turned down. This scenario will be familiar to many architects and clients who are trying to push forward the boundaries of design in an established urban context. It is particularly galling when second-rate 'pastiche' extensions to properties nearby, poorly constructed and perhaps overscaled, which can only detract from the quality of the existing architecture, have been given approval.

## Canadian crusader

Some architects may wonder how Alison Brooks manages to persuade planning officers and neighbours to accept her radical and technically challenging domestic extensions. Perhaps it is because she was born, educated and trained in a different country – a different culture – that she maintains such optimism and refuses to compromise. Her training in Canada at the University of Waterloo followed a similar pattern to the RIBA-validated route to professional qualification in the UK with years of study interspersed with periods of practical experience in an architect's office. Although by the time she completed her course Brooks had worked for a number of leading Canadian firms with international status including Jack Diamond, she decided that architectural practice in the country had limited appeal. 'I needed to get away and to find my own way of working in a new place,' she explains, 'a place free of expectations and convention.'

Portfolio in hand, she walked the streets of London and eventually was offered a job with one of the UK's leading talents and free spirits of the 1980s, Ron Arad. Arad had established a high profile amongst the design community with his innovative sculptural furniture, including the Well Tempered chair of 1986. Although he was commissioned for larger interior design projects in the 1980s, he had no experience of large architectural commissions. In 1988, Ron Arad won the commission to design the public spaces of the Tel Aviv Opera House – the city in which he was born. At a time when the project had progressed and Arad needed to establish an architectural studio, Alison Brooks appeared on the doorstep and was immediately offered a job.

**▲ VXO House, 2000, by Alison Brooks Architects.**
One of the practice's earliest domestic projects, the extension is more restrained than later projects. The architects' obsession with building geometry and expressive use of materials is already apparent.
*Photo: Dennis Gilbert/VIEW*

In the Opera House and in projects such as the Belgo restaurant chain, Brooks worked closely with Ron Arad, turning his sculptural fantasies into three-dimensional reality. But, once more, she began to feel creatively constrained. In 1996, she decided to strike out independently, setting up her own practice in north London and working on a succession of domestic extension projects which have become increasingly sculptural.

Like many young architects starting a career in the capital, she found big commissions difficult to come by, relying on a string of smaller domestic refurbishment and extension projects. Into these early projects Alison was to put some of her most advanced ideas and creativity; they were to be an outlet for years of design frustration caused by restricting briefs and inflexible clients. They were to encapsulate and define her design talent and ability and set a new standard for this often humble and overlooked building type.

One of her earliest projects, completed in 2000, the VXO House transformed a dull 1960s home into a dynamic 21st century dwelling with the addition of a series of geometric structures. The Fold, Wrap and Herringbone houses followed, their titles emphasising the three-dimensional forms, complex geometries and unconventional spaces which are adapted to changing lifestyles, the free form of modern living space and the closer interconnection of internal and external spaces. In the Fold House, Wandsworth, south London, 2001, the geometry is rectilinear. Like a piece of structural origami, a single thin skin of brass is 'cut and folded' to form the roof, columns, walls, light reflectors and benches. In later projects, two of which are featured below (Wrap House, pages 51-5 and Lens House, pages 57-63), the forms become more sculptural, the interventions ever more ambitious.

Alison Brooks Architects' approach may be too radical for some clients and a wide range of approaches are examined below, from technically advanced low-energy, sustainable refurbishments to more passive renovations and remodellings. Achieving excellence through close teamwork is, however, a theme common to every single successful construction project and the clients, contractors and specialist consultants, tradesmen, building product suppliers and craftsmen deserve equal mention to the lead designers responsible for the work which follows.

---

**KEY SELECTION CRITERIA**

- Design excellence.
- The level of enhancement that the design brings by adapting traditional house types to modern ways of living.
- The effectiveness of spatial reorganisation of the interior to suit contemporary lifestyles.
- Success in fulfilling the clients' brief.
- Innovation in construction techniques including new methods of upgrading existing external fabric whilst retaining historic character and features.
- The ability of the interventions to achieve energy savings and ecological improvements.
- The effective incorporation of enhanced energy saving and environmental technologies.
- Recycling and sustainability of new building materials.

# SECTION 1

# Low-energy retrofits

## Introduction

Achieving the Passivhaus EnerPHit standard – the highest international standard for a low-energy domestic refurbishment project – is not always technically possible in the renovation of a listed house or in a period house in a conservation area; the structural work necessary to incorporate high levels of insulation, to integrate a MVHR (mechanical ventilation heat recovery) system within the existing structure, and to achieve an airtight building with no cold bridges to external walls generally requires the stripping down and substantial reconstruction of the building. In the process, many architectural features and details are lost, particularly if external insulation is considered to be necessary. The four projects included in this section have all been selected for the excellence of their approach in creating a low-energy house within the fabric of a traditional dwelling whilst respecting and enhancing its historic architectural character.

Not surprisingly, two of the four projects are for architect/designer, owner/occupiers – John Christophers and Kit Knowles – who have made their homes – in Birmingham and Manchester, respectively – the test bed for new ideas, design concepts and technologies, as well as lifestyle statements underlining their commitment to sustainable building. The two remaining low-energy schemes are in London: the refurbishment of a Victorian villa in Brent carried out by Bere Architects headed by Justin Bere, one of the UK's leading Passivhaus practitioners and a founder of the UK's Passivhaus Trust, and a terraced house in Hackney refurbished by Passivhaus designers Prewett Bizley Architects. One of the clients for the latter project is a carbon analyst, building physicist and climate change adviser. Achieving a low-energy, eco home within a solid-walled Victorian urban dwelling is a big challenge. A successful outcome is only possible with teamwork involving the complete unity of client, architect/designer, contractor and other consultants, craftsmen and suppliers.

*Turning a solid-walled Georgian or Victorian urban dwelling into a low-energy home utilizing sustainable building methods and materials is a big challenge. But as the examples featured here demonstrate this can be achieved without compromising the architectural character of the historic fabric.*

◄ Figure 1.1

**Tindal Street, Balsall Heath, Birmingham**
by John Christophers
*Photo: Martine Hamilton Knight*

Figure 1.2 ▶

**Internal insulation, improved traditional window design and other energy-saving methods have transformed this Victorian house into a low-energy home whilst, on the street façade, the original character has been restored.**
*Photo: Jefferson Smith*

# Dyne Road,
# London Borough of Brent
by Bere Architects

- Victorian semi-detached house
- Low-energy retrofit by one of the UK's leading Passivhaus designers

Established in Germany in the 1990s, Passivhaus has become the international comfort and energy performance standard for both housing and non-domestic buildings (for further information on Passivhaus, see page 208). The key criteria are excellent thermal performance and exceptionally draught-free construction with heat recovery ventilation. The aim is an ultra low-energy home that requires a minimal amount of energy for space heating or cooling and also has very low electrical consumption requirements. The standard is more easily achieved in a new-build than in a refurbishment project.

Architect Justin Bere is one of the leading proponents of Passivhaus design in the UK. Formed in 1994, Bere Architects was the first practice in the UK to have a specialised Passivhaus design team and was responsible for the first new-build certified Passivhaus to be built in London, completed in 2010. In 2010, the practice won a BRE competition for the design of two Passivhaus, low-cost social housing prototypes which form part of BRE's Welsh Future Homes project at Ebbw Vale, Wales. Bere Architects went on to win BRE's Passivhaus competition in 2012 for two Passivhaus homes at the BRE Watford Innovation Park but these were not constructed due to lack of funding.

### Non-domestic retrofit

Passivhaus principles can also be applied to non-domestic projects. Completed in 2011, the Mayville Community Centre became the first certified Passivhaus non-domestic retrofit in the UK. Built in the 1890s, the building was originally a generating station for London's tram network. Bere Architects has transformed the industrial structure to create a number of community offices and spaces. The firm's own office was housed there from 2012 to 2015. Energy savings of more than 90% have been achieved by more efficient energy use through improved levels of insulation, draught-free construction and triple-glazed windows, heat recovery

◀ Figure 1.3

**The rear and side of the house have been externally insulated and rendered to give the highest possible levels of energy performance. The clients did not require a rear extension, though this remains a future possibility.**
*Photo: Jefferson Smith*

ventilation and low-energy lighting and appliances. All junction details are designed to prevent or minimise thermal bridging. Energy consumption is so low that photovoltaic panels generate more than enough electricity for the building's annual heating and regulated energy usage (excluding unregulated socket loads), solar panels provide hot water and a ground-source heat pump supplies warm water to radiators, although the latter has not been used for the last two years. Additional features include rainwater harvesting, two native wild flower meadow roofs and ecologically sensitive gardens for community food growing projects.

### Passivhaus principles

However, can the Passivhaus principles be applied to the refurbishment of the existing housing stock with all the planning restrictions of a designated conservation area? Bere Architects has completed a number of domestic renovation projects utilising Passivhaus principles. One of the most recent is a semi-detached Victorian house in Dyne Road in the London Borough of Brent. The house had been divided into three bedsits and the brief was to turn it back into a family home and, at the same time, to achieve significant energy savings following Passivhaus principles.

The house was not extended in this phase of work. There were minimal structural alterations of the ground and upper floors; a master bedroom suite was created with a bedroom, dressing room and en-suite bathroom on the first floor, and a family bathroom was created on the second floor. On the lower ground floor, a number of small, dark rooms were knocked into a large open-plan, living/dining area and kitchen, with a new WC and utility room. The lower ground floor floats on a deep bed of insulation and, to minimise thermal bridging, all of the new steel columns at this level were

insulated with Schöck thermal insulators. Walls were insulated internally to the front, externally to the rear and externally to the side a year later.

There are four key elements to Passivhaus design: superior levels of insulation, triple-glazed windows, natural ventilation in summer and ventilation via a heat recovery unit in winter, and thoroughly draught-free construction. Additionally, Bere Architects provided for a clean filtered water supply and a vacuum-tube solar panel to supply hot water. The Dyne Road house is in a conservation area so the street façade, with its decorative brickwork, three-storey high bay window, projecting partly glazed porch and Flemish gable, had to be preserved as a planning requirement, and was carefully restored using traditional lime mortar, wire brushed to expose a gritty texture that complements the existing facing bricks. While it was not permitted to insulate the front of the house externally, it was proposed that a high level of external insulation would be applied to the side wall and to the rear of the house. Planning permission for this was refused by the London Borough of Brent but this decision was overturned on appeal.

### Internal insulation

UdiIN RECO wood fibre insulation, 100 mm thick, was applied to the inside of the front façade (see Materials and technologies chapter, page 197). Although it is possible to increase this to 150-200 mm, Bere Architects believes that this may increase the risk of interstitial condensation within the building fabric. 'It is possible to increase the thickness with careful moisture analysis utilising a program such as WUFI,' says Sarah Lewis, a director at Bere Architects. To minimise the risks of interstitial condensation as far as possible, an invisible water-based, hydrophobic cream called Stormdry was applied to the external London stock brickwork in order to reduce rainwater absorption without affecting the vapour-breathability of the fabric.

To enhance the moisture-buffering qualities of the Sika-rendered basement, Calsitherm Climate Board was applied at this level. Ideally suited to applications in older buildings, Calsitherm Climate Board is manufactured from calcium silicate, a microporous mineral building material with good insulating properties. Its high capillary action ensures humidity regulation and the nature of the material means that mould cannot form on its surface (see Materials and technologies

Figure 1.4

**Bere Architects' subtle approach – low-energy lighting, an insulated and airtight front door, the glass balustrade to the stairs to the lower ground floor – retains the character of the original Victorian interior whilst upgrading the energy performance of the house.**
*Photo: Jefferson Smith*

chapter, page 193). Chris Brookman of Back to Earth, a consultancy specialising in 'natural building issues' from design and materials specification to construction skills, visited the site and provided advice on the internal insulation.

External insulation maintains the thermal mass of the building, as the fabric of the building remains warm and external insulation has no interstitial moisture risks. At Dyne Road, 100 mm of PermaRock phenolic external insulation, finished with PermaRock K-finish textured render, was applied to the side and rear of the house. As part of the overall energy-saving strategy for the house, including roof and floor insulation, this has reduced energy use by an estimated 88%, at the same time as providing exceptionally warm and comfortable winter conditions without a trace of dampness or condensation, even on the windows. The house was made

as draught-free as possible, particularly important in winter. Traditional sash windows on the front elevation have been fitted with security glass and incorporate high-performance weather seals. The insulated front door is very unusual because, while it looks exactly like the original, it is completely new and closes very tightly against its double-seals that wrap right around the door, including the threshold. It is fitted with advanced automatic multipoint locking which is operated from a single key, so there is no need to secure multiple locks.

A high standard of workmanship was paramount to achieve a pressure air test performance which is more than five times better than that required by the Building Regulations for a new building. New windows at the rear of the property, manufactured by Mumford & Wood, are triple-glazed. These can be opened in the summer to supply fresh air; in winter, an

◄  Figure 1.5

**The most significant improvement to the layout of the house is on the lower ground floor where an open-plan kitchen and dining space has been created.**
*Photo: Jefferson Smith*

Figure 1.6 ▶

**The minimalist white kitchen/ dining area opens out into the garden. A modernist space has been created in a previously dark basement.**
*Photo: Jefferson Smith*

efficient heat recovery unit keeps the air fresh without wasting heat.

Bere Architects stresses the fact that, in 2010, housing accounted for around 13% of all UK carbon emissions and the firm believes that reducing this is a national priority. The UK government had a pledge that all new homes in the UK would be zero carbon by 2016 – but recent government legislation has made it impossible for this to be achieved, and emissions are now set to rise steeply, even though it remains relatively easy to achieve the zero carbon target in new-build houses if the Passivhaus principles are followed. When it comes to the refurbishment of the existing housing stock, the practice takes a balanced and carefully considered approach to individual projects, with increased comfort often being a deciding factor. The Dyne Road owners comment on how warm and

comfortable the house is. Originally they decided to fit the external insulation on the side wall in a later phase but during their first winter they noticed how much warmer their daughter's room was compared to their son's room, which is on the corner between the insulated back wall and the uninsulated flank wall. The noticeable improvement due to the external insulation persuaded them to bring forward their plans to install the flank wall insulation.

## Sustainable development

The principles of sustainable development are at the core of the work of Bere Architects and strict ecological, environmental and sociological criteria are applied to all projects undertaken by the practice. Retaining and upgrading an existing structure is, in itself, a sustainable approach, but some compromises are required in the treatment of an historic structure. A stated aim of the practice is 'to create a bridge between the past and the future, bringing together the historic and the contemporary as far as possible'.

A craftsman-like approach is applied to all aspects of the building process; whilst traditional techniques are respected, this does not prevent the practice from using advanced, sustainable materials and techniques. The practice takes advantage of indigenous materials, techniques, traditions and industries when they can be sourced locally, as long as there is no compromise on cost, environmental concerns or the appearance of the finished product.

If the government's 2050 carbon reduction targets are to be met, Bere Architects estimates that around 13,000 'deep energy-saving retrofits' will have to be completed every week. 'The question that many social housing providers are currently asking is how to improve the energy efficiency of "difficult to treat" solid-walled homes,' says Sarah. The £17 million Retrofit for the Future (RtF) programme, launched in 2009, sought to answer this question. 'All the RtF projects adopted a "whole house" approach to retrofit,' says Sarah. 'In these projects, internal insulation is particularly difficult to install due to the cost and disruption.' The RtF projects that Bere Architects was involved in used external insulation entirely and were completed while the occupants remained in their homes.

*From top to bottom*
**Section**
**Second floor plan**
**First floor plan**
**Ground floor plan**
**Lower ground floor plan**

**Key**
1    **Kitchen**
2    **Dining area**
3    **Hall**
4    **Reception**
5    **Bedroom**
6    **Dressing room**
7    **Bathroom**
*Images: bere:architects*

## KEY FEATURES

- Upgrade of insulation to exceed current Building Regulation standards;
- Triple-glazed, fully openable windows with insulated frames (at Dyne Road, all new sash windows in existing openings were double-glazed due to planning restrictions and only new windows in new openings were triple-glazed);
- Creating a draught-free building envelope;
- Natural ventilation via opening triple-glazed windows in summer;
- Heat recovery ventilation to provide plentiful fresh air in winter;
- Solar thermal panels for heating hot water;
- Photovoltaic cells for electricity generation (not applicable to Dyne Road);
- Water filtration for pure water supply;
- Natural paints and materials for a healthy environment;
- Incorporation of biodiverse features such as wild flower meadow green roofs, native planting for gardens and so on.

**Site:** Dyne Road, London NW6
**Start on site:** June 2011
**Completion:** May 2012
**Client:** Confidential
**Contract value:** Confidential

*The practice takes advantage of indigenous materials, techniques, traditions and industries when they can be sourced locally.*

Figure 1.8 ▶

**The original façade of the Arts and Crafts semi-detached house has been thermally upgraded without altering its appearance – particularly difficult as it had to match its pair next door.**
*Photo: Colin Poole*

## Chorltonville, Manchester
by Kit Knowles

..................................................................

• 1909 Edwardian semi-detached house in conservation area
• Solid brickwork construction

..................................................................

In the early 1900s, Chorltonville was an experiment in social housing, one of several garden suburbs built in the UK before the First World War. The charitable trust set up to create and run the 40-acre estate aimed 'to provide beautiful, healthy, conveniently planned homes, with plenty of light and an abundance of fresh air, at reasonable rents'. With their gables, white-washed render, pebbledashing, decorative porches, bay windows, stained glass, pitched roofs and chimneys set at differing angles, this type of semi-detached house became an archetype for much larger suburban housing developments in the decades following the war and forms a large percentage of the existing housing stock in the UK.

Kit Knowles and his wife were attracted to the social ideals of the suburb and spent many months searching for a renovation project in the village which could be used by Kit as an experimental laboratory for his newly established Ecospheric consultancy, as well as a home for his young family. Although Kit comes from a family of architects, he trained as a chemical engineer and worked for large multinationals such as AstraZeneca and BP. He became skilled at scaling up laboratory experiments into a production model. 'There's nothing really new any more,' says Kit. 'It's all about hybridisation, combining technologies to create something innovative.'

Ecospheric is a sustainability consultancy set up to advise the

◀ Figure 1.9
..................................................................

**A large extension to the side of the house has allowed the creation of an open-plan kitchen/dining area overlooking the garden. Light floods in through the triple-glazed doors and rooflight.**
*Photo: Colin Poole*
..................................................................

domestic construction industry. 'I enable private homeowners to reduce their carbon footprint, energy bills and maintenance and enhance the internal environment to remove any discomfort and to control building and occupancy health,' says Kit. Having found a suitable house in need of substantial renovation in the garden suburb, he set to work transforming it into a 21st century 'eco' home whilst retaining its historic character.

## Show home on trial

'The brief was to select one of the most difficult property types for eco renovation and turn it into a show home with three goals,' says Kit. 'Firstly, the house was to be an educational facility, working with national charities such as Sustainable Energy Academy, the SuperHomes Network and

Action for Sustainable Living to get as many members of the public to see what can be done, truly understand what technologies and techniques are available, and transform their own properties; secondly, to trial technologies, acting as a live laboratory. We currently have up to six world-first trials being carried out on site; finally, we set out to improve the performance of this traditional dwelling significantly.' SuperHomes are older properties refurbished by their owners to cut fuel bills and to reduce carbon emissions by at least 60%. There are currently more than 160 SuperHomes in the UK and owners have to commit to hosting open days so that experience can be disseminated and the network expanded. For more information, see page 209.

Chorltonville is a conservation area so there could be no alterations to the front elevation of the semi-detached house. The house also had to match its pair and the other semis grouped at the end of a small cul-de-sac. From an initial inspection, there is little difference between the Knowles' house and its unimproved pair, but Kit has managed to upgrade the façade to the highest possible performance levels. The outer walls of the house are of solid brick so cavity wall insulation was not possible. Indeed, Kit prefers external insulation as this keeps the fabric of the house warm and means that valuable internal floor area is not lost.

However, external wall insulation can often destroy the character of a period house. Kit came up with a super-thin solution which retains the look of the existing façade. The original render and pebbledash were stripped off and the pointing of the exposed brickwork removed. A thin coat of lime render was then applied, thrown across the wall by hand so that it penetrated the brick joints and then smoothed to create a finish which is airtight but permeable to moisture. On top of this was applied a 50 mm thick aerogel insulation board – a hybrid of Spacetherm and Kooltherm K5 EWB phenolic foam which gives a U-value of 0.263 W/m$^2$K (see pages 192-3); the outer surface of the board provides a suitable key for the new external render. Insulation was similarly applied to the exposed brick plinth to the house and a thin outer skin of brick slips attached which matches the original brickwork. Leaded glazing and stained-glass panels were encapsulated in triple-glazed units set into replacement timber window frames. Kit generally prefers to retain existing timber frames but, in this case, they were too rotten to be reused.

Behind the front façade, a more radical renovation has taken

Figure 1.10 ▶

**The matt finish, black slate flooring acts as a heat sink during the day. Kitchen units and other fittings and finishes throughout the house are manufactured from recycled or recyclable materials.**

*Photo: Colin Poole*

place. The house was stripped back to its bare structure, although all original features – cornices and so on – were retained. This meant that new energy-saving systems and services could be installed more easily. At the rear, a new super-insulated, timber-framed extension, housing the kitchen and a dining area under a glazed mono-pitch roof, was designed by Kit's architect father. The extension is comparatively large but Kit found the local planners supportive of his plan to turn a traditionally-constructed property into an 'eco' home.

## Gadget-less approach

Although, according to Kit, the house includes around 100 energy-saving features, he tries to avoid expensive eco technologies, particularly those that use electricity. Kit's initial

advice to clients is always to reduce electricity consumption as much as possible. 'Electricity is the most expensive form of energy and its production has a huge carbon footprint,' he explains. So he tends to adopt a more passive, gadget-less approach to energy use. 'People are distracted by certain technologies such as solar panels and wind turbines but often they are not the most efficient solution.' At the start of any project, a thermal-imaging camera is used to identify where energy loss is greatest and the areas where the most cost-effective improvements can be made.

Passive solar gain is key to the low-energy approach to heating the house. The rear of the house faces south to capture as much as possible of the sometimes elusive Manchester sunshine. The dining area under the glazed mono-pitch roof is designed to capture and to store heat. Kit calls the room, 'the

◀ Figure 1.11

**Opening off the rear reception room is the dining area with its glazed mono-pitch roof, designed to capture and to store heat. Kit calls this room 'the solarium, the engine room of the house'.**
*Photo: Colin Poole*

solarium, the engine room of the house'. He is a big fan of mono-pitch roofs as they are very efficient in terms of the use of materials and maintenance. Here he has angled the roof as steeply as possible so that, at the top, it is tucked under the window sill of the window to the first-floor bedroom. This allows the largest possible panel of brickwork to be exposed internally, above the opening to the former dining room. The panel is exposed to the maximum amount of sunlight during the day so is an effective heat store. Heat peaks at midday and is released into the house during the night.

Matt finish, black slate is used to pave the new dining area. 'Slate has excellent heat absorption properties which is improved even more by the matt finish,' says Kit. The slate is laid on an insulated concrete floor. Kit now regrets placing the insulation on top of the concrete instead of beneath it, as the latter arrangement would have improved the floor's effectiveness as a heat store as the thermal mass of the floor

slab would be significantly increased. In this case, a closed-cell insulation should be laid on top of the damp-proof membrane as it is impervious to water and will not compress under the weight of the concrete. Kit further recommends doubling up on the membrane to ensure watertightness. A deep layer of perimeter insulation in the footings is also important when using a floor as a thermal store. 'Lateral heat loss, rather than heat loss into the ground, should be more of a concern,' says Kit. 'You don't have to go down far before the ground temperature is a steady 10-12°C. Heat loss going down will stop at around 700 mm depth.'

## Heat recovery for health

Warm air from the 'solarium' is circulated throughout the house by a heat recovery unit installed in the attic. At the rear of the house, air is supplied to the family room and circulates through the dining area around to the kitchen and is

▶ Figure 1.12

**On a few days during the winter months, the energy-efficient wood-burning stove in the living room supplies supplementary heating.**
*Photo: Colin Poole*

extracted close to the back door and the utility room. 'This has the advantage of preventing cooking smells from entering the rest of the house,' explains Kit. There are also extracts in the bathroom and en-suite shower room to the new first-floor bedroom above the kitchen.

Warm extracted air is drawn into the heat recovery unit where the heat is recovered to heat fresh air and foul air is expelled. This was the first installation of Passivent's iHybrid whole house Mechanical Ventilation Heat Recovery system (MVHR) (see Materials and technologies chapter, page 196). 'Passive cooling is an important tool in overcoming the overheating potential of most passive solar designs,' Kit explains. 'Use of the iHybrid ventilation system means that we have heat recovery for the winter and passive – no electrical consumption – ventilation in the summer.' Hot high-pressure air at the bottom of a vertical pipe with cold low-pressure air at the top creates passive stack ventilation. If a hot water coil

is placed at the base of a stack – this can be powered by excess energy from the solar thermal system – then the temperature differential is increased and the ventilation rate increases considerably. Any increase in extract rates will increase infiltration rates and aid cooling.

Kit aims to improve the effectiveness of the MVHR even further, achieving an 85% carbon reduction for the house. Working with Newform Energy, he has developed a hybrid photovoltaic thermal (PVT) system that combines electricity and hot water production in one panel, with a new technology to preheat air coming into the house and provide cooling in the summer time. 'The Achilles' heel of normal photovoltaics is the drop in efficiency occurring at the height of the day due to the panels overheating,' says Kit. 'By running cool water through the panels, a lower temperature is maintained, greatly increasing electrical output and providing hot water as a by-product.' To further enhance this new

Figure 1.13 ▼

In the master bedroom, a headboard and bed surround have been upholstered using fabric remnants and natural latex from rubber plants. The original stained glass panels in the windows to the front of the house have been encapsulated within double-glazed units.
*Photo: Colin Poole*

Figure 1.14 ▶

**The family bathroom has a beach pebble floor. Moist air is extracted and processed through the heat recovery unit.**
*Photo: Colin Poole*

technology, a zeolite module is to be installed alongside the heat recovery unit. Zeolite is a naturally occurring mineral which gives off heat when exposed to humid conditions. In winter, as humid air is extracted from the property, it passes through the zeolite which absorbs the moisture and gives off heat. This supplies a greater pre-heat to the incoming air as it passes through the heat exchanger. The zeolite is then dried out, utilising heat from the solar thermal panels.

Kit explains that the ventilation system has other important benefits: 'Research has shown that we spend around 90% of our time inside buildings and only 10% in the fresh air. The air we breathe in buildings should be as fresh as possible for our own health and for the health of the building itself. The circulating warm air prevents any areas of condensation or dampness in buildings and removes dust and bacteria. Pollen is also removed which is an advantage to those that suffer from hay fever or other allergies.' The only maintenance required is regular vacuuming of a removable filter; the fans which drive the air flow use a minimal amount of electricity.

Walking around the Knowles' house reveals that Kit has analysed every detail, every single material used, to assess its performance, its sustainability and its suitability for this period

property. Inventive thinking and hybrid concepts are to be found in abundance – and the detailing is often very subtle. The units to the dining area mono-pitch roof, for example, are triple-glazed but the top layer of glass projects forward on the lower edge so that, externally, it appears like traditional patent glazing used at the time the house was originally constructed. From below, only the glass is visible as the units are fixed on top of the supporting pine rafters. Accoya wood has been used for the cover caps to the glazing units. This hardwood has a relatively short life cycle making it more sustainable and is pickled in acetic acid – vinegar – to make it more durable (see Materials and technologies chapter, page 192). Kit is experimenting with various timber finishes which will extend its durability even further.

In the kitchen, cupboard doors are of recyclable glass and the worktops are made of a recycled material which looks like granite. Developed by Consentino, a Spanish manufacturer, the ECO worktops are made from 75% recycled glass and 25% quartz, natural stone, resin and pigments. Fallen timber is used for the floors, desks and shelving. The unusually grained timber flooring in the guest bedroom above the kitchen is from an ancient diseased oak tree felled on a National Trust estate. Pebbles from the seabed form the floor to the family bathroom. Wallpaper is manufactured from recycled paper and printed with eco ink. Reclaimed elm is used for the dining table and bench, and the living room sofa and master bed utilise natural latex from rubber plants. Material offcuts are used for the bedhead and surround and the living room rag rug is made entirely from second-hand silk scarves and ties.

## Halting heat loss

To save as much energy as possible and meet the SuperHomes standard, the house has been designed to be as airtight as possible. The flues from all the original fireplaces – apart from that housing the super-efficient wood-burning stove – have been sealed. To prevent dampness, the flues are filled with porous LECA – light expanded clay aggregate – which absorbs any moisture. Kit explains that unused chimneys have a cycle of becoming damp during the winter and then drying out during the summer. The flue filling aids this cycle, and air circulating through a vent on the chimney pots helps to keep the chimneys dry.

The house has a rainwater harvesting system to collect water for use in the WCs, baths and outdoor taps. But the WC in the downstairs' cloakroom is another example of Kit's simple, direct sustainable approach. As the room is very small, there was not the space for a wall-mounted basin on the wall facing the WC. Sourced from an Australian manufacturer, the WC incorporates a hand basin on the top of the cistern. When the toilet is flushed water flows through a spout into the basin above, on its way to filling the cistern. This water can be used for hand-washing and the grey water is then used for subsequent flushing (see page 193).

Kit has already hosted a number of open days as part of the concept of the SuperHomes project, in order to explain his experience of the cost-saving benefits of living in this period eco home. During the past cold winters the wood-burning stove has provided the majority of the additional heat required for the house and the conventional condensing gas boiler has been used for as little as five days a year for heating, more regularly as a source of hot water. The combined annual gas and electricity bill has been reduced from £2,500 to £550 and the water bill has fallen from £600 to £220 with a 'purely passive, fabric-first approach – no renewables. Now the active phase has been completed, we see the bills tumble to just £200 per annum'.

The early garden city pioneers who were behind the creation of Chorltonville would be proud of their new residents. In 1910 the houses were some of the first properties in Manchester to have both a centralised hot water and heating system and electricity – an early example of rapidly advancing technology on the domestic front. Kit has taken innovation another century forward and turned an Arts and Crafts home into a 21st century SuperHome.

### KEY ECO FEATURES

- Upgrading of original front elevation using super-slim aerogel external wall insulation without altering appearance;
- Super-insulated timber-framed rear extension;
- Passive solar heating utilising heat store in 'solarium' and hybrid heat recovery system;
- Rainwater harvesting system;
- Extensive use of sustainable materials.

**Site:** Chorltonville, Manchester
**Start on site:** November 2009
**Completion:** January 2011
**Client:** Kit and Ellie Knowles
**Contract value:** £175,000

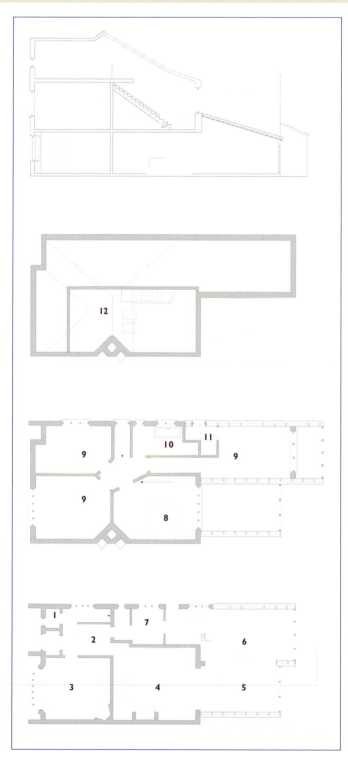

◄ Figure 1.15

*From top to bottom*
**Section**
**Second floor plan**
**First floor plan**
**Ground floor plan**

**Key**
1   WC
2   Hall
3   Study
4   Living room
5   Dining area
6   Kitchen
7   Utility room
8   Master bedroom
9   Bedroom
10  Family bathroom
11  Shower room
12  Walk-in wardrobe
*Images: Kit Knowles*

▲ Figure 1.16

**A new super-insulated, timber-framed extension has been added to the rear of the house. Glazed roofs and large windows maximize solar gain to the kitchen and dining area.**
*Photo: Kit Knowles*

Figure 1.17 ▶

**The rear elevation was rebuilt utilising the reclaimed bricks. Additional space gained on the lower floors compensated for floor area lost through internal insulation.**
*Photo: Kilian O'Sullivan/ www.kilianosullivan.com*

# Culford Road, London Borough of Hackney

by Prewett Bizley Architects

- Victorian terraced house
- Conservation area

Only a few domestic refurbishment projects in the UK have been able to achieve Passivhaus standards which are, understandably, easier to gain on a new-build. Turning a period property into an energy-efficient home can result in the total loss of the original building fabric, including all the historic features. Recent projects by PBa and others have shown that even listed buildings can in certain circumstances be retrofitted to very low energy standards too. Of course any intervention needs to be very carefully considered and justified during the planning and listed building approval process. This level of intervention is not allowed in listed buildings, and houses in conservation areas are subject to many constraints particularly when it comes to alterations to the street façade. Like many small firms of architects, Prewett Bizley was wary about working on a small refurbishment project, but decided to accept the challenge. 'I was tempted by the opportunity to investigate just how low the energy demand could be made,' in a typical Victorian terraced house, Robert Prewett explains.

Graham Bizley and Robert Prewett met at Bath University and both studied and worked abroad for a period before returning to England to set up in practice together. Graham has experience of designing innovative contemporary architecture in historically sensitive urban and rural locations. At Fielden Clegg Bradley, Robert worked on a number of award-winning housing schemes.

PBa was shortlisted in the BRE's Passivhaus design competition 2012 and has received both a local and national RIBA award (Dundon Passivhaus). Typically, their work involves individual responses to constrained sites or circumstances and includes a number of new-build projects which attempt to balance the client's requirements with practical considerations and the ideal of a green approach to construction. A house in Newington Green, London was the first completed project.

## Low-energy, eco approach

Although the partners were reluctant to take on a domestic refurbishment project, when they were approached by two clients with a low-energy, eco agenda – Robert Cohen, a carbon analyst, building physicist and climate change adviser, and Bronwen Manby, a human rights legal adviser – they were persuaded by the commitment of the couple. 'Our clients stated specifically that they wanted to avoid "eco-bling", referring to clichés such as green roofs and wind power,' says Robert. 'We were all interested in what has been referred to as eco-minimalism – as expounded by the likes of Nick Grant. This is based on the elimination of energy demand through well considered design.' The house the clients wanted to transform is a Victorian terraced house in the De Beauvoir Conservation Area in the London Borough of Hackney. The De Beauvoir Estate was developed from the mid-19th century onwards and comprises a mix of villas and terraces built for the prosperous Victorian middle classes at a time when London was expanding at an unprecedented rate.

The three-storey house has a simple plan with two main rooms on each floor: kitchen and service rooms on the lower ground floor with some later rear additions; two reception

◀ Figure 1.18

**The existing street elevation was in relatively good condition. It was insulated internally and the sash windows double-glazed, preserving its appearance.**
*Photo: Kilian O'Sullivan/ www.kilianosullivan.com*

rooms on the ground floor; and two bedrooms on the first floor, so internal reconfiguration was relatively minimal. The existing street elevation with its sash windows, stucco window and door surrounds and stucco cornice was in relatively good condition. As no alteration could be made to this façade – the house is in a conservation area – it was insulated internally and the sash windows double-glazed, preserving its appearance.

A more dramatic intervention was made on the rear elevation. Over time the rear façade had been significantly altered and later additions were of poor structural quality. The decision was taken to completely demolish the rear wall and to rebuild it utilising the reclaimed bricks. The new extension projects 2 m beyond the rear of the house across the full width of the plot. Although there was some initial resistance to the size of the extension from the planning officers – it was larger than other rear extensions in the same terrace – this proposal was eventually approved. Space gained on the lower floor compensated for floor area lost by internal insulation.

The two-up, two-down layout of the original house has been significantly improved. In place of the original gloomy kitchen – daylight being blocked by the later rear additions – a large and light-filled new kitchen/dining room has been created on the lower ground floor which opens on to the garden. At the street front of this level is a bedroom and en-suite shower room. The existing staircase with half-landing has been reconfigured into a single flight opening off the ground floor living room, gaining a large amount of additional width in this relatively narrow terrace. The stairs lead to a master bedroom and large rear bathroom on the first floor and tucked into the attic is a study/bedroom with a large west-facing dormer window.

Turning a solid-wall, Victorian house into a low-energy house can involve stripping down much of the existing structure with the inevitable loss of original features and materials. The conservation of historic fabric has to be balanced against the potential gain in conservation of energy and resources. One of the advantages of a more intrusive approach to refurbishment

Figure 1.19  ▶

**A light-filled kitchen/dining area opens on to an outdoor oasis in north London.**
*Photo: Kilian O'Sullivan/ www.kilianosullivan.com*

is that this facilitates structural alterations such as the elimination of cold bridges and makes it simpler to install services such as ventilation ducts for a heat recovery system. At Culford Road, the decision was made to completely gut the house, retaining some salvaged timber for reuse.

### Insulating the front façade

To meet the clients' brief of achieving the best possible energy efficiency, major works were required to upgrade the thermal performance of the existing building structure. To prevent timber rot and eliminate cold bridging, wall plates were removed from the front façade and replaced with concrete. Reinforced concrete 'elbows' tie the façade to the party walls so that the outer skin can stand as an independent structure. A highly-insulated inner wall was then constructed, leaving a 25 mm minimum ventilated cavity to prevent interstitial condensation. Steel I-beams span between the party walls parallel to, but independent from, the original outer skin. These support the new floor joists at each level. To achieve

airtightness on the front wall, the new insulation incorporated an OSB (oriented strand board) sheathing layer which serves as a robust airtightness layer. Elsewhere in the house, airtightness is provided by new wet plaster or parging as appropriate. The U-value of the front façade has been improved from 2.1 W/m$^2$K to 0.2 W/m$^2$K, significantly better than the statutory 0.3 maximum value required by Building Regulations for new-build. This has been achieved by building a new internal wall utilising Knauf Insulation's ThermoShell internal wall insulation system. Knauf EcoStuds – extruded polystyrene bonded to OSB (see Materials and technologies chapter, page 195) – were used as battens and counter battens within a layered construction. Three layers of OSB were used around these fatter layers of glass mineral wool insulation. The middle OSB layer acted as the airtightness plane and every board joint was carefully taped.

### Super-insulated rear elevation

An even higher standard of insulation – 0.15 W/m$^2$K – was

◀ Figure 1.20

**On the upper ground floor the living room overlooks the garden. Glazed folding doors connect the space to the studio at the front of the house.**

*Photo: Kilian O'Sullivan/ www.kilianosullivan.com*

achieved on the new rear elevation which comprises an external skin of reclaimed London stock bricks, a central core of two layers of 100 mm thick Knauf DriTherm glass mineral wool insulation and an internal 100 m thick skin of lightweight concrete block. All cold bridges are eliminated utilising Foamglas Perinsul blocks (see Materials and technologies chapter, page 194) at critical junctions and TeploTie wall ties from MagmaTech (see Materials and technologies chapter, page 195).

Window openings have also been carefully designed to avoid cold bridging with a separate lintel for the outer skin of brickwork and a plywood box lining for the window, which creates an effective air seal. Sash windows are often the weak point in the energy-conscious refurbishment of a period house, as it is difficult to reconcile aesthetic considerations with thermal performance. Achieving higher standards of airtightness and insulation in sash windows is one of the big challenges faced by architects working on houses in conservation areas. It is not possible to incorporate triple-glazed units in sashes with small panes of glass whilst retaining the slim and elegant glazing bars. Later Victorian sashes with

larger panes of glass and fewer glazing bars are easier to upgrade. Bere Architects (see pages 23-27) has been working closely with window manufacturers Mumford & Wood to investigate the possibility of producing a triple-glazed sash window which would be acceptable to conservation officers. Achieving the thin glazing bars, typical of the Georgian period, is particularly difficult due to the depth of the glazing units.

### Carbon emissions analysis

At Culford Road, heat savings from making the house airtight and using heat recovery dwarf the very modest electrical energy required to drive the fans. The designers estimate the ratio to be about 20:1. An embodied carbon analysis was carried out by PBa based on the ICE index of carbon emissions for common building materials developed by Craig Jones at the University of Bath. 'The 25 tonnes used in this refurbishment is less than half that required for new-build and creates a very low usage building in a context where it would not have been possible to do otherwise,' says Robert Prewett. 'Whilst this project is invasive, the embodied carbon will be paid for within six years. After that point the house will be

Figure 1.21 ▶

**The hall opens into the living room and studio. Stairs lead down to the kitchen and dining area on the lower ground floor.**
*Photo: Kilian O'Sullivan/ www.kilianosullivan.com*

saving carbon compared to its neighbours.' As well as reducing energy demand through the passive means described above, the house also utilises a small PV installation on the roof that generates over half of the electrical energy required by the house and benefits from the FIT – Feed-in Tariff – subsidy, achieving an annual fuel bill estimated at £100. Recent readings show that annual gas usage has decreased from 28,082 kWh to 4,660 kWh.

It may also be worth noting that actual energy use has been monitored during the five years since the works were completed. The results shows that the average annual heating demand is just below that predicted by the energy modelling done by the designers (24 kWhr/m²yr measured compared to 27 kWhr/m²yr calculated). Maximum and minimum annual heating demand varies between 20–29 kWhr/m²yr and correlates with milder and colder winters.

## KEY FEATURES 🗝

- Innovative internal insulation system to front façade;
- Floor space lost from insulating internally has been regained in a rear and roof extension;
- Elimination of cold bridging, making the house airtight, and a heat recovery system have significantly reduced energy use close to the Passivhaus EnerPHit standard used for retrofits;
- Rear elevation rebuilt to exceed current Building Regulations insulation standards – the house achieved an airtightness test of 1.1 m³/m²hr (very close to Passivhaus level); the current UK requirement for new-build is 10 m³/m²hr.

**Site:** Culford Road, Hackney, London N1
**Start on site:** February 2009
**Completion:** February 2010
**Clients:** Robert Cohen and Bronwen Manby
**Contract value:** Confidential

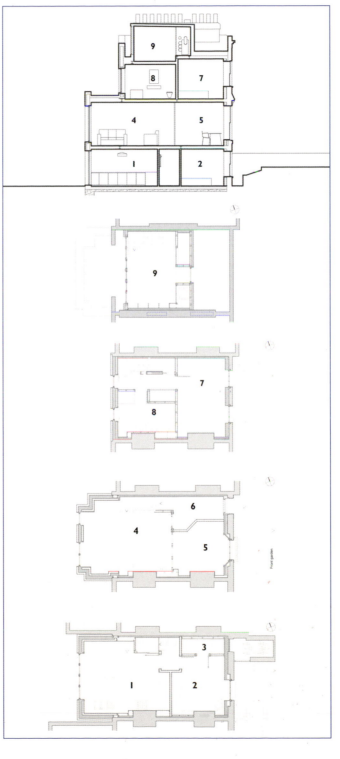

◄ Figure 1.22

*From top to bottom*
**Section**
**Second floor plan**
**First floor plan**
**Upper ground floor plan**
**Lower ground floor plan**

**Key**
1   **Kitchen**
2   **Guest bedroom**
3   **Shower room**
4   **Living room**
5   **Studio**
6   **Hall**
7   **Master bedroom**
8   **Bathroom**
9   **Study**
*Images: Prewitt Bizley Architects*

◄◄ Figure 1.23

**At the top of the house is the study. Long-distance views are gained through the V-shaped gables of the rebuilt rear elevation.**
*Photo: Kilian O'Sullivan/ www.kilianosullivan.com*

Figure 1.24 ▶

**Reclaimed bricks frame a white-rendered panel punctuated by an angled oriel window; above this a square 'dormer' clad in untreated sweet chestnut projects beyond the façade.**
*Photo: Martine Hamilton Knight*

# Tindal Street, Balsall Heath, Birmingham

by John Christophers

• Victorian semi-detached house
• Conservation area

A modest early Victorian, two-up, two-down semi-detached house in Birmingham has been transformed into a beacon 21st century eco design by its architect owner John Christophers. The aim was to achieve 'true zero carbon' as defined by the now obsolete Code for Sustainable Homes Level 6, a code which applied only to new-build houses. Purchased in 2007, the property benefited from a plot of land to the side which allowed the construction of a three-storey extension, more than doubling the existing floor area. The extension wraps around the rear of the existing house, presenting a modern façade to the back garden.

John set out to create the first zero-carbon, retrofit project in the UK and 'to inspire others, demonstrating that green does not have to be dull'. The new street elevation is certainly not dull; it makes a dramatic statement and enriches the varied streetscape. The planners were fully supportive of the new intervention, wanting to encourage this important green refurbishment initiative. The existing street scene is a varied mix of Victorian architecture, of differing styles and differing scales. Opposite the house is a large Victorian primary school. The new addition fits well into this context. 'Although the scale and materials are contextual, the architecture is modern, not pretending to be Victorian pastiche,' John explains.

## Highly articulated façade

The façade of the new extension is highly articulated and a range of building materials has been used to differentiate the various forms, reflecting the interior spaces. Reclaimed bricks frame a white-rendered panel punctuated by an angled oriel window; above this a square 'dormer' clad in untreated sweet chestnut projects beyond the façade. Completing the composition is a rooftop studio with a mono-pitch slate roof angled perfectly to catch the sun.

This dynamic, sculptural, deconstructivist approach extends to the design of the interior. The rectangular form of the

existing reception rooms is penetrated by a curving staircase to the first floor. In the new extension this curve is echoed in the curving wall of the hallway, creating a womb-like, elliptical form at the very centre of the house.

Spaces on all levels of the house revolve around this radiating stair with the curving form extending vertically and emerging at roof level to form one side of the 'dormer'. As well as being penetrated by the staircase, the existing volume of the house has been cut away to form a double-height, top-lit living room. The master bedroom and en-suite bathroom occupy the existing first floor. In the extension are the kitchen/dining area on the ground floor and two bedrooms plus shower room on the first floor.

The new bedrooms have shutters which open into the living space and more shutters screen the staircase. These are used to alter the dynamics of the space and to control the flow of air and the penetration of light. 'The shutters create introverted spaces when closed and extrovert ones when left open,' says John. 'I've been inspired by the windows in Elizabethan theatres.' On the top floor is a large studio.

▼ Figure 1.25

**The highly articulated new side extension bridges the differing scales of the two adjoining Victorian semi-detached houses. It adds interest and enlivens the street scene.**
*Photo: Martine Hamilton Knight*

Figure 1.26 ▶

**The new garden façade is a crisp composition recalling the work of early Modernist architects.**
*Photo: Martine Hamilton Knight*

In contrast, the rear garden elevation is calm and elegant; the restlessness of the front elevation has been resolved. Crisp white planes are punctuated by horizontal strips of sliding glass doors and windows. Inserted panels of bold colour recall the experiments of early Modernist architects such as Le Corbusier. John sees himself as working in 'an alternative English modernist tradition', inspired by the work of Alvar Aalto and Hans Scharoun. 'I aim to enrich the possibilities of modernism, creating richness not complexity.'

### Exploiting natural light

The manipulation of daylight was a key factor in the genesis of the design. Natural daylight floods into the heart of the house through rooflights – 'five times more effective than windows,' says John – and openings with mirrored reveals. 'Better natural light reduces the reliance on electric light and energy use, but designing with top lighting also has interesting design implications, leading to more vertical internal spaces.'

Thicker external construction, necessary to achieve the highest standards of insulation, has meant that windows and other openings have larger reveals. John has exploited the increased wall thickness, using splayed angles to frame views, form window seats and to modulate the daylight. The splayed reveals echo those of one of Edwin Lutyens' best-known restoration projects, Lindisfarne Castle in Northumberland, a favourite destination for John and his wife.

Mirrors reflect the light into the interior. 'The mirror linings are purposely thin; they ripple slightly, reflecting shimmering patches of sunlight. Honeycomb panels in the lobby door, staircase screen and landing floor, in combination with the mirrors, intensify the daylight and bounce sunlight deep into the interiors.'

### Reclaimed materials

In addition to the skilful manipulation of daylight, John's interest in the use of a wide range of new and reclaimed building materials is apparent in the project. Fourteen different reclaimed materials are used in the construction. Structural timber was reclaimed from an old school building; drainage pipework and roof decking are also recycled; insulation is recycled cellulose; Canadian honeydew maple boarding was salvaged from a factory floor and used for the staircase, an internal shuttered balcony, kitchen units, window seats and the internal lining of the top floor timber 'dormer'.

Figure 1.27 ▶ ▶

**At the heart of the house is a double-height living room with a wood-burning stove. Apertures with timber shutters open off the staircase; the shutters can be opened and closed to control the flow of heat and to vary the access of light.**
*Photo: Martine Hamilton Knight*

Hemp rope is used for the staircase handrail. There is a fascination with craftsmanship inspired by the masters of Arts and Crafts architecture.

Structural walls are built from unfired clay blocks, one of the first applications in the UK. The hydraulically compressed blocks have very low embodied energy, high thermal mass and hygroscopic qualities which help to regulate the internal humidity. New internal walls are finished in natural, self-coloured lime plaster. The addition of ground recycled-glass aggregate gives it a lustrous sparkle. Recycled glass is also used for the kitchen worktops and wet room floors. Even the Arne Jacobsen-designed brass ironmongery – an architect's favourite – is also reclaimed original 1960s vintage.

### Rammed earth floors

One of the most innovative Arts and Crafts architects, Edward Prior, utilised building materials sourced from the site itself for iconic houses such as Home Place at Holt in Norfolk. Similarly, in Birmingham, John has used material from the site excavations to make floors of rammed earth with some additional clay, a finish with ultra-low embodied energy. The ox-blood coloured floors undulate softly and are finished in beeswax. An earlier domestic project in Worcester, also designed by John Christophers, with cob – compressed clay and straw – walls, gained an RIBA Sustainability Award in 2005. In this project John used sand excavated from the site as a component of the floor screed.

'This approach is inspired by Japanese philosophy,' says John. 'Together with other reclaimed materials, the floor creates a "wabi-sabi" aesthetic in sharp contrast with mechanistic modernism. Wabi-sabi was popularised in the 16th century by Sen no Rikyu who believed that the tea ceremony had become ossified and dead, so he subverted it by introducing imperfect tea utensils.' John also refers to an article in an issue of the *Architectural Review* dating back to the 1940s, 'Pleasing Decay' by the artist John Piper. 'There is a beauty in aged, used materials,' says John, 'compared with the perfection of modernist materials. The 200-year-old Canadian timber has nail holes, traces of previous uses, which add another layer of interest.'

### Fossil fuel use reduction

The energy required to heat the house and to supply hot water has been substantially reduced. U-values of 0.11 W/m²/°C for the walls and 0.08 for the roof have been achieved. The

triple-glazed windows have a U-value of 0.65 W/m²/°C. 'Our walls and roof are 16 times better, windows 14 times and airtightness 28 times better than the existing building,' says John. South- and west-oriented glazing maximises passive solar heating; an existing mature ash tree provides useful shading in the summer. Ash comes into leaf late in the season so solar gains are still possible in a cooler springtime. High thermal mass and natural stack ventilation allow night cooling for warm summer nights. The house is extremely airtight and a heat recovery and ventilation system which operates in the winter months reclaims up to 93% of waste heat. To achieve the high

level of airtightness, technical information and a system of membranes, advice was sought from Ireland-based Niall Crosson of Ecological Building Systems. Solar hot water panels mounted on the perfectly angled studio roof have an annual yield of 5,150 kWh; solar electric photovoltaic panels yield 4,000 kWh and a 7 kW high-efficiency, clean-burn wood stove by Lenius Wodtke provides top-up heating and hot water for the coldest weeks of the year. Wood from the necessary tree surgery of the adjacent ash tree should last for up to seven years. Ecological Building Systems supplies a number of natural insulation and airtightness products.

Figure 1.28 ▶

**Natural and reclaimed materials and finishes are used throughout the house. The dining table formed from reclaimed materials sits on the undulating, ox-blood coloured, rammed earth floor which is finished in beeswax.**
*Photo: Martine Hamilton Knight*

A 2,500-litre rainwater harvesting tank in the cellar serves WCs, the washing machine and a dedicated kitchen tap. Low water-use fittings – 4/2.6 litre dual-flush cisterns, for example – reduce water usage to an estimated 80 litres per person, per day. A gravity-fed grey water harvesting system allows bathwater to be used for watering the garden.

John sees the project as a community resource as well as a home. Seven open days were held during construction, each attracting up to 600 people, and he holds regular open days. For eco pioneers such as John, the dissemination of knowledge is paramount.

### KEY FEATURES 🔑

- Radical addition to a traditional street;
- Innovative use of materials: unfired clay blocks, rammed earth floors;
- Manipulation of natural lighting using rooflights, shutters and mirrors;
- Extensive use of reclaimed materials;
- Rainwater and grey water usage;
- Whole house ventilation.

**Site:** Tindal Street, Balsall Heath, Birmingham
**Start on site:** October 2008
**Completion:** November 2009
**Client:** John Christophers and Jo Hindley
**Contract value:** Confidential

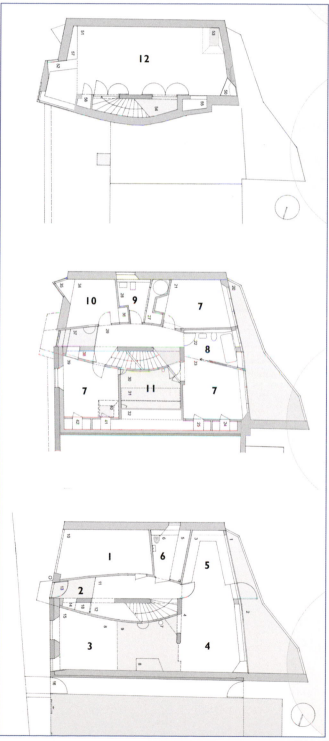

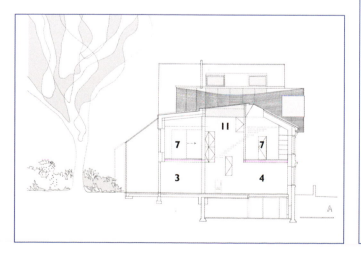

◄ Figure 1.29

*From top to bottom*
**Second floor plan**
**First floor plan**
**Ground floor plan**
**Bottom left, section**

**Key**
1   **Garage**
2   **Hall**
3   **Living room**
4   **Dining room**
5   **Kitchen**
6   **Cloakroom**
7   **Bedroom**
8   **Bathroom**
9   **Shower room**
10   **Bedroom**
11   **Void**
12   **Studio**
*Images: John Christophers*

# SECTION 2

# Space for family living

## Introduction

Semi-detached villas and end of terrace houses with sufficient space at the side of the house and large rear gardens offer the best opportunity for the extension of the ground floor living space. Four projects are featured in this section. These are all in London; the high value of property in the capital justifies the level of expenditure required in these schemes. In urban areas in the rest of the UK, it is unlikely that the value of a property would be increased by such a large contract sum.

The work of Alison Brooks Architects has been discussed in the Introduction. Wrap House in Chiswick and Lens House in north London are two of her most accomplished domestic refurbishment and extension projects. Sculptural form, unity of building material and the connection between inner and outer space are three of the key elements of her design approach. Ground and lower ground floors of the existing houses are adapted and remodelled, fully integrated into the angular rooms on the garden side. From street façade to garden elevation, the plans evolve from a rigid geometry into fluid form, from traditional to contemporary.

Hairy House in Hammersmith by Hayhurst and Co takes a similar radical approach to the reshaping of a traditional ground floor layout to create an open-plan living/dining/kitchen space which has become the essential hub of the contemporary home. Forms and materials are carefully chosen to enhance rather than detract from the existing architecture, and to unify the interior finishes with external cladding and garden structures.

In all the schemes featured in this section, planning officers have been supportive of more radical interventions. Robert Dye recognised the opportunity presented by a house with serious structural problems in Dunollie Place in Camden; the planners were more receptive to a modernist extension as the house was at risk. The façade and a proportion of the supporting structure at the front of the house were kept intact; towards the garden, much of the existing house was dismantled and reconstructed using reclaimed materials. On the garden side, a modernist two-storey extension has been created which takes full advantage of the site levels and distant views.

*An open-plan kitchen/dining/living space where today's families can cook, eat and relax together is the key element of the majority of the projects featured here. This can be achieved most effectively by extending semi-detached and end of terrace houses with large rear gardens.*

◄ Figure 2.1

**Recycled House,
Dunollie Place,
London Borough of Camden
by Robert Dye Architects**
*Photo: JCTPhoto.com*

Figure 2.2 ▶

The flat roof of the new
addition extends and folds
down to create an open loggia
at the side of the house.
*Photo: Paul Riddle/VIEW*

## Wrap House, Chiswick, London Borough of Hounslow
by Alison Brooks Architects

- Edwardian detached house
- Conservation area

This extension to an Edwardian house in Chiswick is one project in a series of commissions which have enabled Alison Brooks to redefine the nature and form of the domestic extension in the UK. Her early career and design approach are discussed in the Introduction (see pages 18–19). She is one of a handful of architects who have rethought and reinvigorated this building type. 'The Wrap House is an example of how a humble "house extension" can act as a fertile testing ground for an experimental architecture,' says Alison. 'The project is a form of research into ideas and technologies not often realised at a larger scale, and is a demonstration of what is possible when there is cohesion of ambition, dedication and communication between architect, client and contractor. The building's formal complexity is not a stylistic conceit but emerged from an open-ended process of responding to the particular conditions of the site and brief with a fully integrated architectural concept. The scheme reflects in equal measure the client's open-minded approach, adapted construction techniques, structural finesse and unparalleled craftsmanship, bound together by a shared understanding of the potential of the project.' Alison only has one domestic project in progress at any one time in her practice due to the time demands of this type of contract.

◄ Figure 2.3

**Designed as a 'floating pavilion', the new extension appears to hover; it sits on piled foundations which preserve the protected tree's roots.**
*Photo: Paul Riddle/VIEW*

Figure 2.4 ▲

**Glass doors slide back to open the living/dining space to the terrace and garden.**
*Photo: Paul Riddle/VIEW*

The folded form of the large, 100 sq m new rear addition is designed to read as an 'autonomous timber envelope', a separate 'pavilion'. It is a spatial, structural and technical tour de force. Roof, ceiling and walls are angled, creating a series of 'triangulated folds' that define the internal spaces. The 'pitched and rolling' roof is partly a response to the existing gabled and hipped roof of the existing house and of the varied roof forms of the neighbouring Edwardian properties.

## Three-dimensional design

Computer modelling software has transformed the nature of architectural design. Projects such as Foster and Partners' central courtyard at the British Museum in London, with its undulating roof composed of individually sized geometric glazed panels, would not have been possible without it. Alison Brooks has exploited the potential of this relatively new technology and introduced it to the simple house extension with dramatic and exciting results.

At some stage, the ever-evolving form on the computer screen was 'frozen into a single ribbon-like element that resolves structure, planning constraints, internal spatial conditions, existing views, and drainage flows' – a combination of design genius and prosaic practicality. The folding roof was conceived as a single element which merges into the garden decking. Through the use of a rainscreen cladding system it was possible for the timber boarding to wrap around the entire structure, emphasising the ribbon effect.

Views from the first floor of the existing house have also had an impact on the design. On the north side of the extension, the roof is folded down to enclose an 'intimate' low-ceilinged dining area with a window focusing on one close-up view of the garden. The 'compressed' form at this end of the extension allows views of the garden from the master bedroom over a 'crumpled timber landscape'.

Light enters the new space through an angled linear rooflight which separates the new structure from the old. The separation is achieved through some structural brilliance which appears effortless and invisible. Alison works closely with a number of talented engineers, in this case with Akera. The metal structure of the extension is completely separated from the existing house. This means that the continuous rooflight, composed of a series of structural double-glazed units, rests on a steel edge beam to the new extension and then on the brick wall of the existing house.

## Geometric discipline

Being in a conservation area, there were a number of restrictions to the possible height and footprint of a rear extension. The illusion of a much larger space has been created by exploiting the full width of the plot and by closely integrating covered external space and garden decking with internal floor space. The plan of the refurbished house evolves from the front door towards the new rear extension.

Opening off the traditional hallway of the double-fronted house are a formal dining room, on the right, overlooking the street and, on the left, a study, downstairs WC and shower room and side entrance. Adjoining the dining room is a formal sitting room. At the far end of the hall past the staircase, double doors open into the kitchen which breaks through the rear wall of the existing house, past an island unit, into the dynamic and liberated new living/dining extension and beyond into the garden.

Internal space is subtly defined without the use of physical partitions and a series of views are opened up – upwards through the rooflight, where the rear wall of the existing house is visible, and out into the garden. At the south-facing corner of the pavilion, the roof folds upwards, opening up wider views into the garden and into the branches of an existing mature copper beech tree which penetrates the external decking.

Light entering the interior from above and through the windows highlights the angled wall and ceiling planes. This light is constantly changing, depending on the seasons and the time of day. In summer, the tree shades the extension from excessive solar gain and dapples the light in the interior, introducing an additional dynamic quality.

## Floating pavilion

High technology and refined aesthetics converge in the construction of this unique project. Techniques not often found in smaller projects have been used to improve construction speed and efficiency. Making a minimal impact on the ground, the extension sits on an elevated concrete slab supported on 24 100 mm-diameter concrete mini-piles, a system more commonly found in large-scale commercial buildings. Benefits included the reduction in time-consuming groundworks, particularly crucial as construction was carried out in the winter, waste from the site was practically eliminated, and any potential disturbance of the existing foundations avoided. The root system of the protected copper beech tree was also preserved.

◄ Figure 2.5

**Angled ceiling planes merge into the walls and incorporate the dark gash of a fireplace highlighting the flickering flames deep in its heart.**
*Photo: Cristobal Palma*

Within a week of commencing groundworks, a dry working platform had been formed. The primary steel superstructure comprises a 10-m long, single-span beam, raked in plan and elevation, whose only visible means of support are two delicate columns clad in mirror-polished stainless steel. Braced by a skin of structural plywood, the frame is infilled with timber studwork and roof joists, allowing space for thermal insulation in the roof and walls. A fibreglass waterproof membrane was laid on plywood – similar to the construction of a boat's hull – to form the shallow pitches of the roof. This was overlaid with a rainscreen cladding of Ipe, a Brazilian hardwood sourced from sustainable forests which will slowly weather to a silvery-grey.

The raised floor slab also has an aesthetic rationale. Alison Brooks sees the extension as a free-standing 'pavilion', separated to allow natural light to penetrate the existing house, and lifted clear of the ground to float above the lawn. 'By treating the roof, floor, and walls as a continuous wrapping surface this "floating pavilion" attempts to express ethereal weightlessness and dramatic lift.' Boundaries between house and garden are blurred and this 'dematerialization is reinforced by placing polished steel columns either side of the glazing like a grove of slender tree trunks, a kind of structural camouflage. The linear rooflight which separates new and existing structures and the apparent thinness of the timber enclosure enhance the effect of dematerialization'.

Figure 2.6  ▶

..................................................

**An angled linear rooflight separates the new structure from the old. It rests on a cantilevered steel edge beam to the new extension and on the brick wall of the existing house.**
*Photos: Cristobal Palma*

..................................................

## Traditional craftsmanship

The construction of the roof form was particularly complex and Alison Brooks pays tribute to the standard of craftsmanship achieved by the main contractor, John Stidworthy, which comfortably matches that of the Edwardian joinery of the existing house. 'Using a combination of lasers and traditional string techniques, the converging planes of the timber and internal plastered surfaces were lovingly set out and constructed,' says Alison. John is a joiner by trade and an experienced boat builder, experience which proved useful when it came to constructing the roof.

The homogenous skin of the new extension wraps down to the side of a centrally located fireplace to merge into an outdoor timber deck which extends out into the garden. Internal timber flooring is completely level with the external decking so that, in summer, when the sliding doors are open, indoor and outdoor space are united. The copper beech tree spears the decking, anchoring the floating structure to the natural landscape. At its midpoint, the undulating internal surface wraps down to incorporate a fireplace which forms a focus to the interior between the dining space and the seating area. The fireplace is a deep horizontal black gash in the angled white walls. At night, in winter, a fire glows, casting its flickering light over the geometry of the interior.

Within the planning restrictions of the Chiswick Conservation Area, Alison Brooks and her team have created a building which generates 'an immersive experience of light, surface and landscape'. It is formally spectacular yet creates calm spaces with a refined palette of materials, scrupulously detailed and crafted.

### KEY FEATURES 🗝

- Dynamic geometric form with skilful manipulation of daylight;
- Illusion of larger extension created by unifying internal space with external dining area and decking;
- Concrete raft on mini-piles to facilitate construction, minimise waste and preserve site;
- Sustainable super-insulated timber construction for walls and roof.

**Site:** Wrap House, Chiswick, London W4
**Start on site:** 2004
**Completion:** November 2014
**Client:** Confidential
**Contract value:** £180,000

### AWARDS

Winner RIBA National Award 2006
RIBA Stephen Lawrence Prize 2006
Wood Awards Commendation 2006
Shortlisted Manser Medal 2006

◄ Figure 2.7

**Ground floor plan**

**Key**
1 Formal dining room
2 Study
3 Living room
4 Kitchen
5 WC
6 Living room
7 Dining room

*Image: Alison Brooks Architects*

Figure 2.8 ▶

**Through the conventional front door is a spatial surprise. The existing structure has been cut away leaving the rear reception room as a balconied mezzanine in a soaring double-height space. A sheer glass screen allows a view down into the kitchen below.**
*Photo: Paul Riddle/VIEW*

## Lens House, Canonbury, London Borough of Islington
by Alison Brooks Architects

• Victorian house
• Conservation area

Transforming a restrained Victorian villa into a dynamic 21st century live/work space utilising modern forms and advanced building technologies requires a great deal of skill, a sympathetic client and a good budget. Alison Brooks has honed her skills over a number of innovative domestic refurbishment projects. She appears not to be constrained by the limitations of working within some of central London's most protected areas; seemingly insurmountable obstacles

inspire her to ever more exciting creations. At Lens House – the two sculptural elements added to the classical 19th-century semi-detached house focus like lenses on to views of the garden – the lower ground and upper ground floors have been radically transformed, completely remodelled into one of London's finest contemporary homes.

### Live/work space

The brief was to restore the derelict building as a family home with an independent workspace for the client's photographic agency. Sited in the heart of the Canonbury Conservation Area, the house was locally listed. It had been vacant for ten years and was suffering major structural problems. The poor condition of the building meant that the local planning department was more sympathetic to ABA's adventurous proposals, as this would give the building at risk a new and sustainable lease of life. A sensitive approach was adopted

◄ Figure 2.9

**At the rear of the 19th-century villa, the remodelled interior bursts out into sculptural forms which spring down into the garden.**
*Photo: Paul Riddle/VIEW*

Figure 2.10 ▼

**New additions create a series of lenses which focus on views of the garden. The new bay window at upper ground floor level angles away from the neighbouring garden, focusing on the protected walnut tree.**

*Photo: Jake Fitzjones Photography, on behalf of DuPont Corian www.dupont. co.uk and Alison Brooks Architects*

with the project being divided into three phases which would be carried out over a six-year period. Firstly, major remedial work was undertaken to stabilise the gable wall and the roof was replaced to make the building watertight. The next phase was the conversion of the house on the lower and upper ground floors and this was followed by the construction of the extensions and garden landscaping.

The first phase commenced while detailed design proposals were prepared. These were submitted for planning in June 2006. However, a Tree Preservation Order was placed on the walnut tree in the rear garden, requiring the designs to be

amended and resubmitted in November 2006. Planning consent was granted in January 2007. The major addition to the house was the office area. There was sufficient space at the side of the house to accommodate a large extension. Planning officers advised that this should be set back as far as possible so that it would be imperceptible from the street.

On the garden side, the protection area for the roots of the walnut tree set a limit on the length of the new side extension. The glazing to the new bay window at upper ground floor level was angled away from the neighbouring garden, focusing on the walnut tree.

## Double-height living

Being in a conservation area, only limited modifications to the original house were possible on the street elevation, so the existing steps to the entrance door were retained. Visitors will not be aware of the spatial surprise which awaits them as they enter through the conventional front door. The lower ground floor has been excavated and the ground floor of the former front reception room removed, leaving the rear reception as a balconied mezzanine in a soaring double-height space. On the right of the hallway, a sheer glass screen allows a view of the kitchen below and, from here, most of the living space of the house can be seen in a single view. On the left, the existing staircase has been preserved, curving up to the bedrooms on the first and second floors. It stands like a historical exhibit in a modernist art gallery.

A staircase with a minimalist glass balustrade leads down to the double-height kitchen which can also be accessed through the traditional service entrance. 'This space draws south light deep into the house and, like a "great hall" overlooked by a minstrels' gallery, creates a powerful visual connection between the original upper ground floor entrance hall and the kitchen/dining space,' says Alison. 'The folded geometries of

Figure 2.11 ◄

The front section of the upper ground floor has been removed to create a soaring double-height space like a great hall overlooked by a minstrels' gallery.
Image: Paul Riddle/VIEW

Figure 2.12  ▲

**An external staircase leads down from the pavement to the entrance to the single-storey workspace side extension.**

*Photo: Paul Riddle/VIEW*

the extensions continue into the house to become surfaces punctuated by steel fireplaces, a cantilevered kitchen and other "inhabited walls": a variety of framed settings for modern life.'

Walls are white and the concrete floor with underfloor heating is highly polished to maximise the natural daylight from the two levels of south-facing windows at the front of the house. A hint of luxury is added by the use of walnut veneer on the kitchen units. 'In open plan spaces, we detail kitchens as pieces of furniture,' says Alison. 'This makes the space more multi-purpose.' The worktops are simply detailed; continuous stainless steel incorporating inset sinks and marble for the island unit. Deeply recessed polished stainless steel

plinths make the island appear to float. A bright yellow panel gives a 'pop' feel to the space and the colour contrasts well with the walnut veneer. The lower ground floor extends past the fireplace into a dining area and through sliding glass doors into the garden.

At the rear of the upper ground floor living room is the first of the two tapered volumes which have been added to the house: a sculptural angled bay window. Here and in the work space extension, the three-dimensional design skills of the architect come into play. 'The extension was designed as a series of large apertures framed and connected by large trapezoidal planes,' Alison Brooks explains. 'These openings capture light throughout the day, draw the garden into the

◄◄ Figure 2.13

**The rooflight to the workplace highlights the sculptural dynamism of the expressionist ceiling as light of varying intensities reflects off the angled planes.**
*Image: Paul Riddle/VIEW*

◄ Figure 2.14

**Opaque and glass planes collide in the modernist bay window to the upper ground floor sitting room.**
*Image: Paul Riddle/VIEW*

house, and frame precise views of the spectacular walnut tree. Each plane is either fully glazed or fully solid; there are no "punched" windows. This approach creates an architecture without mass and weight. It is more like the folded surfaces of origami.'

## Computer-aided design

As in projects such as the Wrap House (see pages 51-55), computer design technology has enabled complex geometric volumes to be constructed. Where the first floor and side extension converge, seven planes come together at one point. The trapezoidal office extension has ten sides. It has a separate entrance from a new sunken courtyard accessed

from the street via external steps. A huge hinged wall panel can be swung back to connect the space with the kitchen/dining area of the main house. Daylight floods into the office space through a rooflight, the light bouncing off the various angled planes of the ceiling which merge into the walls.

Looking at the house from the garden, the rigid geometry of the classical Victorian villa dissolves from the eaves to the lower ground floor. The two geometric additions are in harmony and yet create a dynamic tension. They appear to advance and project into the garden; the variously angled planes create the feeling of movement. Unity of material is key to achieving this sculptural quality. 'Roof and wall planes are one material,' says Alison, 'and follow their own geometric

Figure 2.15 ▶

**Daylight from the south-facing street elevation is drawn deep into the house. Minimalist detailing and the use of luxury materials – marble and walnut – make the space multi-purpose.**
*Image: Paul Riddle/VIEW*

logic, so that they touch the ground, and the brick house, lightly.' Utilising a rainscreen cladding system has allowed wall and roof covering to be unified. The Corian panels have a rich metallic finish and were specified, as they are dimensionally stable and easily cut to complex shapes. Rainwater downpipes and gutters are concealed behind the rainscreen cladding.

## Responsible sources

The architects adopted a passive approach to the sustainability of the refurbishment and extensions. All timber is from sustainable sources through FSC and PEFC certified schemes; insulation levels exceed the minimum Building Regulations' standard; a high level of airtightness has been achieved in the new build work; and the internal planning, the orientation of rooms and windows, was designed to maximise passive solar gain and to minimise the requirement for artificial lighting.

### KEY FEATURES    🔑

**Site:** Lens House, Canonbury, London N1
**Start on site:** 2007
**Completion:** 2013 (work carried out in three separate phases)
**Client:** Confidential
**Contract value:** £700,000

### AWARDS

RIBA London Regional Award 2014
Grand Designs Award: Best Extension 2014

▼ Figures 2.16

From top to bottom
**First floor plan**
**Ground floor plan**
Bottom left, **section**

**Key**
1   **Hall**
2   **Living room**
3   **Kitchen**
4   **Dining area**
5   **Workspace**
6   **WC**

*Images: Alison Brooks Architects*

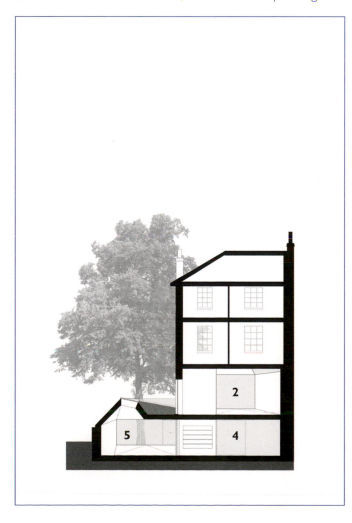

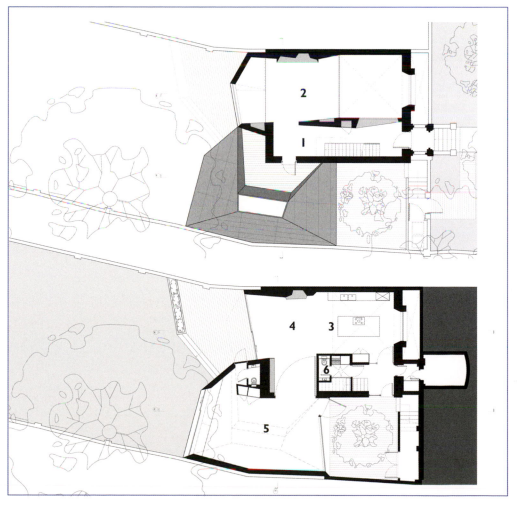

Figure 2.17 ▶

The green roof softens the
impact of the extension.
Timber perimeter seating/
decking to the sunken terrace
angles into the lawn where
strips of slate of differing
widths merge the man made
and the natural.
*Photo: Kilian O'Sullivan/
www.kilianosullivan.com*

## Hairy House, Dalling Road, London Borough of Hammersmith and Fulham

by Hayhurst and Co

....................................................................................

• Victorian end-of-terrace house
• Conservation area

....................................................................................

Runners-up in the Autodesk Young Architect of the Year Award 2012, Hayhurst and Co was established in 2004 and operates from a studio in historic Fournier Street, Spitalfields

in the East End of London. The firm has built up an excellent record of work in the education sector and has also produced a number of award-winning, smaller-scale residential conversions and extensions.

Two of the practice's most innovative domestic projects were both commissioned in 2010 and completed the following year. Hairy House is an extension to an end of terrace, two-storey Victorian house in Hammersmith and Fulham. The clients were Lucy Carmichael, a design adviser at CABE, and her husband Gareth Langdon, a furniture maker, and the potential of the angular shape of the site presented a number of design opportunities which they wished to explore in partnership with their chosen architect. They were keen to avoid the

◄ Figure 2.18

....................................................................................

**The angular plan of the end-of-terrace house is reflected in the modelling of the new extension. Vertical slate cladding is a reference to the existing roof covering. It is laid in courses of varying width to create an effect of stratification and layering.**
*Photo: Kilian O'Sullivan/ www.kilianosullivan.com*

....................................................................................

ubiquitous 'glass box' or minimalist white-rendered cubic addition and were seeking a more contextual, sensitive but, at the same time, more radical approach.

Although Lucy is an architect, she is more familiar with advising on larger-scale projects such as the development of the Olympic Park so, due to the complexity of the project and the likely planning issues, the couple commissioned Nick Hayhurst. With two young daughters, the family spends a great deal of time in the kitchen. When they bought the house 'there was a tiny breakfast room and the kitchen was a 2 sq m scullery at the back of the house,' says Lucy. They wanted a family-size kitchen opening on to the garden with plenty of space for all ages to relax and play.

## Angular plot

Addressing a curve in the road, the end of terrace property is cranked around, creating a triangular-shaped house on a triangular plot. The original two-storey rear extension is also set at an angle to the main body of the house. This unusual configuration results in some interesting room shapes, none of which is perfectly rectangular, and it is the development and extension of this geometry that makes this project so interesting and stimulating.

The garden widens from a narrow 1.5-m wide strip along the gable end of the house to 12 m at the widest point, so the architects had ample space to extend the ground floor. However, the clients were keen to retain as much of the usable sunny garden as possible and the new additions only extend the existing floor plate by an additional 10 sq m.

The existing staircase is the fulcrum of the new ground floor plan. Space from a small trapezoid-shaped room at the rear, now used as a study, has been sacrificed and incorporated in a larger hallway adjacent to the staircase with an adjoining utility room and downstairs WC.

The hall steps down, widens out, then narrows as you enter the single-room extension which houses the kitchen, dining area and living space. 'This kink in the circulation reorientates the route through the house towards the centre of the garden and allows a slow and staggered transition from the Victorian house into its new extension,' says Nick Hayhurst. 'The twisted staircase, the lowered floor, the angled plan and the raking ceiling open up a sequence of carefully controlled spatial relationships with the existing house.'

## Liberating space

The existing ground floor room of the original rear extension has completely disappeared; the upper first-floor structure is supported by some invisible structural steel gymnastics. Just a slender tubular column at one end of the kitchen island indicates the position of the loadbearing steel above. The steel frame has liberated the space, allowing the architects a free hand in the design of the new interior.

Privacy was an issue on this overlooked site and lowering the internal floor level by 500 mm has helped to screen views into the interior. This also allows a high ceiling, giving the room Victorian proportions and sufficient height so the ceiling profile can be angled upwards to the south-west to catch the afternoon sun. The rear of the house faces north so that the extension is angled to make the most of the restricted sunlight from the south-west. Three full-height glazed sliding doors on the side of the rear extension open on to a sunken paved

▲ Figure 2.20

**A trapezoidal-shaped picture window in a sculptural iroko frame incorporates a window seat at the same height as the lawn outside.**
*Photo: Kilian O'Sullivan/ www.kilianosullivan.com*

◄◄ Figure 2.19

**Glazed doors slide away to open up one wall of the living space to the external terrace. White floor tiles extend out on to the terrace.**
*Photo: Kilian O'Sullivan/ www.kilianosullivan.com*

Figure 2.21 ▲

**A larger hallway has been created with steps down to the new living space to form a slow and staggered transition from the Victorian house into its new extension.**

*Photo: Kilian O'Sullivan/
www.kilianosullivan.com*

into full play in the iroko island unit which is a cabinetmaking *tour de force*. At the rear of the extension is a trapezoidal-shaped picture window in a sculptural iroko frame with a timber window seat at the same height as the lawn outside, emphasising the differential in levels.

The new extension merges into its surroundings through the subtle detailing and landscaping. The timber perimeter seating/decking to the sunken terrace angles into the lawn and strips of slate of differing widths set into the lawn help to merge the man-made and the natural. Vertical slate cladding continues on to the garden wall, locking the new building into its context.

## Contrasting materials

Although slate forms the roof of the existing terrace, the vertical use of slate – Heather Blue Welsh slate from the Penrhyn Quarry – and timber is in contrast to the existing building methods and materials of the house. 'In contrast to the constructional logic of the existing house, the use of slate and timber are both conceived as "thick" in function but "thin" in material application,' says Nick. 'The slate cladding on the soffits and window reveals helps to give the appearance of a thick material whereas the coursing clearly conveys it is thin cladding. Equally, the timber is conceived as a thick ribbon carved to form steps, shelves and seats; however, as a surface treatment, it is clearly formed from timber boards.' The differently sized slates are laid in courses of varying height to create a textured effect in contrast with the regular brickwork of the existing house and creating a sense of stratification and layering.

Iroko timber, selected for its stability, cost and variation in grain, has been used for the frame of the three sliding doors, the internal shutters, interior and exterior cladding, decking and bench, unifying these disparate elements. 'The internal/external timber lining weaves around the awkwardly-shaped plot, activating a ribbon of domestic functions; thinning, thickening and twisting to create spaces with differing scales of intimacy fit for modern family life,' Nick explains. The use of a steel frame has made this possible.

## Sustainable roof

The green roof is finished with a layer of wild flower turf. During the summer, the mixture of tall-growing grasses, herbs and flowers becomes visible over the parapet as a dense, colourful meadow, an effect which gives the project its name.

terrace which is surrounded by decking forming continuous perimeter seating. In summer, the wall of glass disappears as these doors can slide away into a timber-clad pocket. On the inside, there are three iroko shutters which also slide away into a similar pocket.

White floor tiles laid in a herringbone pattern extend from the kitchen/living space out on to the terrace, uniting inside and outside space. The horizontal reflective white plane maximises the available light and continues beyond the iroko island unit, vertically up the white kitchen units and wall, and wraps around on to the ceiling. Gareth's craftsman skills come

## KEY FEATURES

- Sweeping away dark cellular rooms to create free-flowing space;
- Light-reflective planes around which sculptural elements and furniture are placed;
- Design with wit: hairy roof, inventive hard landscaping;
- Co-ordinated detailing of joinery extending from inside to outside.

**Site:** Dalling Road, London W6
**Start on site:** January 2011
**Completion:** October 2011
**Client:** Lucy Carmichael and Gareth Langdon
**Contract value:** Confidential

## AWARDS

RIBA National Award 2012
RIBA London Small Project Award 2012

In addition to the environmental advantages, views of the roof from upper windows and from neighbouring properties are enhanced, softening the impact of this new intervention in a conservation area. Despite the radical external treatment of the new extension, there were no problems with the local planning department which was fully supportive of the proposals. The use of natural materials, such as the timber and slate cladding, combined with a green roof seeded with meadow flowers, speeded the design through the planning process and permission was granted in only eight weeks.

Nick pays tribute to his 'enlightened, design-literate clients' who supported and contributed to the design process and allowed the architects a rare opportunity to pursue an uncompromised design approach to one of the most common, but also much-maligned, types of architectural work: the kitchen extension.

▼ Figure 2.22

Below left, **detailed section showing the green roof construction and sunken ground floor**
Below right, **lower ground floor plan**

**Key**
1 Hall
2 Living room
3 Study
4 Kitchen
5 Utility room
*Images: Hayhurst and Co*

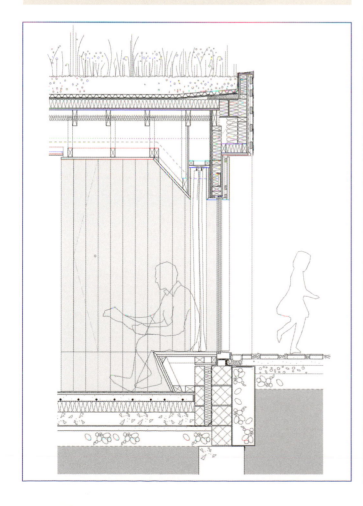

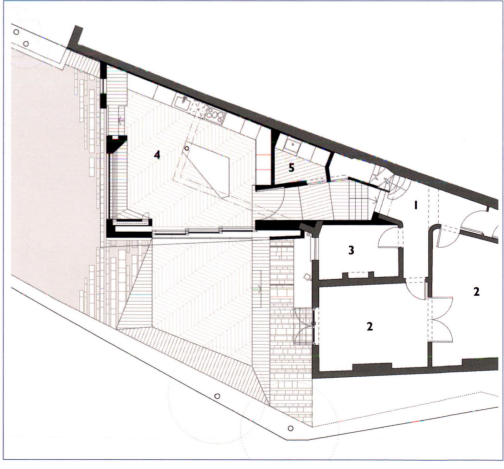

Figure 2.23 ▶

Simple detailing, geometric forms and a limited palette of materials set up a contrast between the existing architecture and the modernist interventions, strikingly apparent in this view of the rear elevation at night. A traditional house has been skilfully and sensitively transformed into a residence for modern urban living.

*Photo: Gabriel Haidau, commissioned by main contractor Ship Shape Construction:*

*www.shipshapeconstruction.com*

## Recycled House, Dunollie Place, London Borough of Camden
by Robert Dye Architects

- 1880s end of terrace house
- Major structural problems

After eight years working with James Stirling, Robert Dye set up his own practice in north London and has won a number of awards for smaller-scale projects. Several of the young architects featured in this book look up to this experienced architect who claims that a mix of 'adrenaline and fantasy' get him through the week. Teaching at the Bartlett School of Architecture brings him into contact with a lot of new talent and he runs a small, cosmopolitan architectural studio which is a hotbed of new ideas.

Innovative new-build homes and challenging domestic refurbishment projects are the lifeblood of the practice. Not least of the latter was Dunollie Place in London. This was, possibly, a project which the majority of architects would persuade their clients not to take on. But after reviewing a number of potential properties for this particular client, Robert was committed to providing a solution, a realisation of his client's vision.

The chosen house, an end of terrace on a steeply sloping site, was suffering from severe structural problems. However, its location, the views to nearby focal points and the aspect were all factors that swayed the client. She fell in love with the defective property and threw the gauntlet down to Robert: 'Turn this derelict house into the home of our dreams.'

### Structural problems

On an initial inspection, Robert saw that the house had 'broken its back'; there was settlement on the party wall and on the vertiginous end gable. Somehow a central wall had not subsided so that floors on either side sloped away; the refurbishment costs would be substantial. Before Robert could dissuade his client, the house was purchased. 'It was perched on the edge of a cliff with a 1.5-m drop down into the adjoining garden,' says Robert. 'But I saw the appeal; it is in a charming cul-de-sac and the fall in the ground provides excellent views to the surrounding urban landscape.'

At the rear of the existing house was a brick extension, the 'closet' wing with a kitchen on the ground floor and steps down into the garden. Robert saw the potential of the site. The slope of the land meant that the ground floor of the house could be extended into a new rear extension at garden level, taking advantage of the views to the west of a large established tree and, beyond, to a distant church spire.

The existing house had remained untouched for 30 to 40 years, so many of the original features were intact. At some time it had been divided into two units. Robert considered the options. 'We could have stabilised the walls as they stood, and lived with the funny slopes and angles, including the

▼ Figure 2.24

**Full advantage has been taken of a drop in level at the back of the house to create a lofty rear extension accommodating a new kitchen/dining/living space. The minimalist first-floor study follows the outline of an existing rear wing.**
*Photo: JCTPhoto.com*

Figure 2.25  ▲

**The new family room cuts back to incorporate the rear reception room of the existing house. Tall units at the back of the kitchen form an upstand to a small mezzanine. A large rooflight illuminates the centre of the plan and light also enters from above the open staircase.**
*Photo: JCTPhoto.com*

vertiginous slope in the floors, or we could completely gut the building and start again on the inside. The more we investigated the existing structure, the more difficult it seemed to adapt it to meet the client's requirements.'

### Demolish and rebuild

Once the house sale was finalised, the client did not want to compromise on the finished project; it was decided to substantially demolish the house behind the front façade and to reuse as many of the building materials as possible, retaining the majority of the original architectural features and joinery. In this way all the defective elements of the house could be removed entirely and a new structure rebuilt from a lower

level on deeper foundations. Essentially, the brief was to create a new-build house behind the existing façade whilst not losing the character of the original interior. Robert did not baulk at the challenge.

He has always been interested in the way Victorian and Edwardian housing stock can be regenerated. 'With solid wall construction, load-bearing brickwork, it is difficult to take this type of property into the 21st century.' There are also the issues of sustainability and energy efficiency. 'A developer would, most likely, knock the house down, the materials would all go to landfill, and the replacement products would be of lesser quality than the original.' Retaining existing fabric keeps continuity and anchors the house in its historic timeline.

## Recycling and reuse

As Robert explains, he believes that there is a big distinction between recycling and reuse. 'Reuse is the most sustainable approach; recycling requires energy input as the reclamation process adds transportation miles on to the material. There are also economic reasons for the encouragement of recycling rather than reuse as the reclamation industry contributes to GDP growth; it is a measurable part of the construction industry.' Planning officers are usually resistant to the demolition of houses with historic character in conservation areas but, in this case, such a degree of demolition was allowed due to the severe structural problems. However, the planning process was not easy. At the time the house was purchased, an extension could have been achieved under permitted development, but delays in approval meant that new legislation required full planning permission. Although the large rear ground floor extension was approved, consent to extend at first-floor level was discouraged; the volume and outline of the existing 'closet' wing had to be retained.

Robert had previously reused existing materials on other projects. Bricks from earlier extensions have been used for hard landscaping and paving roof terraces, for example. At Dunollie Place, however, a more comprehensive whole-house reuse approach came into play. Behind the retained façade, the house was carefully demolished whilst retaining as much salvageable building material on site as possible. Some features were dismantled and removed from the site for restoration, including the existing staircase, then reconstructed in their original position. Original skirting boards were removed and then replaced on to new walls. The house benefits from new construction methods whilst retaining the quality, detailing and character of key existing elements. 'This approach is more sustainable,' says Robert. 'You don't have to cut down more trees, for example. The 19th century handrail is made from slow-growing mahogany. Today, there is a limited supply of accredited, sustainable hardwood.'

## Linking house and garden

The layout of rooms at the front of the house has been retained. But the transformation of the house is immediately apparent on opening the front door; beyond the existing hallway, the refitted staircase is flooded with light. Rebuilding the house has meant that a very high standard of finish has

▲ Figure 2.26

**Extensive glazing has opened up distant views to existing trees and landmark buildings and also formed a connection between house and garden which previously did not exist.**
*Photo: JCTPhoto.com*

been achieved. Lime plaster has been used on the staircase; it is more sustainable and more flexible. It has a slightly raised, stucco-like texture which catches the slanting sunlight. Shadow gaps where the plaster meets other materials define the planes of white plaster and highlight the quality of the finish.

As you move forward, the space opens up into a central hallway where there is a study area overlooking the rear kitchen and dining room. Double doors connect the front and rear rooms. The ground level has been cut back into the

Figure 2.27 ▶

**The formal sitting room at the front of the house opens on to a mezzanine/study area which overlooks the family room.**
*Photo: JCTPhoto.com*

Figure 2.28 ▶▶

**The crisply detailed first-floor study has wide-ranging views. The glass has been etched to indicate the position of a no longer existing window, a ghostly apparition of the former closet wing.**
*Photo: JCTPhoto.com*

▼ Figure 2.29

**The street elevation prior to restoration.**
*Photo: Robert Dye Architects*

house, incorporating the rear reception room to form this large room with its high ceiling. Above the minimalist white kitchen is a large rooflight and fully glazed sliding doors attract the eye out to the garden and to the distant views. Remodelling and extending the rear reception room to create a spacious cooking, eating and living space means that the house is now more well connected with the garden, which has been kept as a simple grass rectangle without borders. The transition between house and garden has been blurred.

Viewing the house from the garden, the different elements are easily read: the London stock brick original three-storey structure, the modernised 'closet' wing and the large rear extension. Here, Robert is playing what he refers to as a 'formal game'. Brick fin party walls project out of the existing structure, one two-storey and one single-storey, both constructed from reclaimed bricks which are exposed on the interior. The roof of the rear wing follows the outline of the

original structure and folds over to form the vertical side wall, which sits on the large flat roof to the kitchen/dining room. This roof projects beyond the angled sliding glass doors to prevent solar glare. Here, Robert has used one of his favourite building materials, Marley Eternit fibre cement board. 'This relatively sustainable, very thin and lightweight, easy to cut and drill, fairly inert, man-made "slate" will not rot and does not patinate,' Robert explains. The flat sheets on the pitched roof are effectively a rainscreen cladding fixed to battens mounted on a roofing membrane. The sheets continue on to the vertical side wall. Here, one panel, perforated to allow pinpricks of light to enter the first-floor study, is hinged to allow maintenance access to the flat roof.

At Dunollie Place, Robert has successfully merged old and new, combining the best elements of a traditional Victorian terraced house – the quality of materials, decorative features, formal spaces – with the characteristics of an innovative

new-build house – free-flowing informal living spaces, plentiful natural light, advanced building services and construction techniques – to create a unique dwelling. To him it is an exemplar project, a demonstration of how to reinvigorate the traditional housing stock.

### KEY FEATURES

- Front façade retained, majority of house demolished and reclaimed materials reused retaining original features;
- Neatly detailed roof structure utilising Marley Eternit board;
- Skilful handling of natural light to illuminate the centre of the plan;
- Integration of house and garden and exploitation of distant views.

**Site:** Dunollie Place, London NW5
**Start on site:** June 2009
**Completion:** August 2010
**Client:** Catherine Kanter
**Contract value:** Confidential

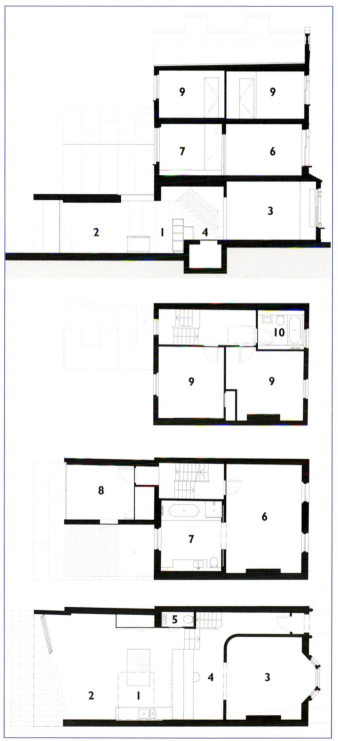

◄ Figure 2.30

From top to bottom
**Section**
**Second floor plan**
**First floor plan**
**Ground floor plan**

**Key**
1  **Kitchen**
2  **Living/dining room**
3  **Sitting room**
4  **Mezzanine**
5  **WC**
6  **Master bedroom**
7  **En-suite bathroom**
8  **Study**
9  **Bedroom**
10  **Family bathroom**
*Images: Robert Dye Architects*

# SECTION 3

# Reinventing the closet wing

## Introduction

Long life, loose fit, low energy was a concept pioneered by a former president of the RIBA, Alex Gordon (1917–99). It was the title of a paper presented at the RIBA Conference in 1971, following which publications such as *The Architects' Journal* promoted the cause. There can be no better example of a building type with more flexibility and, therefore, longevity than the Georgian and Victorian terraced or semi-detached house.

Over the centuries, these houses have been simply and easily adapted to accommodate new living patterns and technologies. A rear extension containing service rooms including kitchen, scullery and wash house allowed easy updating without disturbing the living and sleeping rooms in the main body of the house. When the water closet began to be introduced to homes in the 1850s, it was housed in this rear extension, replacing an earth closet at the bottom of the garden or yard.

More recently, this rear accommodation offers opportunities of further updating with larger kitchens, contemporary bathrooms, utility areas and so on. This section of the book profiles four refurbishment projects illustrating a range of 21st century reinterpretations of the 'closet wing'. In two neighbouring terraced houses in the London Borough of Camden, Knott Architects has completed two very different new wings, each individually tailored to suit the lifestyle of the owners. In the first, the existing wing had to be retained, so it was clad in an insulated timber-clad skin to give it a contemporary look and finished with an environmentally friendly sedum roof. In the second, the existing wing was demolished and replaced with a high-tech, rubber-clad extension. The other two projects, also in London, feature three-storey tower additions. Vicco's Tower in Hackney houses a kitchen, study and a bathroom with a reassuring Scandinavian feel for the owner who is a leading Norwegian artist. In Westminster, Henning Stummel has added a 'reversible' tower housing bathrooms and a utility room to a listed building. At night it transforms into an amazing illuminated art installation – enhancing the Georgian terrace rather than detracting from it – a beacon for the concept of contemporary additions to historic buildings.

*There can be no better example of a building type with more flexibility and, therefore, longevity than the Georgian and Victorian terraced or semi-detached house.*

◄ Figure 3.1

**Shouldham Street, London Borough of Westminster**
by Henning Stummel Architects
*Photo: Nigel Rigden*

Figure 3.2 ▶

**At night the 'reversible' rear tower turns into an illuminated garden sculpture.**
*Photo: Luke Caulfield*

# Shouldham Street, London Borough of Westminster

by Henning Stummel Architects

• Grade II listed Georgian terrace
• Conservation area

Small Georgian terraced houses can be difficult to adapt to modern-day requirements as the incorporation of bathrooms and other services may compromise the traditional room layout. Understandably, conservation officers want to see the rooms and historic features of listed Georgian houses retained or restored to their original form. Clients, on the other hand, can only compromise so far when it comes to balancing modern-day comfort with historical accuracy. Architect Henning Stummel came up with a radical solution for the refurbishment of a listed Georgian terrace house. He added a 'reversible' timber-framed tower on the rear which allowed the historic rooms of the house to be restored to their original form.

The south-west side of Shouldham Street in Paddington is a remarkable survival of a terrace of '4th rate' houses dating from the early 19th century. The three-storey houses with basements and attics have only two rooms on each floor. Wash houses and, at a later date, WCs were housed in a rear 'closet' wing projecting out into the back yard.

## Reversible service tower

To bring one of these houses firmly into the 21st century, Henning came up with the radical concept of building a service tower at the rear. This would allow later alterations to be removed from the Georgian interior, restoring the house to its original form, and for contemporary bathrooms and service spaces to be 'plugged in' at each floor level. Henning proposed a lightweight timber-framed structure clad in horizontal timber boarding which would be 'reversible'. The planning officers, however, wanted a more traditional solution, utilising London stock brick and sash windows.

As a young architect working on one of his first commissions, Henning refused to compromise. There are a number of precedents for timber-clad additions to Georgian houses,, as a walk around the historic centres of Hampstead and Highgate

in nearby north London reveals. Timber-clad structures appear in the form of bay windows and in side and rear additions, often cantilevered out at first-floor level, housing service staircases or closets. The studio of artist George Romney in Holly Bush Hill in Hampstead, constructed in 1796, is a more extensive example of a timber-clad Georgian house which inspired Henning's design. He also cites 18th-century 'mathematical' tiles as an example of lightweight cladding of the period.

## Two-stage planning route

To gain planning permission in the face of opposition from the local authority, Henning adopted a two-pronged approach. He first applied for permission to build a traditional version of the service tower, utilising conventional brick and sash windows. This was approved. He then applied for permission to build the more radical, timber-boarded version. Although this was initially refused, it was finally granted permission on appeal, as the inspector found that the intervention 'enhanced' the listed building and was an example of good workmanship and design.

*Henning wanted the ship-lapped surface to 'give the impression of a homogenously clad timber box'.*

◄ Figure 3.3

**Shouldham Street façade: the rear extension has allowed the original layout of the Georgian house to be restored.**
*Photo: Nigel Rigden*

Figures 3.4  ▶

From top to bottom
**Second floor plan**
**First floor plan**
**Ground floor plan**

**Key:**
1   **Shower room**
2   **Garden store**
3   **Utility room**
4   **Bathroom**
*Images: Henning Stummel Architects*

Figure 3.5   ▶▶

**Kitchen looking into the ground floor utility room. An opening has been cut through an existing rear chimney breast to connect each floor of the existing house to the new rooms in the tower.**
*Photo: Nigel Rigden*

New openings were formed through an external chimneystack to connect the three-storey service tower to the Georgian house at each level. On the lower ground floor is a shower room and WC, together with a small garden store accessed from an external 'secret' door. Above this are a utility room and WC connected to the existing ground floor room, and the uppermost floor contains a bathroom.

The party wall is of London stock brick and the two remaining sides of the tower are timber-framed, highly insulated, with horizontal weatherboarding. There is no access to the backyard from the street. This meant that all building materials had to be brought through the house so lightweight timber construction was an ideal solution. Carpenters could also carry out the majority of the building work, limiting the number of building trades. The tower is topped off with a traditional lead roof.

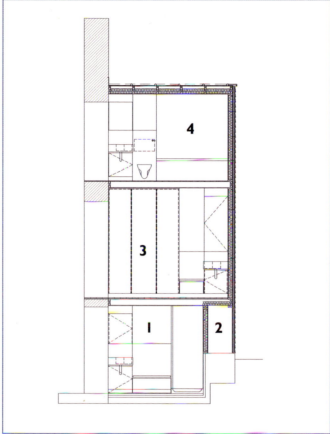

◀ Figures 3.6

**Section**

**Key**
1   **Guest shower room**
2   **Garden shed**
3   **Utility/Cloakroom/WC**
4   **Master bathroom**
*Image: Henning Stummel Architects*

◀◀ Figure 3.7

**Bathroom on the first floor.
The Perspex strip windows
give an ethereal light to the
interior.**
*Photo: Nigel Rigden*

## Homogenous timber box

The new tower has no conventional windows. The rooms are not permanently habitable, so discreet trickle ventilation, together with mechanical extracts, was sufficient to comply with Building Regulations. Henning wanted the ship-lapped surface to 'give the impression of a homogenously clad timber box'. Sanded Perspex boards distributed randomly follow the horizontal rhythm of the timber weatherboarding, admitting slits of diffused light to the interior. The interiors are bathed in an 'ethereal light', says Henning. 'They have a spiritual quality.'

To 'camouflage' the tower so that it blends in with the surrounding London stock brick and white-painted stucco structures, the timber boards are painted three different shades of grey, which does present a challenging decorating regime. 'During the daytime, the Perspex appears to be grey and we played with this, choosing to paint each board in a different shade of grey,' Henning explains. 'The colours were carefully chosen to create a dialogue between new and old.' The exterior is most dramatic at night when the Perspex boards become illuminated, giving the tower the appearance of a Turner Prize-winning art installation, an innovative new addition to the 200-year-old terrace.

**KEY FEATURES**

- Highly insulated timber-framed addition;
- New service tower enabling full restoration of listed interior;
- Fast, lightweight timber construction minimising building trades;
- Innovative façade treatment;
- Dramatic night-time illumination.

**Site:** Shouldham Street, London W1
**Start on site:** Spring 2003
**Completion:** Autumn 2004
**Client:** Beatrice Tan
**Contract value:** £70,000

Figure 3.8 ▶

The sleek, timber-clad, lightweight, three-storey extension to the rear of the Victorian villa has opened up the kitchen on the lower ground floor and provided a raised ground floor study and a first-floor bathroom.
*Photo: Vegar Moen*

## Vicco's Tower, Queensbridge Road, London Borough of Hackney
### by 51% Studios

• Victorian semi-detached house
• Conservation area

Queensbridge Road runs parallel to Kingsland Road, the A10, which stretches north from London's East End towards Cambridge. It is a mixed urban landscape with 20th-century development sitting alongside the remains of a once prosperous Victorian suburb. One of these semi-detached, mid-Victorian villas was purchased by Norwegian artist Anne Katrine Dolven. The three-storey villa was relatively spacious with two rooms on each floor. Queensbridge Road is very wide and the house has a front garden, quite large for central London, and a sizeable rear garden so there is plenty of light on the upper floors, but the kitchen and dining room on the lower ground floor were small and dark. Anne Katrine is one of Norway's best-known living artists and her photographic and video work draws on the dramatic rocky landscape of the Lofoten Islands, north of the Arctic Circle, where she has a house and studio. The restored rooms of the original Victorian London house with their high ceilings and simple detailing would make the perfect background for her artwork. But she needed a more modern kitchen and bathrooms to bring the house into the present century and to create a clean, contemporary, Scandinavian-inspired interior.

*Architectural expression is something we would regard as part of artistic expression in general.*

◄ Figure 3.9

**The timber-framed lightweight tower sits on a steel beam supported by an elegant, asymmetric 'stiletto'. Both the beam and stiletto are split so that the large glazed sliding door slips between the two halves, opening up the previously dark, cramped kitchen to the garden.**
*Photo: Vegar Moen*

## Rejecting pastiche

The brief from Anne Katrine to her architects, Catherine du Toit and Peter Thomas of Camden-based 51% Studios, was to produce an example of 'good contemporary architecture' which would sit happily alongside the existing house. They designed a sleek, timber-clad, lightweight, three-storey extension which opened up the kitchen on the lower ground floor and provided a ground floor study and a first-floor bathroom – it answered the client's brief perfectly.

However, this proposal was rejected by the London Borough of Hackney planning department in 2002. They suggested that a 'pastiche' design would be more acceptable. An international artist of Anne Katrine's calibre was unlikely to compromise; she had seen many schemes similar to hers on her travels around the world where contemporary additions

Figure 3.10 ▶

**The ground-floor, plywood-panelled study is a calm retreat away from the working rooms of the house.**
*Photo: Nigel Rigden*

sit happily alongside historic buildings. She was also aware of the many poorly designed and badly constructed extensions, many close to her own house in London, which the planning authorities had approved. The battle lines were drawn. 'As we passionately believed that such a pastiche design leads to further corrosion of the very buildings the planners seek to preserve, through mediocre and poorly constructed brick extensions, blurring and dissolving the elegance of the original buildings, we sought guidance from CABE and English Heritage,' Catherine explains.

## Design review

CABE undertook a full design review of the project and found in favour of 51% Studios' proposal in 2003. Peter Stewart, who was at the time CABE Director of Design Review, stated: 'One of the benefits of a clear contemporary design is that it indicates constructive growth and change. Architectural expression is something we would regard as part of artistic expression in general and in this case, given the applicant is an artist, we think this proposal is doubly to be encouraged.' Sadly, Anne Katrine's husband died soon after planning permission had been granted but, following a three-year pause in the project, she decided to proceed with the ambitious renovation plans, naming it Vicco's Tower in his memory.

## Responding to the landscape

Anne Katrine's artistic output is a response to the landscape of Norway and the extension to her London home was also to be a response to 'nature in the city'. There is a large London plane tree on the pavement immediately outside the house and a mature horse chestnut tree in the back garden. These natural features, together with the sky, were to play a part in the design of the extension. 'Each space is designed as much by what happens inside it, as by the space outside,' explains Catherine.

The timber-framed lightweight tower sits on a steel beam supported by an elegant, asymmetric steel 'stiletto'. 'The stiletto provides drama and lightness,' says Catherine. 'It was important that the views were undisturbed by structure, and also that the relationship between the existing building and the new extension felt very easy and comfortable.' The exposed galvanised steel structural beam doubles as a gutter and the hollow steel stiletto serves as a downpipe, reinforcing the clean and simple lines of the new extension. Both the beam and stiletto are split into two so that the large glazed sliding door slips between the two halves when it is opened.

## Framing nature

The existing dining room has been opened up and the space flows into the new kitchen at the base of the tower. Full-height glazing floods the previously dark dining room with light and unites the open-plan room with the garden. On the raised ground floor of the tower is a plywood-lined study and on the upper floor is a large bathroom. Glazed slots focus the attention on specifically framed views of nature outside. 'In a dense urban environment, the two mature trees and the garden behind the house gain in focus and beauty: architecture as lens,' Catherine explains. 'Vicco's Tower frames four specific views and creates particular qualities of light in each space.' The first view is from the study, a room entered directly from the entrance hallway. Here a 'panorama' window frames the garden as a landscape viewed from the artist's desk. Where the tower abuts the side of the existing house, there is a second view extending over two floors. This vertical glass slot frames the London plane outside, one of the original avenue of trees planted around the time the houses were built. The third view is from the bathroom through a horizontal slot window set at bath height to allow bathers glimpses of the garden. The fourth view is the sky; natural light floods into the room through the glazed roof without overlooking the neighbours.

## Sustainable construction

The architects adopted a timber-framed solution for its sustainability. It was also lightweight, requiring minimum excavation and was quick to erect, an important

▼ Figure 3.11

**The rear timber-clad tower projects slightly beyond the end gable allowing a full-height slot window which gives views to the London plane tree at the front of the house.**
*Photo: Vegar Moen*

◄ Figure 3.12

**Over the bath, a horizontal slot window allows views of the mature trees in the garden whilst bathing.**
*Photo: Vegar Moen*

Figure 3.13 ▶

**Rooflights flood the first-floor bathroom with ethereal daylight, enhancing the natural Scandinavian feel of the interior.**
*Photo: Vegar Moen*

Figure 3.14 ▶▶

**Detail of supporting steel structure comprising a horizontal beam which doubles as a gutter and an angled 'stiletto'.**
*Photo: Nigel Rigden*

consideration in a dense domestic environment. The client was able to live in the house during construction which meant that she could supervise the work closely as well as avoiding additional expenditure on alternative temporary accommodation. Materials were used 'intelligently', says Catherine, 'to wear well and to age gracefully'. This was both cost effective and sustainable. For example, the structural plywood in the study was left exposed, a warm and appropriate finish for a workroom and an economic one.

Exterior walls are highly insulated, substantially improving the energy performance of the existing house. All glazing is low-E, double-glazed and argon-filled to minimise heat loss. The heat-treated larch cladding, ThermoWood from Finnforest, has weathered to a soft silver colour. Interiors are white – simple white kitchen units with a white composite marble

worktop, white porcelain sink, white porcelain floor tiles, and white-painted plaster in the kitchen. Other materials are natural with a Scandinavian feel: Danish oiled plywood on the walls in the study, reclaimed timber flooring in the bathroom. A full house water purification system from the Pure H2O Company has been installed.

Houses are a refuge from the stresses and strains of everyday life. Anne Katrine escapes to north of the Arctic Circle for artistic inspiration and renewal. But, in the very heart of London, with the help of her architect, she has created a small oasis of Scandinavian calm. 'To be able to bathe in the moonlight and shower under a tree is something I thought was only possible in the remote place I come from in Norway,' she says. 'With this inside-outside space, I can continue these elemental experiences in East London.'

## KEY FEATURES

- Sustainable, lightweight timber-frame construction of rear three-storey tower;
- Interaction with surrounding natural features;
- Natural materials in harmony with Scandinavian client;
- Use of natural light to create a calm oasis remote from the city.

**Site:** Queensbridge Road, London E8
**Start on site:** June 2006
**Completion:** February 2007
**Client:** Anne Katrine Dolven
**Contract value:** Confidential

◄ Figure 3.15

*From top to bottom*
**Section**
**First floor plan**
**Ground floor plan**
**Lower ground floor plan**

**Key**
1    Dining area
2    Kitchen
3    Office
4    Sitting room
5    Study
6    Bedroom
7    Closet
8    Bathroom
*Images: 51% Studios*

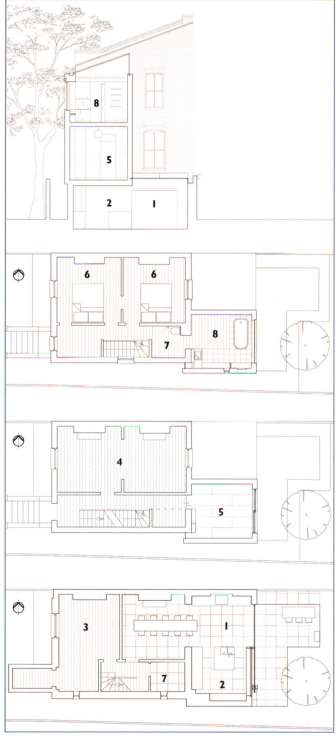

◄◄ Figure 3.16

**The new extension seen from the street. A full-height slit window allows views of the mature London plane tree on the pavement.**
*Photo: Vegar Moen*

Figure 3.17 ▶

**The 'fish bone' roof structure of the garden room/study is a consciously playful element emphasised at night by the tubular light fittings fitted between the individual rafters.**
*Photo: Jefferson Smith*

# Kelly Street, London Borough of Camden
## by Knott Architects

- Victorian terrace
- Grade II listed
- Conservation area

The room layout of artisan houses in inner city areas changed very little in the 18th and early to mid-19th centuries. In the smaller class of housing, there were, typically, two reception rooms on the ground floor and two bedrooms on the first floor. In the basement would be the kitchen and scullery. Services in the form of WCs and laundry were housed in a 'closet' wing to the rear of the property. Knott Architects has refurbished a pair of two-up, two-down houses in Camden, adopting different approaches for each, adapted to planning requirements and also the differing lifestyles of the clients.

Kelly Street is a little oasis off noisy Kentish Town Road. It is a remnant of mid-19th-century housing built between 1840 and 1870, in an area which was previously occupied by pleasure gardens extending south from Parliament Hill Fields along the River Fleet. The façades of the small terrace houses are surprisingly elaborate with arched first-floor windows and a riot of stucco decoration, rusticated ground floors, moulded window surrounds and decorative ironwork, now painted in a series of candy colours. Space is limited at the rear with narrow closet wings extending into tiny gardens.

### Stripped interiors

The client of the first project is a marketing statistician and this is her main residence. She has a weekend retreat in Hastings. When the interiors of these houses are stripped down, modern spaces can be created. Although the original features are simple, the quality of materials is very high. Sanded and polished pine floorboards, white walls and black cast-iron fireplaces form the perfect background for modern furniture and light fittings. Large windows flood the interiors with light.

The brief was to create a new 'sumptuous' bathroom in the closet wing – the owners had had enough of the existing, unheated, unfinished bathroom extension – and a functional utility area. The living room and kitchen would be on the first floor to benefit from the improved natural daylight and the main bedroom was to be on the ground floor. Although the architects and clients would have preferred to rebuild the closet wing to a contemporary design, the planners insisted that the original fabric should be retained, even though it was a later addition to the Victorian house. It would have been unlikely, in any case, that any expansion of floor area would have been permitted.

Figure 3.18 ▼

**The modest houses in Kelly Street are surprisingly elaborate with a riot of stucco decoration now painted in a series of candy colours.**
*Photo: Jefferson Smith*

Figure 3.19  ▶

**Shadow House. Black rubber wraps around this contemporary version of a closet wing. The garden room opens on to a terrace paved with black slate.**
*Photo: Jefferson Smith*

## Encasing existing structure

Knott Architects came up with the solution of encasing the original structure, cladding it externally with a layer of insulation and oak boarding, to improve its thermal performance and to signal that this was a modern intervention to the period building. 'We wanted to create a contemporary extension that sits well with the historic house. The timber-clad box harmonises with the small courtyard garden. We left a small strip of the original wall exposed where it joins the back of the house,' says George Knott, 'a subtle hint of the history of the building.' The vertical oak boarding, a rainscreen cladding fixed over a waterproof membrane, is in four varying widths 'to soften its appearance, avoiding the regimental feel of regular spaced planks'.

Timber double-glazed windows were carefully inserted, retaining as much of the original fabric as possible and sized to reflect the new use of the spaces inside. Cills and drip

mouldings are of minimalist stainless steel, forming a neat detail which protects the end grain of the timber and prevents staining. Stainless steel is similarly used for the parapet detail.

The internal focus of the refurbished extension is the purpose-made Japanese style bath, which sits in the far corner of the room. A slit window allows views of the garden whilst bathing, and daylight to enter, but privacy is protected. Increasing the luxurious feel of this interior are the glass mosaic tiles used for the bath and the surround and the rubber flooring which is 'soft and safe'.

## Living roof

The extension, which also houses a utility room, has a completely new 'living' roof. 'This is an extension of the garden,' says George. 'It is part of the eco approach to the project; the existing extension has been recycled, not replaced, and the green roof replaces the portion of the

◀ Figure 3.20

**Shadow House. Minimalist detailing of the white kitchen units complements existing period features such as the elegant sash window. The use of a strong colour on the outer wall creates a contemporary feel.**

*Photo: Jefferson Smith*

garden that it covers. The roof also improves the view from the first-floor kitchen and the views of neighbours.'

'The ultimate sustainable development is to reuse a building and prolong its life, rather than to demolish and rebuild,' says George. Replacement building materials are often not of the same quality as those being stripped out and disposed of. 'The old windows in Kelly Street have functioned for 160 years, with a bit of loving attention they have many more years of life left in them.' Where new windows were required, these are triple-glazed and to current Building Regulation standards.

The neighbours must have been impressed, as Knott Architects was commissioned by the owner of one of the adjoining houses to rebuild their rear closet wing. In this case, the planners allowed the demolition of the original structure. These clients – two retired academics living in Glasgow – had a completely different brief; they wanted to retain the living room and kitchen on the ground floor and a main bedroom

and bathroom on the first floor. Whilst the rear extension was deemed to be expendable, the planners were keen that as much of the original fabric of the modest interior was retained as possible, including areas of original lime plaster. The opening between the two ground floor rooms was enlarged and a small area of original panelling was removed and reinstated. One cast-iron fireplace was also relocated.

## Rubber-clad addition

As with next door, the stripped-down interior with its new polished timber floorboards, white painted walls and generous windows forms a perfect backdrop for modern furniture. These clients have a small collection of 20th-century art and furniture and they wanted a modernist approach to the design of the new extension incorporating some high-tech finishes, particularly black rubber. Knott Architects stepped up to the challenge and designed a rubber-clad extension

Figure 3.21 ▶

**Shadow House. The modernist theme continues in the dark ink blue and white bathroom with its rubber flooring and black fitted cupboards.**
*Photo: Jefferson Smith*

Figure 3.22 ▶▶

**Shadow House. Simple modern finishes and muted colours highlight the beauty of the original staircase with its polished treads and turned balusters.**
*Photo: Jefferson Smith*

Figure 3.23 ▶▶▶

**The purpose-designed Japanese bath looks out on to a small oasis in central London.**
*Photo: Knott Architects*

totally in keeping with the historic house. 'We wanted to respect the original building,' says George. 'A high mark of respect is to avoid mocking or competing with the historic fabric. Our approach is to be overtly 21st century when adding to the building so that the two eras are visually distinct from one another. The forms of the new addition are monolithic and austere on the outside, balanced by a playfulness on the interior seen in the "fish-bone" ceiling.'

The wrap-around rubber, Prelasti EPDM sheeting was cut and formed off-site and welded together in-situ. Dark ink blue rubber was also used in the refurbished bathroom of the existing house where the walls are also painted a complementary matt black. 'Materials are used in a raw or pure condition – unpainted galvanized steel and exposed timber,' George explains. 'These materials are assembled with an honest, no-nonsense approach, expressing how they are put together.' The roof panels are an insulated plywood sandwich which rest on softwood rafters supported by a central galvanized steel I-beam. Knott Architects refers to the project as the 'shadow house' due to the use of black rubber and because the gull-wing form of the extension roof reflects the roof of the Victorian house with its central valley gutter.

The form of the roof is also dictated by the need to restrict the height of the extension where it adjoins the party wall, so the form is 'partly practical, partly sculptural'. Furthermore, the client is very tall, so maximising the available headroom was critical. Recessed lighting highlights the form of the roof, completing this unique and innovative extension.

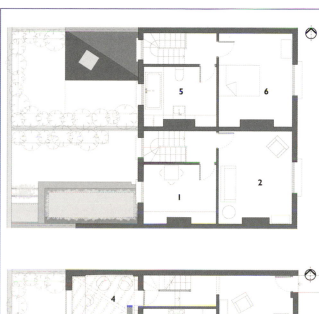

◀ Figure 3.24

*From top to bottom*
**First floor plan**
**Ground floor plan**

**Key**
1   **Kitchen/dining room**
2   **Sitting room**
3   **Bathroom/utility**
4   **Garden room/study**
5   **Bathroom**
6   **Bedroom**
*Images: Knott Architects*

◀◀ Figure 3.25

**The corner window allows views into the small courtyard garden from the bath.**
*Photo: Knott Architects*

## KEY FEATURES

- Skilful adaptation of two 'closet' wings to suit varying planning requirements and client briefs;
- Green roof;
- Innovative use of rubber cladding on insulated ply panel construction.

**Site:** Kelly Street, London N1

**Project 1**
**Start on site:** February 2010
**Completion:** May 2010
**Contract value:** £49,000 – a proportion of work zero rated for VAT due to listed status
**Client:** Confidential

**Project 2**
**Start on site:** September 2012
**Completion:** February 2013
**Contract value:** £98,000
**Client:** Confidential

◀ Figure 3.26

**An existing closet wing has been clad in vertical timber cladding in varying widths to express the fact that it is a contemporary intervention to a period building.**
*Photo: Knott Architects*

# SECTION 4

# Sustainable timber framing

## Introduction

Timber from sustainable sources is one of the most environmentally friendly materials to use for house construction. It lends itself particularly well to house extensions, as it is a fast method of construction; where access to the rear of a property is difficult, timber can be easily transported through existing rooms or through narrow passages; and it is light, requiring minimal foundations. Many of the best-constructed extensions featured in this book have a high content of specialist joinery and carpentry, and carpenters make some of the best site agents in the UK due to their attention to detail and pride in their work.

David Mikhail won a well-deserved Wood Award in 2012 for his refurbishment of, and extension to, a major Georgian listed house in east London. Demonstrating that the best contemporary design can sit harmoniously alongside the finest 18th century architecture, David has created a large and lofty living space and library, which runs the entire length of the garden elevation of this double-fronted Georgian townhouse. From the restored central hallway, the visitor enters a first-floor gallery housing a library. The fine detailing in timber is immediately apparent, offset by the use of luxury materials, such as the patinated bronze balustrade. Views open out on to the terraced garden and to the less formal lawned area beyond; truly *rus in urbe*.

Timber Fin House in Walthamstow, a one-room-deep artisan's cottage, was extended and refurbished by Neil Dusheiko. The client, a film-maker, asked for a timber extension and Neil has produced a new addition which demonstrates the beauty and flexibility of the material. Key to the design was the play of light in the interior, a feature of Neil's other domestic projects. On a suburban street in Winchester, lined with uninspiring 1940s' detached houses, Dan Brill has produced a contemporary home for a professional couple and their family. The plain but functional existing house has been gutted and transformed into a double-height living space. Bedroom accommodation has been added in a linear, timber-framed single-storey extension which runs down one side of the garden like a luxury *wagons-lit* setting off for some romantic destination.

At Goldhawk Road in Shepherd's Bush, west London, Waind Gohil + Potter Architects has remodelled a simply detailed classical villa, sitting a lightweight timber-framed structure on top of an earlier extension. The upper ground floor living space has been extended on to the former terrace, creating an impressive *piano nobile* looking out over its own private landscape, just a short walk from one of London's busiest traffic junctions.

◀ Figure 4.1

**Long House, Woodfield Drive, Winchester by Dan Brill Architects**
*Photo: Edmund Sumner/VIEW*

# East London House
## by Mikhail Riches

- Grade II listed Georgian terrace
- Conservation area

The most desirable Georgian properties in central London rarely come on to the open market. The clients waited many years to secure their ideal family home. Finally they acquired one of the finest houses overlooking one of the most desirable garden squares in east London. The property had originally been one, very large 18th-century house but had been subdivided into three units: two basement flats and one house on the upper three levels. At 16 m in width, the property occupies the space of three more conventional Georgian terrace houses. Alterations to the lower levels of the house provided an opportunity to create a modernist double-height living space.

Since establishing his practice in Clerkenwell in 1992, David Mikhail has worked on a series of domestic refurbishment projects in central London, adding modernist extensions to listed buildings and houses in conservation areas. David has developed a refined and elegant modernist style which has enhanced several of the capital's historic houses. He has gained an excellent reputation and the practice has won a string of awards.

### Sustainable public housing

David is also interested in extending his skills to the design of public housing and, in 2005, he co-founded sister practice Riches Hawley Mikhail, which specialised in public projects,

◀◀ Figure 4.2

**The double-height, timber-framed extension forms the central element of rear extensions to the Georgian house. A sedum roof and refined detailing soften the impact of the new addition and disguise its bulk.**
*Photo: Tim Crocker*

◀ Figure 4.3

**The design of the terraced rear garden is an integral part of the unification and reconfiguration of the previously disjointed Georgian house.**
*Photo: Tim Crocker*

Figure 4.4 ▶

**The formal Georgian entrance hall opens on to a mezzanine in the large double-height dining area and library with views across the garden through floor-to-ceiling glazing.**
*Photo: Tim Crocker*

Figure 4.5 ▶▶

**A staircase with a patinated bronze balustrade leads down to the lower level and the junction between old and new is highlighted through the use of linear rooflights.**
*Photo: Tim Crocker*

including the RIBA Award-winning Clay Field social housing development, 26 sustainable homes completed in Suffolk in 2008. In this project, David and his partners advanced the concept of sustainable construction for this building type. The houses are constructed using a structural timber frame filled with Hemcrete, a sprayed mixture of lime and hemp. This innovative insulation is not just carbon neutral but carbon negative, locking in $CO_2$. Surface finishes include lime render and red cedar shingles and boards.

The site layout is designed to reflect ancient field patterns and to promote diversity of habitat. 'Public space is a vital part of larger village life,' says David, and RHM provided three low-maintenance communal gardens including a wild flower meadow, allotments and an orchard of traditional varieties of Suffolk apples in the landscaping of the development. In 2009, Riches Hawley Mikhail Architects was awarded Building

Design Housing Architect of the Year 2009. The firm carried out other work in the education and commercial sectors.

Such a sustainable approach is not always possible in the refurbishment of an inner-city listed house. However, at the East London House, David Mikhail won a Wood Award in 2012 for his use of sustainable timber in the construction of a large rear extension which, in one airy, lofty room reunites the original Georgian house, creates a relaxed and uplifting living space in the centre of London, and reinstates the connection between house and garden.

## Uniting house and garden

At the start of the project, David was faced with a divided house and garden. A modern glass conservatory gave the only rear access via an internal spiral staircase. Alterations over time had gradually changed what was once a grand home

▲ Figure 4.6

**The architect's elegant detailing is well demonstrated in the minimalist white kitchen island and units and in the thin, stretched, linear stainless steel cooker hood.**
*Photo: Tim Crocker*

into a jumble of dark, disconnected rooms, with no meaningful access to the garden. The brief was to reinstate the original interior and to design a new kitchen/dining/living room overlooking a redesigned garden. In the first phase, recent additions such as access stairways and extensions were removed. The original hall and curving Georgian staircase were restored as the central feature to the entrance front of the house. On the upper floors, the original layout was largely intact and bedrooms and bathrooms were refurbished.

Moving beyond the original fabric of the house, passing either side of the staircase, a new contemporary realm is entered. The hall opens on to a mezzanine in a large double-height library and living space with views across the garden through floor-to-ceiling glazing. 'We were keen that this journey from the old to the new was explicitly experienced,' David explains. A staircase with a patinated bronze balustrade leads down to the lower level and the junction between old and new is highlighted through the use of linear rooflights. The basement and rear garden were excavated to give a level access and 'a sense of openness to the landscape while the gentle terracing of the garden avoids the sense of being underground,' says David. The garden, also designed by Mikhail Riches with planting by Jane Brockbank, is divided into two zones: a formal walled garden with water features and raised beds and, beyond it, a more informal area with mature trees and a lawn for outdoor activities.

## Timber structure

In contrast to the traditional brick construction of the existing house, the extension is a predominately timber and steel structure. The central double-height library and dining space is formed from glulam laminated larch portal frames from

Figure 4.7

**The lighting of the different interior spaces has been carefully considered so that the house comes alive at night.**
*Photo: Tim Crocker*

Figure 4.8 ▲▲

**Formal terracing close to the house leads to an informal area of grass with mature trees: a city-centre oasis.**
*Photo: Tim Crocker*

Finnforest. The floor to the upper library gallery was designed to be as thin as possible. All the timber used in the project is white-oiled Siberian larch, including the purpose-made sliding doors, the floors, joinery and external cladding.

A white brick with light grey lime mortar was specified for new interior walls and for retaining walls, raised beds and terracing in the garden. The white finish reflects and maximises the available light. Pale-coloured Pietra Serena stone has been used for wall copings and terracing to complement the white walls. 'These materials were chosen to provide texture and scale, to achieve a domestic intimacy,' says David. 'They also mediate between both the feel and the construction of the new and the older parts of the house, the inside and the outside.'

## KEY FEATURES

- Sustainable timber construction;
- Creation of large kitchen/dining/living/library space;
- Reintegration of house and garden;
- Limited palette of quality materials ties together old and new building.

**Site:** East End of London
**Start on site:** January 2012
**Completion:** August 2012
**Client:** Confidential
**Contract value:** Confidential

## AWARDS

Wood Award Private Category Winner 2012
NLA 'Don't Move, Improve!' Award 2015

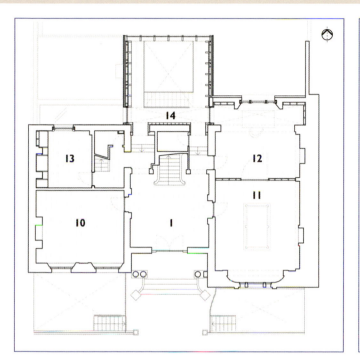

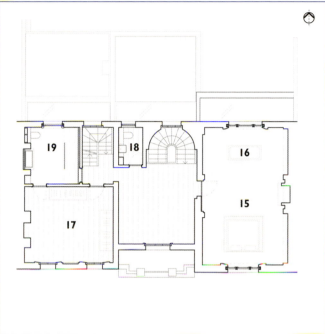

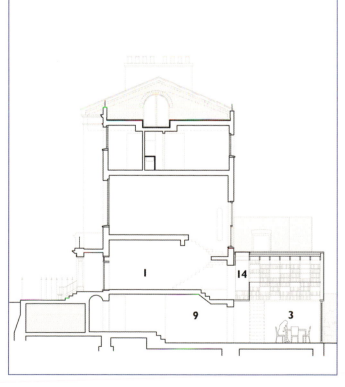

◄ Figure 4.9

*Clockwise from top left*
**Ground floor plan**
**First floor plan**
**Section**
**Lower ground floor plan**

**Key**
1   Entrance
2   Sitting room
3   Dining area
4   Kitchen
5   Bedroom
6   Shower room
7   Wine store
8   Larder
9   Hall
10  Snug
11  Billiard room
12  Study
13  Cloakroom
14  Library
15  Master bedroom
16  Bath
17  Dressing room
18  WC
19  Shower room
*Images: Mikhail Riches*

## Timber Fin House, Winns Avenue, Walthamstow, London Borough of Waltham Forest
by Neil Dusheiko Architects

• 19th century end of terrace house

In contrast to the deep-plan terraces of Victorian cities, some 19th-century artisan housing was built with larger gardens to allow for an element of sustainability; the growing of vegetables, space for livestock and the recycling of waste. Typically, these houses are only one room deep, presenting a double front to the street with living rooms on either side of a central entrance door. Neil Dusheiko has transformed an example of this modest type of dwelling in Walthamstow, adding a timber-framed, single-storey extension and flooding the interior with light.

Neil studied at the University of Witwatersrand, Johannesburg, South Africa and practised in Sydney. He found relocating to London a real contrast. 'Moving to England was a definite culture shock,' says Neil. 'The privileged in South Africa live in detached houses set in large plots in gated communities in a blockaded streetscape. In direct contrast, houses in London are largely open to the street with front gardens forming a line of defensive space that is essentially public. London is bound by strict planning laws to protect the dense historic fabric but there are also special cases where there is the opportunity for innovation.'

 ◀◀ Figure 4.10

**Hinged and sliding/folding doors open up the new accommodation to the garden. Sunlight streaks across the vertical timber cladding, creating ever-changing textures and light effects.**
*Photo: Daryl Dusheiko*

◀ Figure 4.11

**The single-storey rear extension is timber framed and clad in timber in keeping with existing structures in adjoining gardens. Different functions and volumes are reflected in the 'informal stack' of three boxes.**
*Photo: Daryl Dusheiko*

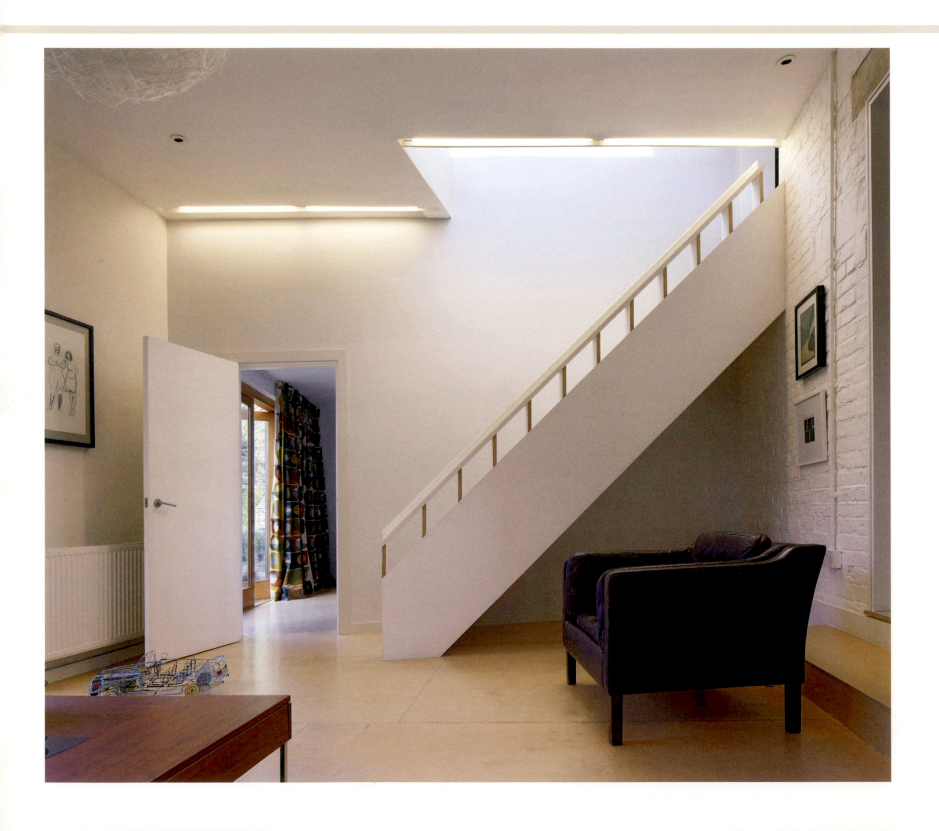

## Collaborative approach

'The project began one afternoon while sitting with the client on their existing terrace discussing ideas about how to create more space for the family in the tiny terrace house,' says Neil. 'We thought it would be interesting if the existing central staircase in the double-fronted house somehow continued up and over into the garden from the mid-landing and so the idea of extending the house came about.'

A combination of a series of enlightened clients, appreciative planning officers, unusual building types and Neil's creative approach has resulted in a series of innovative domestic projects which have helped him to establish a growing architectural practice in London's Clerkenwell, an enclave of several emerging firms. One of his first projects, the Timber Fin House in Waltham Forest, is the result of collaboration with his clients. The resulting house is an exemplar of how to breathe new life into a tired building.

The original cottage is one room deep, arranged lengthways on to the street. On either side of the entrance door are the sitting room and dining room, above these on the first floor are two bedrooms and a two-storey side extension houses the kitchen on the ground floor and bathroom on the first floor. The benefit of this configuration was that there is a sizeable garden but also plenty of space for a large extension.

## Sustainable timber construction

The local planners insisted that any extension should utilise the building materials of the original house: brick walls and pitched slate roof. However, Neil's client wanted a timber-framed and timber-clad extension as it was more sustainable and Neil convinced them that a timber structure in the leafy rear garden was more in keeping with the existing timber structures – sheds, fences and so on – in the gardens of adjoining properties. 'The concept was to create a series of different volumes to accommodate the various functions in an informal stack of boxes placed next to each other like packing crates,' Neil explains. 'The extension exists as three timber containers sitting next to and on top of one another with a singular nature borne out of using one material.'

A brick extension may have been possible under permitted development but Neil's clients were set on an all timber addition and the scheme was submitted for planning permission. Due to the early consultation Neil carried out

◄◄  Figure 4.12

**A new staircase in the living room gives access to two first-floor bedrooms and a bathroom. The master bedroom is on the ground floor, opening on to the garden.**
*Photo: Dennis Gilbert/VIEW*

◄  Figure 4.13

**Existing door and window openings have been retained between the kitchen and the new living room so that the original form of the building is still apparent.**
*Photo: Daryl Dusheiko*

with the planning department, his designs were supported by the conservation officer and the plans were approved with no amendments to the initial design. The project later received an award for best residential extension from the local authority as part of their annual design awards.

## Doubling the footprint

Neil used the proportions of the existing rooms to work out how large to make the new extension so that the new living space would have a hierarchy but also relate well to the smaller spaces. New accommodation on the ground floor more than doubles the original footprint of the house. The former sitting room is now a study/guest bedroom and the

Figure 4.14 ▶

**The vertical timber cladding is designed to catch the slanting sunlight, creating interesting patterns of light; this inventive handling of light is continued on the interior of the house.**
*Photo: Neil Dusheiko*

Figure 4.15 ▶▶

**Rooflights and artificial light strips illuminate the top of the staircase. The manipulation of light is one of the key elements of the new intervention.**
*Photo: Dennis Gilbert/VIEW*

rear extension houses the new living area and the master bedroom, together with a new staircase to the first-floor landing. New openings have been formed between the kitchen and dining room and the living area, although the original form of the building is still apparent.

The rear of the house faces north and manipulation of light is one of the key elements of the new intervention; Neil's client is a film-maker, someone who plays with light, with images, with effects to create his very special art form. 'He was interested in the cinematic qualities of light,' says Neil. 'So I designed a staircase "funnel" to catch the light, to create amazing light effects internally as the sun moves around in the afternoon and evening.'

## Sustainable materials

The north-facing rear façade is asymmetrical with two cranked planes clad with vertical timber fins angled to catch the evening light, creating a magical and ever-changing effect as the light flickers through the surrounding trees, distorting and disturbing the shadows. Carpentry skills came to the fore in the building of the single-storey extension. The main

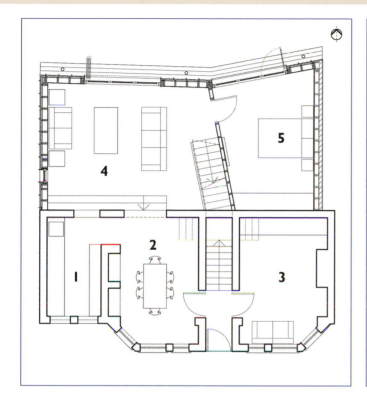

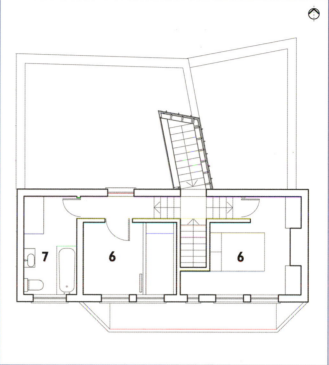

◀ Figure 4.16

**Ground floor plan,** *far left*
**First floor plan,** *left*

**Key**
1 **Kitchen**
2 **Dining room**
3 **Study**
4 **Living room**
5 **Master bedroom**
6 **Bedroom**
7 **Bathroom**
*Images: Neil Dusheiko Architects*

structural framework is built out of oak and the cladding is Siberian larch from local sustainable sources, which will weather to a silvery-grey over time. Wastage was minimised during construction. For example, the height of the extension was regulated by the length of the larch planks so that any wastage from offcuts was virtually eliminated; there are few visible joints. Birch plywood sheets are utilised for the flooring and the staircase is formed from laminated plywood.

The larch planks are mounted on to battens fixed to Panelvent sheathing boards which have a high 'racking' strength but also allow for a water vapour permeable construction. Panelvent is made from wood chips and forest thinnings, utilising a Masonite defibration system to combine low formaldehyde emissions in use and low embodied energy in manufacture. The original Panelvent board has now been replaced with a new version, Panelvent DHF.

'The use of timber gives a warmth and richness and it seems appropriate in the suburban context of this outlying district of London which is close to water reservoirs and Epping Forest,' says Neil. The roof of the extension is designed to allow for a

**KEY FEATURES** 🔑

- Sustainable timber construction;
- Built by a team of highly skilled carpenters as opposed to a traditional building contractor;
- Use of artificial lighting to enhance natural light sources;
- Innovative use of rooflights and windows to flood previously dark interiors with light and to create interesting light effects.

**Site:** Fin House, Walthamstow
**Start on site:** June 2009
**Completion:** October 2009
**Client:** Bella Relph
**Contract value:** £74,000

finishing layer of sedum to be added at a later date, as the initial budget did not allow for this.

The young family was able to live on site during construction of the extension, which saved additional rental costs. Once the new work was completed, a temporary partition was removed, uniting the two ages of the house and extending the use of the house into the following centuries.

## Long House, Woodfield Drive, Winchester
by Dan Brill Architects

- 1950s' detached house
- Suburban street with planning restrictions

In a street of unexceptional 1950s' detached houses, Dan Brill's clients thought that they would be allowed to demolish the property they had acquired and build a new uncompromisingly modern home. But this proved not to be the case; the Winchester planners preferred that the existing house should be retained to preserve the 'uniformity' of the street. If demolition were to be approved, they would then require two new houses to be constructed due to the size of the site. Dan came up with a radical solution. He gutted the original house, keeping the shell as a double-height living space and pierced it through with a long rectangular entrance and bedroom block, which extends from the front driveway far down the spacious garden.

### Twin living space

The design approach is indicated on the restrained front façade. Where there was once a conventional porch with a pitched roof and an integral garage, an elegant, minimalist porch projects beyond the original façade, reflecting the shape of the rear extension. To the right of the large obscured glass screen is a full-height timber entrance door and side panel. At night the glass panel is illuminated, revealing the ghostly outline of the staircase to the first-floor snug and television room

◄◄ Figure 4.17

**The minimalist kitchen is tucked in under the first-floor mezzanine. Existing windows are retained on the front façade to illuminate the double-height space. A diffused glass screen lights the open-plan entrance hall with its sculptural staircase.**
*Photo: Edmund Sumner/VIEW*

◄ Figure 4.18

**Dan Brill's design approach is indicated on the restrained front façade. An elegant, minimalist porch projects beyond the original façade, reflecting the shape of the rear extension.**
*Photo: Edmund Sumner/VIEW*

Figure 4.19 ▶

**A wood-burning stove sits on a concrete plinth to form the hub of the new double-height living space which has been formed from the scooped out interior of the existing house. The remaining section of first floor is clad in vertical timber, harmonising with the timber-clad bedroom extension which runs off down the garden.**
*Photo: Edmund Sumner/VIEW*

Figure 4.20 ▶▶

**All bedrooms in the crisply detailed new extension open on to a paved rear terrace. The slim eaves detail disguises the thickness of the well-insulated flat roof.**
*Photo: Edmund Sumner/VIEW*

located on a small section of the first floor which has been retained. The existing windows of the house on the left of the façade now illuminate the two-storey living space.

On entering the house, the plan can be easily read; there is a view right down the top-lit bedroom corridor to the garden in the far distance. To the left, the spacious entrance hall leads around the staircase into the dining/kitchen area and the large two-storey living room. A wood-burning stove set on an L-shaped, cast-concrete hearth and log-store forms a pivot to the plan. The space flows out into the garden through full-height doors uninterrupted by a change in floor level between inside and the external terrace paving. Alternating panels of vertical timber cladding and glass panels of varying widths create a visual rhythm reinforcing the sense of advancing space and movement along the new linear addition to the existing house.

Dan's clients, Ian and Lucy Golding have three children and wanted a spacious and modern family home with four to five bedrooms. 'They are both keen "foodies", enthusiastic cooks, and wanted a spacious open-plan kitchen at the heart of their home,' says Dan. The detailing is minimalist with a restrained dining table and bench seating and flush white kitchen units. A built-in fridge/freezer and all the usual cooking appliances are set into the dividing wall between the kitchen and the bedroom corridor.

## Minimising waste

'By retaining the existing structure, we were able to minimise demolition and waste,' says Dan. 'This approach also reduced the divergence between client budget and expectation as well as avoiding a conflict with the planning department regarding the streetscape.' The new bedroom wing is constructed of timber – a construction method preferred by the practice for its sustainability, with full-height, flush-glazed windows and doors, interspersed with panels of vertical timber boarding, opening on to the south-facing terrace. At the far end there is a master bedroom with large glazed doors. Hemp insulation has been used in both the new structure and to upgrade the existing house.

Dan wanted the new wing to be clearly distinguished from the original house. Its sleek detailing gives it an abstract sculptural form. Creating a unity between outer and inner space, the materials continue from the external elevation into the interior where they are used to clad the wall to the first-floor snug. Polished cast concrete flooring also extends from the living area on to the external terrace. The eaves detail is particularly slim; the timber and glass panels extend in front of a recessed housing for window blinds, disguising the depth of the roof structure. Dan Brill now lives and works in Los Angeles.

## KEY FEATURES

- Existing structure retained to avoid planning problems;
- Original house gutted to form a single two-storey space and mezzanine;
- New accommodation all in a single wing;
- Sustainable timber construction.

**Site:** Woodfield Drive, Winchester
**Start on site:** January 2011
**Completion:** November 2011
**Client:** Ian and Lucy Golding
**Contract value:** Confidential

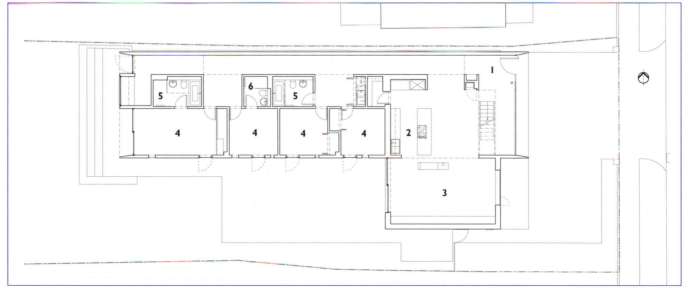

◄ Figure 4.21

**Ground floor plan**

**Key**
1    **Hall**
2    **Kitchen**
3    **Living room**
4    **Bedroom**
5    **Bathroom**
6    **Shower room**
*Image: Dan Brill Architects*

Figure 4.22 ▶

**The new upper ground floor extension sits on an earlier single-storey addition. Lightweight timber-frame construction meant that no additional structural work was required to the existing foundations.**

*Photo: James Potter*

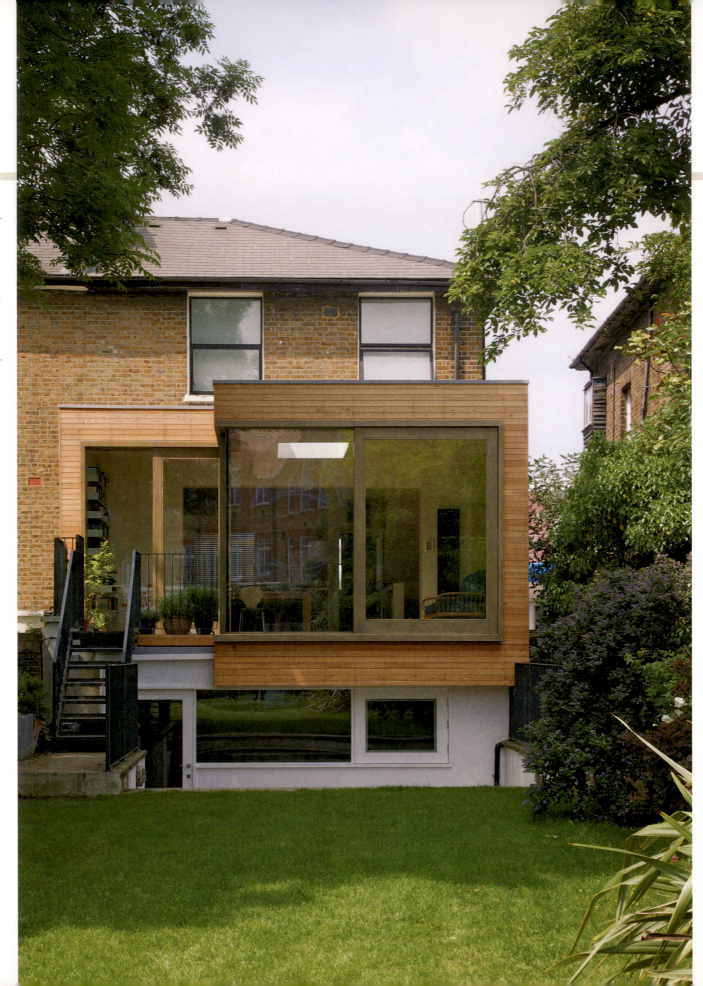

## Goldhawk Road, Shepherd's Bush, London Borough of Hammersmith and Fulham
### by Waind Gohil + Potter Architects

- Victorian semi-detached house
- Conservation area

Refurbishing an existing house and extending its life is, in itself, a form of sustainable construction. In assessing each domestic renovation project, several factors have to be taken into account: structural condition, the clients' aspirations, the available budget and the need to adopt an ecologically sound approach and to increase energy efficiency. Only then can the necessary level of intervention be gauged. Sometimes a less intrusive approach can be the more sustainable, and the most economic solution to the brief.

Waind Gohil is a medium-sized practice in west London. For 10 years, Phil Waind worked for The Manser Practice, a firm founded by Michael Manser in 1960. Michael's first project was a house for his parents and he built his reputation on a series of contemporary houses acknowledging his debt to the work of Mies van der Rohe. The Manser Medal, administrated by the RIBA, was set up by Michael as an annual award to recognize the best one-off modern houses in the UK.

At Goldhawk Road in west London, Waind Gohil + Potter Architects was commissioned to increase the living accommodation of a Victorian semi-detached house dating from the early 19th century. The house was of a simple, classical and practical design with solid stock brick walls and a pitched slate roof. The brief was to extend the living space at the upper ground floor level and to improve the

◄ Figure 4.23

**Glazed doors slide away to open up the sitting room to the views of the mature garden. A sheer glass balustrade protects the drop without restricting sightlines.**
*Photo: James Potter*

Figure 4.24 ▲

**Structural framing and tracks for the doors are recessed into the floor and ceiling so that they do not interrupt the views and flow of space. Butt-jointed glass panels form the corner of the extension so that the building enclosure dissolves.**

*Photo: James Potter*

interconnection between the house and the garden and, on the lower ground floor, to create a master bedroom suite and utility room. It was decided to retain an existing, comparatively recent extension at lower ground floor level and to use the existing structure as the base for the new addition.

The house is not listed but is registered locally as a 'Building of Merit'. No alterations were permitted on the street elevation and the design of the new extension had to take account of views from neighbouring properties and the impact on adjoining houses and gardens. The house had been renovated about a decade earlier. As part of this project, the existing upper ground floor of the original house was converted into an open-plan kitchen/dining/living space opening on to a raised terrace above a new rear extension constructed at lower ground floor level, which housed two bedrooms.

To suit their growing family, the clients decided to embark on a second phase of refurbishment. The children were to be relocated to the top floor; a master bedroom suite and utility room would be created on the lower ground floor; and the living space on the upper ground floor would be increased by building a further extension: a new sitting room in a timber

and glass pavilion which would sit on the existing lower ground floor extension.

## Lightweight timber structure

To avoid any necessary strengthening to the existing foundations, a lightweight timber-framed structure was proposed. The roof to the earlier extension was removed and the masonry walls repaired and consolidated. A new timber floor was then constructed to form the base of the new addition. Cantilevering out over the new extension, the new flat roof at the higher level is supported by a central, single timber column. To maximise natural daylight — the rear of the house faces south — and to take advantage of the views across the garden and into neighbouring gardens, the walls of the sitting room extension are fully glazed.

Purpose-made glass doors with stained Accoya timber frames (see Materials and technologies chapter, page 192) slide away to open up the room to the garden. Structural framing and tracks for the doors are recessed into the floor and ceiling so that they are invisible from the inside and do not interrupt the views and flow of space. Butt-jointed glass panels form the corner of the extension so that the building enclosure dissolves — a favoured modernist device pioneered by Gerrit Rietveld and other masters of the Modern Movement. A frameless glass balustrade guards the terrace edge when the larger glass panel is open. In addition, a linear frameless rooflight allows sunlight to penetrate deep into the centre of the house.

At 2.8 m, the floor-to-ceiling height of the existing ground floor rooms is comparatively generous and this has added to the airy, lofty feel of the extension. Planning guidelines allowed this volume to be continued into the new extension, emphasising the effect of a *piano nobile* overlooking the garden, an appropriate form for this classical house.

The original Victorian architecture is severely geometrical and the modernist extension is in total harmony with this both in form and in the use of complementary building materials. 'We wanted the new addition to be contemporary without being too austere,' explains Phil Waind. Siberian larch cladding was specified to soften the impact of the new structure. This will not require any ongoing maintenance and, over time, it will weather to a silvery-grey. All the timber — both the cladding and the structural frame — is from sustainable sources; no steelwork is used in the construction.

## KEY FEATURES

- Lightweight, timber construction;
- Cantilevered roof;
- Use of existing foundations;
- All timber from sustainable sources.

**Site:** Goldhawk Road, London W12
**Start on site:** August 2011
**Completion:** February 2012
**Client:** Confidential
**Contract value:** Confidential

At Goldhawk Road, a simple and elegant contemporary extension to the *piano nobile* has been created which harmonises with and enhances a cool, classical Victorian villa.

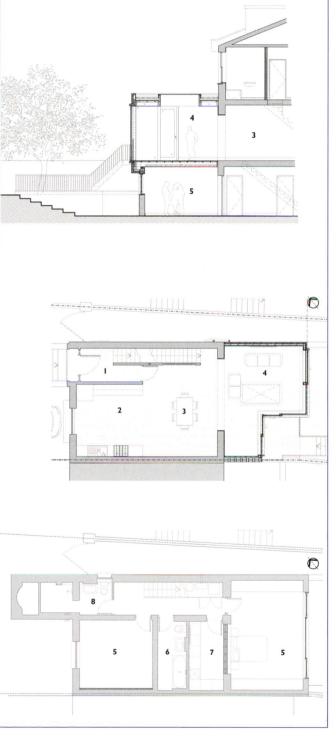

◄ Figure 4.25

*From top to bottom*
**Section**
**Upper ground floor plan**
**Lower ground floor plan**

**Key**
1   Hall
2   Kitchen
3   Dining area
4   Living room
5   Bedroom
6   Bathroom
7   Utility
8   WC
*Images: Waind Gohil + Potter Architects*

◄◄ Figure 4.26

**Detail of the sliding doors.**
*Photo: James Potter*

# Illuminating the basement

## Introduction

High property prices in central London and planning restrictions have meant that the risky and expensive option of converting available basement space is an economic possibility in the capital. However, these developments can be controversial. Ground conditions can be difficult to ascertain in advance and unknown factors can lead to soaring and uncontrollable construction costs once work is under way. Other potential problems are connected with high water tables and the management of ground water and the structural stability of adjoining properties. Several local authorities now also request the analysis of borehole samples, which can require the complete removal of the ground floor, with no guarantee that approval will be granted.

Lowering the lower ground floor and adjoining garden is a more economic and less intrusive option. This can make a huge improvement to the living space of a typical terraced house and there are many firms of architects and contractors in London who specialise in this type of project. Phil Coffey has completed an impressive portfolio of domestic refurbishment projects, mainly in his home borough of Islington, to the extent that he was able to organise a walking tour of half a dozen of his renovation projects as part of London's Open House event held in the capital each autumn. His own house in Whistler Street established the template: a lowered lower ground floor with glazing to the garden admitting light into the centre of an open-plan living space; extensive use of exposed concrete, power-floated and polished for the floor, for upstands, fireplaces and for kitchen worktops; a limited palette of finishes, allowing the occupiers to customise the interior; minimalist built-in furniture to hide the accretions of daily life. At a listed Georgian house a stone's throw from Camden Passage, Phil Coffey has developed this theme, creating new accommodation around a glazed courtyard in place of a dark back garden and garage.

In the more densely developed area of Hoxton in the East End of London, David Mikhail has hewn a double-height living space out of the two lower floors of a narrow terrace house, reducing the level of the garden to admit more light. A similar approach was taken by Paul Archer in a terrace house at the top of Highgate West Hill in north London. The formal ground-floor reception room with its carefully restored original features now opens into a double-height, fully glazed dining space which opens on to the garden. Here the ground level has also been lowered to improve access, establishing an intriguing interface between outside and inside, between old and new.

*Lowering the ground floor and adjoining garden can make a huge improvement to the living space of a typical terrace house; more light will be admitted to a previously dark interior and there will be a stronger connection between the living space and the garden.*

◄ Figure 5.1

**Whistler Street,
London Borough of Islington
by Coffey Associates.**
*Photo: Timothy Soar*

Figure 5.2 ▶

**Dining/living space viewed from the hall. The polished concrete floor reflects light deep into the interior.**
*Photo: Timothy Soar*

# Whistler Street, London Borough of Islington
## by Coffey Architects

- Victorian two-up, two-down terrace house
- Conservation area

Drawing on a spatial awareness, a sensitivity for context and utilising a limited palette of materials, Phil Coffey has created a progression of domestic interiors in central London. His own house in Whistler Street, a few minutes' walk from Highbury Fields in Islington, was used as a test bed for his ideas. A quiet secluded oasis behind the grander Georgian and Victorian houses of Islington, Whistler Street is smaller scale with a mix of 19th century mainly two-up, two-down terraced houses lining the narrow street.

'The Victorian terrace is perhaps the most recognisable and treasured of British period properties,' says Phil, 'offering up a wealth of original features to tempt loving, faithful restorers. But this renovation project is not about restoration, it challenges every design principle from the traditional layout, section and materiality to create a logical and hugely enjoyable family home.

'There are several drawbacks to the traditional terrace home: a tight entrance corridor, lightless back reception room and a small kitchen to the rear with limited connection to the garden. This layout clearly evolved in the 19th century to meet the lifestyles of the workers who inhabited these little terraces. Whether the layout was successful then is difficult to say but it bears little relation to the requirements of the sustainable, modern, open-plan lifestyle that many people aspire to live in today.'

### Letting in the light

Phil was looking for an unimproved house which would be a blank canvas for his emerging ideas. An east-west orientation was also important, west being on the garden side, so that the house could benefit from passive solar gain and be flooded with light during the evening; a house for sale on the other side of Whistler Street with an east-facing garden was rejected. The fall in the ground level at the back of the house that Phil bought means that light is not blocked by nearby

properties. 'Light and heat enter the home creating a symbiotic relationship with the outside and allowing for an enjoyable light and fresh living environment,' says Phil.

The house was bought in 2006 and its transformation took nine months towards the end of 2007. Phil explains his approach: 'The design objective was to transform the typical two-up, two-down terrace into a modern urban space for family living. There were four main aims: to strip back the structure and express it, not to create a decorated box; to create a number of different spaces within a very small volume – long, short, tall and narrow for different uses, connected to the city and the sky; to create a place to rest between journeys, not a retreat; and to create a home that is unique in terms of its context which would also benefit from passive environmental design to the greatest degree.'

### Element of surprise

The pretty, cottage-like street façade with its bay window remains; behind this the entire house was rebuilt and completely remodelled. On entering, the kitchen is immediately on the left and steps lead down to the sunken

◀ Figure 5.3

**Whistler Street façade: a typical Victorian terrace 'the most recognisable and treasured of British period properties'.**
*Photo: Coffey Architects*

Figure 5.4 ▶

**Hinged glazed doors concertina neatly back to open up the living space to the small garden courtyard. The house is cooled on hot summer days by a stack effect up the open stairwell.**

*Photo: Timothy Soar*

Figure 5.5 ▼

**Kitchen: Simple and sophisticated detailing of kitchen units and other built-in furniture is key to Phil Coffey's approach in the creation of a neutral background for itinerant urban living to which the occupant can add his or her personal effects, before moving on.**

*Photo: Timothy Soar*

living area. To create height — and an element of surprise and drama — Phil has excavated the ground floor, a technique he uses in many of his domestic refurbishment projects. The kitchen is partly screened by a peninsula unit and high level cupboards so that visitors do not notice the paraphernalia of everyday life in this working part of the house; instead, their attention is drawn to the full-height glass doors at the other end of the room and to the small garden with its whispering bamboo beyond. The traditional rear service wing and side courtyard have been completely swept away and the space incorporated into the open-plan ground floor.

'The kitchen to the front creates a deep "privacy threshold" to the street, maintaining security on the public façade of the house and also buffering the living area to the back,' says Phil. 'External potted bamboo shades the front bay substituting the ubiquitous net curtain – the equivalent of "turning a blind eye" to the city.'

At the heart of the house, Phil has created a 'grand hall … a tripartite moment, a 3.5 m cube defined by the concrete inglenook fireplace and structural steel beam overhead, the staircase and the wall mounted Prouvé Potence lamp. The middle of the plan has been rejuvenated.' Like an ancestral oil painting, a portrait of his wife, Tamsyn, hangs in the 'hall'. A textured, shuttered concrete stub wall divides the kitchen from the living area. The concrete upstand rises slightly above the oak kitchen worktop, hiding any cooking in progress from dinner guests but allowing the cook to see into the living space and talk to friends.

### Heart of the home

The hearth is at the centre of the house and the cast concrete walls form a modernist 'inglenook'. Neat circular holes in the concrete house the fire irons. Polished concrete extends across the floor and forms the steps up to the raised garden,

◄◄ Figure 5.6

**The open fireplace is at the centre of the house. The shuttered concrete stub wall hides views of the kitchen clutter.**
*Photo: Timothy Soar*

◄ Figure 5.7

**A virtually transparent staircase allows light to flood into the centre of the house from above.**
*Photo: Timothy Soar*

which sits, like a stage, at the far end of the room. This concrete 'bowl' expresses the excavation of the ground floor and the underpinning of the party walls and acts as a thermal store, retaining heat from the evening sunshine which is then released into the house, funnelled up the staircase, during the night. This is supplemented by underfloor heating in the kitchen and living room, the only heating in the house.

The staircase is a delicately engineered assembly of tensioned vertical wires, steel stringers and oak treads, allowing light to flood down into the middle of the house and heat to rise from the ground floor. From the first to the second floor the staircase treads become transparent toughened etched glass invisibly attached to the black painted steel supports with double-sided structural adhesive tape, maximising the light entering the house from above. Off the first landing is a bathroom with walk-in shower and raised spa bath – perfect for bathing small children, a 'heroic bath; you don't have to lie on the floor to bathe', explains Phil. The minimalist main bedroom with sleek flush white cupboards concealing services and the fireplace flue – to gain extra space, the chimney breast was removed – is one of two bedrooms on the first floor.

### Natural ventilation

At the top of the house is a study/guest bedroom with a large horizontal window which folds right back to make the most of the view over the surrounding houses to the Emirates Stadium and the hills of north London beyond. Light also floods in through a large skylight. The rear of the house faces west, catching the evening sun and maximising solar gain in winter. On hot days, the garden doors and the second-floor folding windows can be opened to create a cooling stack effect utilising the stairwell as a ventilation funnel. 'Summer overheating is a typical problem associated with Victorian terrace houses,' says Phil.

Figure 5.8 ▶

**At the top of the house is an airy, light-filled study. Windows hinge away to open up wide-ranging views over north London.**
*Photo: Timothy Soar*

## Limited palette

Materials are kept simple to maximise the feeling of space in this small house, easing circulation through the open-plan ground floor. Purpose-designed kitchen cupboards have simple, white, flush doors with sleek stainless steel handles. The oak worktop angles round and laps over the end of the units to meet the floor – very neat and very controlled. The oak floor in the kitchen extends through into the landing and staircase treads; white cupboards extend from the kitchen into the living room; kitchen extract, fireplace flue and service pipes are all concealed in the cupboards; the living room floor is homogenous power-floated concrete; party walls are exposed London stock brick. Power-floated concrete appears in many of Phil's projects. 'You don't need to finish it; it improves with age, polishes up and gets a patina,' he explains. 'It is also more efficient for underfloor heating.' This is all part of Phil's philosophy of creating urban spaces for living. 'I'm fortunate to be practising in north London where I can create modern, architectural interiors,' he explains. His interiors are practical; they can be moved into and lived in with little decoration required.

This radical remodelling of a small terrace house was completed in December 2007 and would not be possible today. Planning for the scheme was initially refused and eventually the project was carried out under permitted development. Now that the house is in a conservation area, this route is no longer available.

## KEY FEATURES

- Excavation of lower ground floor and removal of internal divisions to admit light;
- Cooling stack ventilation via open staircase;
- Limited palette of materials to create feeling of space;
- Coordinated joinery and cupboards to hide clutter.

**Site:** Whistler Street, Islington, London N5
**Start on site:** April 2007
**Completion:** December 2007
**Client:** Phil and Tamsyn Coffey
**Contract value:** Confidential

◀ Figure 5.9

*From top to bottom*
**Section**
**Second floor plan**
**First floor plan**
**Ground floor plan**

**Key**
1   Kitchen
2   Hall
3   Living room
4   Bedroom
5   Bathroom
6   Study
*Images: Coffey Architects*

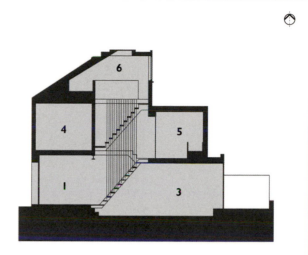

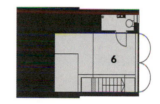

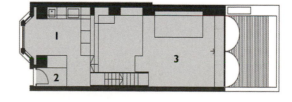

◀◀ Figure 5.10

**The raised bath is perfect for bathing small children. Minimalist white finishes and natural materials create a feeling of calm and enhance the sense of space.**
*Photo: Timothy Soar*

Figure 5.11 ▶

**Timber decking at ground floor level regains the garden space above the new accommodation below. A frameless glass balustrade surrounds the courtyard.**
*Photo: Timothy Soar*

Figure 5.12 ▶▶

**A dark rear garden and garage have been swept away and replaced by a courtyard and bedroom/study. The garden space has been reclaimed on the rooftop terrace and decking.**
*Photo: Timothy Soar*

## Court House, Danbury Street, London Borough of Islington
by Coffey Architects

• Georgian end of terrace house
• Conservation area

Phil Coffey's formula for the creation of exciting urban spaces in a crowded city has been developed and refined in a number of his later projects. The latest of these is at Danbury Street in Islington, a few minutes away from the bustle of Camden Passage. The clients' Georgian end of terrace house had already been refurbished when Phil was asked to introduce new accommodation on the site of a rear courtyard and garage. His solution has far exceeded the expectations of the clients. When the temporary partition was removed

between the existing kitchen and the space beyond, his clients must have thought that they were stepping into another dimension.

As the basement kitchen had already been refurbished, it was not possible for Phil to lower the floor of this room and to introduce more light, as he would have liked, so all his spatial wizardry was reserved for the space beyond. Gloomy courtyard and garage have been swept away and replaced by a magical two-level space where walls dissolve and light dances off polished glass, dazzlingly white render and aluminium.

### Connecting space

Descending from the entrance hall, a glazed slot allows a glimpse into the new living space. Elements of the new room slide into the existing kitchen, meshing the two spaces together. On one side, a stainless steel worktop ends in a neat

*Coffey is pleased that he has re-created a garden in this densely developed part of Islington.*

▼ Figure 5.13

**Danbury Street façade: the elegant classical proportions of a typical Georgian terraced house.**
*Photo: Coffey Architects*

Figure 5.14 ▶

**The sunken living room has a polished concrete floor and upstand incorporating the fire hearth. The bedroom/study can be seen through the glazed central courtyard from which steps lead up to the ground floor external deck.**
*Photo: Timothy Soar*

housing for the flat screen television. On the far wall, three elements merge into an almost cubist sculpture at the fireplace. White lacquered cupboards extend from the kitchen into the family room, culminating as a stainless steel hood over the fireplace; an oak bench for the dining table also extends into the room, angling into the fireplace; the third element is the cast concrete hearth, part of the concrete 'bowl' in the excavated part of the room.

The power-floated concrete floor extends from the kitchen, steps up to the small glazed courtyard and continues into the pavilion-like bedroom beyond. Cast concrete steps lead up from the open courtyard to the ground floor deck with its barbecue area. Moving around the light well with its sheer plate glass balustrade, closer to the house is another seating area with oak decking and a raised planter. A plate glass door opens from the formal ground floor drawing room across a

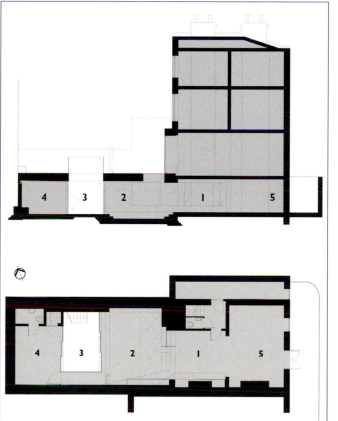

◄  Figure 5.15

**Section,** *top*
**Lower ground floor plan,** *below*

**Key**
1    **Kitchen**
2    **Living room**
3    **Courtyard**
4    **Bedroom/study**
5    **Sitting room**
*Images: Coffey Architects*

◄◄    Figure 5.16

**Three elements merge into an almost cubist sculpture at the fireplace: white laminate cupboards culminating in a stainless steel hood, a built-in oak bench, and the angled concrete hearth, part of the concrete 'bowl' in the excavated part of the room.**
*Photo: Timothy Soar*

toughened glass platform, which admits light to the room below on to timber decking.

## Greening the site

The corner site had a number of advantages. The clients could

### KEY FEATURES 🔑

- Excavation of lower ground floor and creation of glazed courtyard to admit light;
- Garden space regained on upper terrace;
- Limited palette of materials to create feeling of space;
- Coordinated joinery and cupboards to hide clutter.

**Site:** Danbury Street, Islington, London N1
**Start on site:** January 2012
**Completion:** September 2012
**Client:** Confidential
**Contract value:** Confidential

live in the house whilst the new accommodation was under construction; in many projects in central London the only access to the building site is usually through the house itself. Phil is pleased that he has re-created a garden in this densely developed part of Islington, although this aspect was not appreciated by the planners initially. 'The provision of a full-sized garden with areas for planting to the edge restores some green space to this urban site. The removal of the garage also allows more light to penetrate into the rear of the house and especially to the newly formed lower-ground spaces so that the house now enjoys more sunlight during the day and the opportunity for the occupants to enjoy the amenity of significantly improved external space.' The house itself is not listed, although adjoining properties are, so permission for the project was not as difficult to gain as it might have been. Additional accommodation has been created, the basement living space has been extended and revitalised and the garden space has been regained.

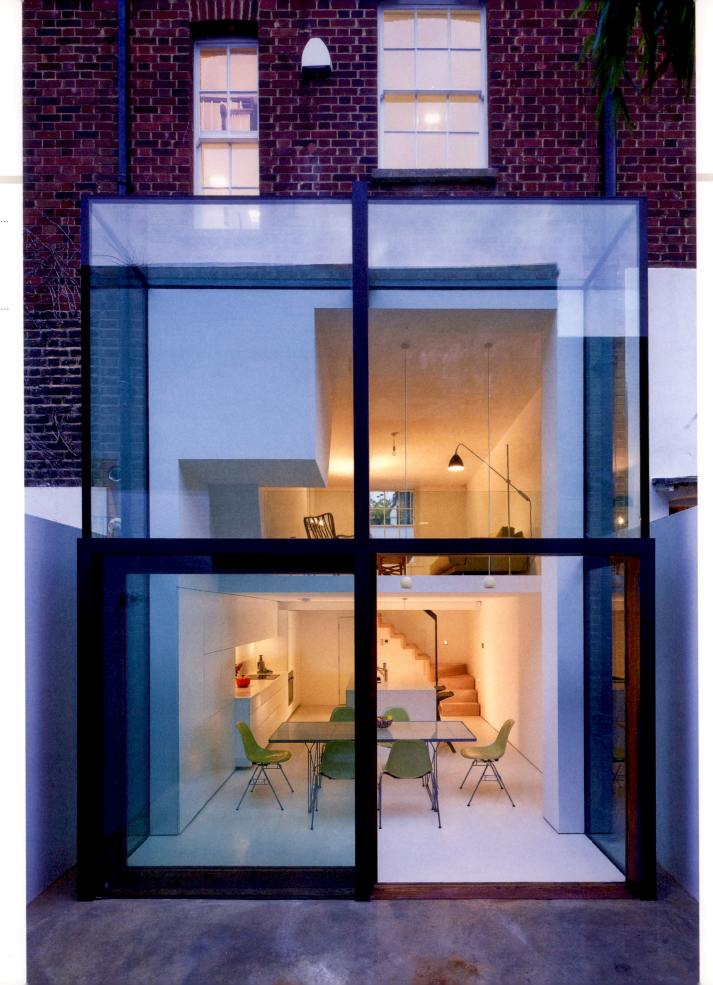

Figure 5.17 ▶

**A double-height glazed extension, just 1 m deep, has been added to the rear of the terrace house.**
*Photo: Tim Crocker*

# Hoxton House,
# London Borough of Islington
by Mikhail Riches

- 19th century terrace house
- Conservation area

Very narrow Georgian and Victorian terrace houses in conservation areas present a particular challenge when it comes to the creation of contemporary living spaces. A series of small rooms arranged vertically around a staircase create a confined cellular layout with some rooms receiving restricted daylight. Traditionally, the basement housed a kitchen and scullery with access from the 'area' at the street front and not much light from a window overlooking the yard at the rear. At a house in Hoxton, Mikhail Riches has added a small glazed rear extension, which has transformed the internal space at the back of the house. Modest in scale, the intervention gives the house 'a grander architectural order and new connectivity'.

## Sensitivity and vision

Working on a historic property requires a certain level of sensitivity and vision to know what to take away and what to add to achieve a harmonious whole suitable for today's lifestyles. 'By taking away fabric as well as adding it, we have been able to carve out a set of new rooms,' David explains. 'The extension to the rear is modest so as not to encroach too much on the garden or to affect the neighbours.' This subtle adaptation has revealed new spatial potential and allowed new ways of living within the historic structure.

In remodelling the two lower floors of the house, a section of the upper ground floor has been entirely removed at the rear of the house to create a two-storey dining area. The space is increased further by the addition of a two-storey glazed extension, which is just 1 m deep. Both the level of the garden and the lower ground floor of the house have been lowered to make the space more practical – the existing head height was only 2 m, to admit as much daylight as possible and to increase the connectivity between house and courtyard garden. On the upper ground floor the rear edge of the room, defined by a frameless glass balustrade, now looks out over the dining area and beyond into the garden.

## Illuminating the plan

From the entrance hall a new staircase descends from the sitting area to the kitchen. A WC has been tucked into the former coal store below the pavement. Light from the ground floor window at the front of the house illuminates the staircase and the rear of the kitchen. All the internal finishes here are white – white units, white polished concrete floor, worktops, walls and ceiling – to maximise light, and the design of the kitchen units is sleek and minimalist. Beyond, the kitchen opens into the dining area and the two-storey glazed extension with its cruciform timber framing.

From the exterior, the glass bay looks like a modern artwork, a Mondrian painting. The frame of Douglas fir is stained to

◄ Figure 5.18

**A double-height dining area has been created by the removal of the rear section of the upper ground floor.**
*Photo: Tim Crocker*

Figure 5.19  ▶

**The white finishes and minimalist detailing increase the sense of space in a previously dark basement.**
*Photo: Tim Crocker*

define its geometry. It wraps around to enclose and anchor what looks like four stacked cubes of glass. At the lower level, the solid dark-stained frame to the sliding door and adjoining panel anchor the composition to the ground. Above, a central timber frame rises and then angles into the existing brickwork of the rear elevation. On either side, the planes of structural glass are butted together so that the construction appears to dissolve, particularly when illuminated at night.

In many of his schemes, David also designs the external hard landscaping, creating a close unity between house and garden. Even in such a small scheme, he has integrated the peaceful courtyard into the living space of the lower ground floor with the design of a beautifully constructed dark-stained timber seat and planter at the end of the garden, which disguises the excavated ground level and reduces the impact of the commercial building which the house overlooks.

### KEY FEATURES    ⚷

- Lowering of basement and garden levels to increase light penetration;
- Simple glass extension transforms the rear accommodation of the house;
- Section of ground floor removed to open up the lower ground floor.

**Site:** Hoxton House, London N1
**Start on site:** July 2009
**Completion:** May 2010
**Client:** Confidential
**Contract value:** Confidential

### AWARDS

RIBA National Award 2011
Don't Move, Improve! Overall Winner 2010

◀ Figure 5.20

**On the upper ground floor, a frameless glass balustrade allows unrestricted views from the living room out into the garden.**
*Photo: Tim Crocker*

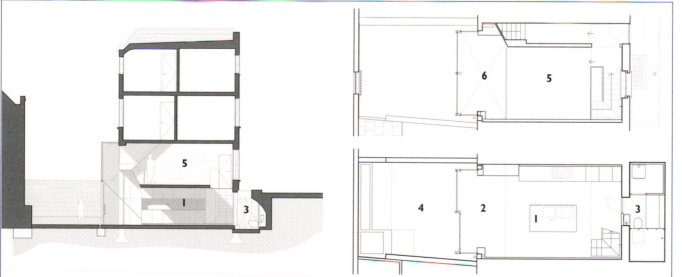

◀ Figure 5.21

**Ground floor plan,** *top left*
**Basement plan,** *bottom left*
**Section,** *far left*

**Key**
1  **Kitchen**
2  **Dining area**
3  **WC**
4  **Garden**
5  **Living room**
6  **Void**
*Image: Mikhail Riches*

Figure 5.22 ▶

The rear wall to the lower ground and ground floors of the Victorian house has been completely removed to be replaced with one of Paul Archer's signature cubic steel and glass extensions. Lowering the garden level also admits more light to the previously dark interior.
*Photo: Nick Guttridge*

# Payne House, Highgate, London Borough of Camden
## by Paul Archer Design

- Victorian terrace house
- Conservation area

Inner-city loft apartments are ideal for a young professional couple, but not so good for a growing family. Myles and Sofia loved their loft lifestyle but, with their first addition to the family on the way, a move was inevitable. Having found a new home on Highgate West Hill in north London, they commissioned Paul Archer to remodel the terrace house, adapting the lower ground and ground floors to provide a large kitchen/dining/living space and to inject the flavour of a loft into the Victorian property.

Paul Archer established his own architectural practice in 1999 and has concentrated on residential work, particularly the remodelling of, and extensions to, existing houses. In 2012 he published a review of more than a decade of his domestic work entitled *Old to New*. Over the years, he has developed a clean contemporary vocabulary for his modernist interventions and he is particularly fascinated by the potential of structural glass, which features in many projects.

## All-glass extension

Although the all-glass extension has, in the opinion of some architects, become something of a cliché, Paul has excelled in the innovative use of glass in domestic refurbishment projects. His key aim in the transformation of dark, cellular Georgian and Victorian terrace houses is to inject as much natural light as possible into the lower floors. Partitions are swept away to create open-plan spaces and as much glazing as possible is incorporated on the garden elevation to admit sunlight.

In Highgate, the rear wall to the lower ground and ground floors of the house has been completely removed to be replaced with one of Paul's signature cubic steel and glass extensions. Despite its modernist credentials, the new intervention sits happily at the back of the Victorian house. 'I wanted to introduce a formal glazed cube as a new element to the composition of the rear elevation,' says Paul. 'In all my schemes I look for a geometric connection with the

neighbouring properties and with the existing elements to be retained on site. The new intervention responds to this context so that the new appears to grow out of the old.'

At the top of Highgate West Hill, the terrain is undulating, so although the upper floors of the house enjoy long views over Hampstead Heath to the south-west, the rear of the house is set into a hillside. The garden was excavated to reduce the ground levels so that there was a stronger connection between the living spaces and the garden. The perimeter of the garden has been terraced with stepped planters.

## Zoned living space

A double-height glazed dining area has been created at the rear of the house, which connects the living rooms on the lower ground and ground floors to the garden and maximises the penetration of natural daylight to the interior. The open-plan lower ground floor is divided into three zones: the kitchen at the front of the house, lit by an east-facing, large pavement-level window; in the centre, a family living space with a fireplace; and, in the double-height space, a raised

▲ Figure 5.23

**Elevation to Highgate West Hill, London.**
*Photo: Paul Archer Architects*

◀ Figure 5.24

**Sliding, folding glazed doors move back to unite the new dining area with the garden. The rear of the garden has been terraced into the hillside.**
*Photo: Nick Guttridge*

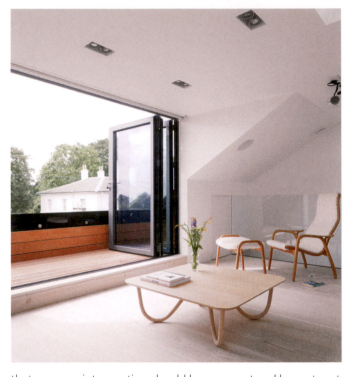

Figure 5.25 ▲

**A gloomy basement has been transformed into an informal, open-plan family living area flooded with light. From the kitchen, parents can supervise children in the living room. The reception rooms on the floor above are 'more formal and adult'.**

*Photo: Nick Guttridge*

Figure 5.26 ▲▲

**At the top of the house is a cinema and family entertainment room. Doors open on to a full-width external terrace which has expansive views over Hampstead Heath.**

*Photo: Nick Guttridge*

dining area which enjoys views over the garden. 'The kitchen is designed so that you can cook and be very much part of whatever else is going on in the space,' Paul explains. 'There is a central play area so that parents can keep an eye on the kids whilst the upper living spaces are kept more formal and adult.'

The glazed extension is one of the first applications in the UK of heated triple-glazed units. Supplied by IQ Glass, the units have a U-value of 0.6 W/m²K. The central layer of the glazing is a plastic film. The outer layer of glass is also self-cleaning which meant that the pitch on the roof sections had to be 30°. Opaque wall panels to the extension are formed from black back-sprayed glass.

## Sensitive repair

From the street, steps rise up to a formal entrance and this formality continues on the interior at this level with the existing hall and staircase. The two ground floor reception rooms have been combined to create one large double-aspect space. As in Paul's earlier projects, original features have been carefully preserved and, where appropriate, reinstated. Paul is a keen supporter of the SPAB's approach to the sensitive repair of historic buildings and the philosophy

that any new intervention should be apparent and honest, not an attempt to reproduce, to fake, the past. When necessary, he calls in conservation experts for specialist advice; his wife is also a conservation architect. 'The old building is allowed to keep its patina of age,' says Paul. 'The new is very new; the old is conserved, enhanced and enriched through contrast.'

This approach is fully expressed on the ground floor of the house where there is a dramatic contrast between the richly detailed original front reception room with its moulded skirting boards, decorative cornice and ceiling rose and the modernist extension beyond. The rear of the room now looks over the double-height dining area. At the interface is a frameless glazed balustrade. At this point, a section of the floor is also glazed so that the formal reception room appears to dissolve into the glazed extension and beyond into the garden and the distant landscape.

On the upper floors, the layout has been reconfigured to suit the clients' requirements. A new master bedroom suite occupies the first floor with the bedroom at the rear of the house away from the traffic noise. At the front of the house is an en-suite bathroom with a freestanding wooden bath, adding a luxurious feel, and a walk-in wardrobe. The second

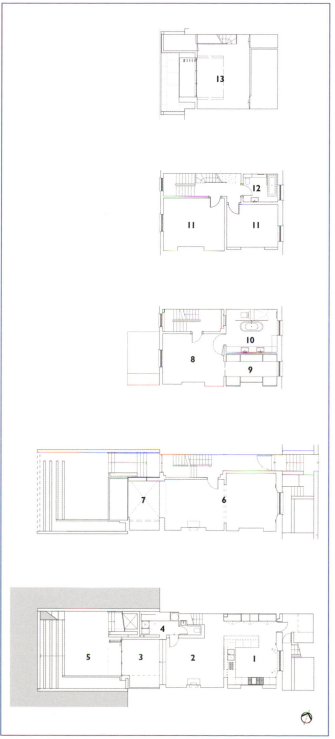

◄◄ Figure 5.27

**An all-glass balcony at the end of the formal living room on the upper floor level projects into the double-height dining area and allows views out into the garden and to the distant landscape.**
*Photo: Nick Guttridge*

floor is the children's domain with a bedroom and a child-friendly family bathroom with ethnic tiles sourced from north Africa and a bench/laundry bin which serves as an ideal perch for sitting on whilst bathing small children. At the top of the house is a cinema and family entertainment room. Doors open on to a full-width external terrace which has expansive views over Hampstead Heath.

A dull Victorian terrace house has been transformed into an innovative contemporary home which forms a perfect background for the clients' large collection of retro Scandinavian furniture and contemporary prints.

## KEY FEATURES

- Remodelling of lower floors to inject natural light into plan;
- Double-height dining space opening on to garden;
- Triple-glazed heated glass units to achieve 0.6 W/m²K U-value;
- Excavation of garden to create stronger connection between living spaces and outside.

**Site:** Highgate West Hill, Highgate, London N6
**Start on site:** May 2011
**Completion:** May 2012
**Client:** Confidential
**Contract value:** £400,000

◄ Figure 5.28

*From top to bottom*

**Third floor plan**
**Second floor plan**
**First floor plan**
**Upper ground floor plan**
**Lower ground floor plan**

**Key**
1   **Kitchen**
2   **Family room**
3   **Dining area**
4   **WC/utility**
5   **Garden**
6   **Sitting room**
7   **Void above dining area**
8   **Master bedroom**
9   **Walk-in wardrobe**
10   **En-suite bathroom**
11   **Bedroom**
12   **Family bathroom**
13   **Media/guest room**
*Images: Paul Archer Architects*

# SECTION 6

# Two-storey additions

## Introduction

All of the refurbishment projects featured in this book involve the complete reconfiguration of the ground floor, sweeping away traditional cellular rooms and creating open-plan living/dining/kitchen spaces which are at the centre of the majority of contemporary homes. Rear extensions at first-floor level are more difficult to achieve, particularly in terraced houses, mainly due to the problem of overlooking adjoining properties and the need to preserve the privacy of neighbours and the benefit of daylight.

Hayhurst and Co has remodelled the upper floor of the rear service wing of a terraced house in Hampstead, making better use of the available floor space in a compact maisonette. Vertical timber cladding and a folding shuttered window give the extension the playful appearance of a beach hut in the centre of north London. In Hackney, Ben Addy of Moxon Architects also uses vertical timber cladding in an extension to an early Victorian classical villa. On the ground floor is an airy kitchen and dining room opening on to the garden; above is an elegant cubic new addition, which harmonises with the refined architecture of the existing house.

End of terrace and semi-detached houses have greater potential for adding extra floor space. In Battersea, Tom Pike of Giles Pike Architects has extended the gable end of a semi-detached Victorian house to create additional space on the ground and first floors. What was once a blank wall has been transformed into a well-designed asymmetrical composition which terminates with a neat gablet in the remodelled roof. Inside is a cool contemporary living space, a hallmark of Tom Pike's work.

Adding a two-storey side extension to a house in one of London's many conservation areas usually faces stiff opposition both from planning officers and local residents. A 'pastiche' approach to the design of a new addition is often suggested as the best route to approval. On the public, street-side face of a structurally ambitious addition to a villa in leafy Twickenham, Andrew Porter has wryly placed a re-creation of one of the existing period windows in a panel which 'floats' above a ground-floor garage. Beyond this, the two-storey extension cuts into the existing house and folds towards the garden so that the rear elevation is suspended from the cantilevered roof structure. The garden elevation is deconstructed; a flight of cantilevered metal staircase treads is sandwiched between the glass wall of the first-floor sitting room and the suspended outer wall which is punctured by a large aperture to allow views over the garden. The new extension dissolves into the landscape and subtly merges with the existing house.

*Rear extensions at first-floor level are more difficult to achieve, particularly in terraced houses, mainly due to the problem of overlooking adjoining properties and the need to preserve the privacy of neighbours.*

◀ Figure 6.1

**Buckingham Road, London Borough of Hackney by Moxon Architects.**
*Photo: Andy Matthews*

Figure 6.2 ▶

Vertical timber cladding to the
first floor of the existing rear
wing continues across the
ground floor of the new side
extension unifying the
elevation and creating the feel
of a beach hut in Hampstead.
*Photo: Kilian O'Sullivan/*
*www.kilianosullivan.com*

## Hampstead Beach House, Roderick Road, London Borough of Camden
by Hayhurst and Co

- Victorian terraced house
- Conservation area

Typical of many rows of terraced houses, Roderick Road, just south of Hampstead Heath, retains its original character on the street frontages whilst the rear of the properties have undergone extension, alteration and adaption over time to suit the individual needs and demands of their occupants. Originally built as a single Victorian house, this four-storey property just south of Hampstead Heath had been converted into a pair of two-storey maisonettes in the 1970s and the lower floors extended to create extra space. These ad hoc extensions created a series of dark, cellular spaces with little sense of fluidity between the existing rooms or connection with the garden.

Hayhurst and Co was commissioned to reconfigure the ground and first-floor maisonette, providing a more effective use of space for the clients and their young family. The brief was to create a new family kitchen which would have a direct relationship with the garden and to rearrange the first floor to provide a guest bedroom and second bathroom.

### Maximising space

The terraced houses occupy relatively narrow plots and the earlier conversion into two separate units meant that further space had been lost on the ground and first floor to allow access to the upper maisonette, so maximising the available

◄◄ Figure 6.3

**Roderick Road in Hampstead retains its original character on the street frontages whilst the rear of the properties have undergone extension, alteration and adaption over time to suit the individual needs and demands of their occupants.**
*Photo: Hayhurst and Co*

◄ Figure 6.4

**At the bottom of the garden is a high wall to an industrial unit, so there were no issues with adjoining neighbours objecting to the radical treatment of the rear facade. With the shutters closed, the windows disappear into the rhythm of the vertical larch cladding.**
*Photo: Kilian O'Sullivan/ www.kilianosullivan.com*

Figure 6.5 ▶

**A huge glazed pivot door can be opened in the summer. Inside and outside are unified by the seamless paving, the similar materials and by lining up the kitchen worktop with the external raised planter**
*Photo: Kilian O'Sullivan/ www.kilianosullivan.com*

Figure 6.6 ▶▶

**Windows in the plywood-panelled study allow views into the kitchen and out into the garden. Light enters the room from a large roof light.**
*Photo: Kilian O'Sullivan/ www.kilianosullivan.com*

space at the rear was a priority. The existing rear two-storey wing was not well built so this was completely demolished and rebuilt. A side extension was continued to the rear wall of the house, increasing the ground floor footprint by just 7 sq m.

From the communal entrance hall, access to the ground and first-floor maisonette is into an inner hall at the centre of the plan. Double doors open into the sitting room at the front of the house and a staircase leads to the first floor. Towards the rear of the ground floor are a small plywood-lined study and an inner hall with adjacent downstairs WC which leads to the rear kitchen/dining area. Upstairs, two interconnecting rooms in the rear wing have been replaced by a guest bedroom overlooking the garden and two bathrooms.

This project ran in tandem with Hairy House (see pages 65–69) and the two schemes have common themes: the creation of a space, a 'stage' around which sculptural elements – walls of joinery, kitchen units – are placed, and the close integration of indoor and outdoor space through careful detailing and treatment of materials. At the Hampstead Beach House, Nick Hayhurst set out to create a 'clear, clutter-free new space in the centre of the plan; like a rug in the middle of a room around which furniture and activities are organised. This rug – the white tiled surface – extends to the outside and pulls the organisation of the internal and external areas together.' A huge glazed pivot door can be opened in the summer; there is a smaller glazed door for everyday access.

## Unifying elements

At Hairy House it was iroko, here white-stained larch cladding wraps around the inside and outside of the spaces to form seats, planting beds, storage areas and the kitchen units. The cladding extends to form the rear elevation of the extension and includes openings for windows with larch-clad shutters. At the bottom of the garden is a high wall to an industrial unit, so there were no issues with adjoining neighbours objecting to the radical treatment of the rear façade. With the shutters closed, the windows disappear into the rhythm of the vertical larch cladding. It is like a beach house and, in the sometimes gloomy light of north London, the bleached timber brings back memories of happy summer holidays.

▼ Figure 6.7

**First floor plan,** *top*
**Ground floor plan,** *bottom*

**Key**
1  **Hall**
2  **Sitting room**
3  **Dining room**
4  **WC/utility**
5  **Study**
6  **Kitchen/diner**
7  **Bedroom**
8  **Family bathroom**
9  **Bathroom**
10 **Guest bedroom**
*Images: Hayhurst and Co*

### KEY FEATURES 🔑

- Sweeping away dark cellular rooms to create free-flowing space;
- Light-reflective planes around which sculptural elements and furniture are placed;
- Design with wit: beach hut-like shutters;
- Coordinated detailing of joinery extending from inside to outside.

**Site:** Roderick Road, Hampstead, London NW3
**Start on site:** May 2011
**Completion:** November 2011
**Client:** Confidential
**Contract value:** £160,000

On both these projects, the architects had the benefit of architecturally trained clients, so their innovative ideas were allowed full reign. One aspect of the recent economic recession is that smaller projects received more attention as opportunities for creative expression on larger schemes became more restricted. Restrictions on government and local authority funded construction projects will continue whilst budget restraint remains a priority. Although Hayhurst and Co is establishing an impressive reputation in the design of buildings for the education sector, it is to be hoped that domestic projects are not neglected as this valuable creative input would be sadly missed.

**A double-height glazed mini atrium forms a central fulcrum between the two main elements of the garden elevation: on the right, a staircase is sandwiched between the inner, plate-glass wall to the living room and an outer suspended solid panel with a large central aperture; on the left, vertical timber cladding extends across the existing rear wing, harmonising the composition.**
*Photo: Andy Stagg/VIEW*

# Cut and Fold House, Amyand Park Road, Twickenham, London Borough of Richmond upon Thames
## by Ashton Porter Architects

• Victorian semi-detached villa
• Conservation area

With a growing family, many parents face the dilemma of whether to move to a larger property or whether to stay put and exploit the potential of their existing home. Maddy Darrall, Simon Reay and their two young sons needed more living space than was available in the house they had occupied for a number of years. They spent a great deal of time looking at alternative houses but these were either outside their financial budget, in a less desirable area or had already been 'improved' in a way which they found unsympathetic. They decided instead to commission Ashton Porter Architects to completely redesign and extend their existing house and, in the process, to create a modern, contemporary living space.

Amyand Park Road is in a leafy residential area of Twickenham, just a short walk from Marble Hill House and the River Thames. A range of Victorian and earlier houses line the meandering road, punctuated by more modern infill. As this is now a conservation area, there were to be some obstacles to the contemporary additions proposed to the existing three-storey 1870s semi-detached villa: the extensions had to be scaled back and an additional room on the third floor had

◄◄ Figure 6.9

**The discreet two-storey extension to a Victorian villa in Twickenham incorporates a large sitting room above a basement garage. A replica of one of the existing windows has been set into a 'floating' panel of white brickwork.**
*Photo: Andy Stagg/VIEW*

◄ Figure 610

**The deconstructed, layered façade to the new side extension.**
*Photo: Andy Stagg/VIEW*

Figure 6.11 ▶

**The double-aspect sitting room has views to the garden at the rear and on to the street at the front. The 'cut and folded' design of the new structure is emphasised by the linear rooflight and the punched-out apertures.**
*Photo: Andy Stagg/VIEW*

to be abandoned. This meant that the bedroom accommodation for a family of four is restricted but the compromise has been that Ashton Porter's proposals for extending the first and ground floors, significantly increasing the living space, were eventually approved.

### Structural gymnastics

Little has altered on the street façade apart from a discreet side extension incorporating a lower ground floor garage with a new double-aspect living room on the first floor. The ramp down to the garage is evidence that the basement area of the house has been excavated to provide the necessary

headroom on the lower ground floor. The architects have made a playful design statement on the façade of this new addition, possibly a wry comment on the planning constraints; a smaller-scale replica of the three-light sash window on the ground floor of the existing house has been placed in a panel of white painted Suffolk stock brick which also mimics the original building fabric.

A stainless steel trim frames this panel, which is separated by strips of glass on all sides so that it appears to float. The panel is pinned back to the structural steel frame which continues to the rear of the extension where more dramatic architectural gymnastics are in evidence.

◀ Figure 6.12

**View from the sitting room into the atrium. Dissolving corners and differentiated planes recall the geometric mastery of Gerrit Rietveld.**
*Photo: Andy Stagg/VIEW*

## Design philosophy

'The strategy to increase the volume of the house was firstly to increase the basement depth to a habitable size and introduce a vertical volume that would connect this newly developed space to the other living spaces of the house,' Andrew Porter explains. 'All the new elements were carefully articulated as separate components by making them explicitly contemporary in their architectural language and always with an interstitial glass condition. Even the front façade to the addition which is 'cut' from the existing façade is framed with stainless steel to emphasise its "artifice" as a new non-load-bearing element. The architectural language becomes more

explicitly contemporary towards the rear as the requirements of planning become less onerous. The cut-out imprint of the house, framed in stainless steel and hung like a picture, was the starting point of the design. That inspired a series of rectilinear frames that fold around the building.'

On the north-facing garden elevation the new interventions wrap around the existing house, creating a unified composition. The two-storey side extension dissolves into a deconstructed layered façade. Full-height glazing to the living room is set back behind a suspended white rendered panel with a large open aperture. Between these two vertical elements, a staircase with cantilevered galvanized steel Tread

Figure 6.13 ▶

**The layering of building elements – the 'cut and fold' of the new extension – creates interesting and ever-changing light effects on the interior.**
*Photo: Andy Stagg/VIEW*

Plate steps descends to the garden level. Lowering the basement floor level has allowed the creation of a fully glazed, double-height interstitial space between the new side extension and the existing rear façade of the house, connecting old and new. Vertical timber boarding of varying widths is used on the lower part of the side extension and on the existing structure, unifying the composition of the rear elevation, blending old and new. The new extension hangs suspended in space; it has an ethereal quality, dissolving the interface between inside and outside.

## Central glazed fulcrum

The fully glazed, double-height central glazed element is the fulcrum of the plan at the rear of the house. Kitchen and dining areas are at the lowest level with views through to the garden. The rear of the house faces north, so maximising natural light levels on the interior was paramount. Sitting at the dining table, lawn-level views of the garden are enjoyed through a large square window.

The refurbished and reinvented house is a composition of new and existing elements which form a composite whole. The design philosophy extends to the finishes and furnishing of the interior. The clients are a television producer and a film cameraman. Possibly due to their work on film sets, they have acquired an eclectic collection of art, artefacts and furniture which enrich the interior. Furniture and materials, some acquired from the ebay auction website, are reclaimed, reused and refinished adding to the richness and interest of the interiors.

As a background to the colourful and unusual contents, materials used on the fabric of the house have been restricted to existing brick and masonry, plain stucco, timber cladding and glass. The sedum roof softens the impact of the new extension for neighbours and enhances views from the upper floor bedroom windows. 'Each material is given an explicit role, whether to separate other elements – such as glass, articulate the new volumes – stucco, or to resurface the existing fabric – timber,' Andrew explains. A Victorian villa with a conventional plan has been given a radical makeover, providing a contemporary home for a young family which should serve their needs for decades to come.

◄ Figure 6.14

*From top to bottom*
**Section**
**First floor plan**
**Ground floor plan**
**Basement plan**

**Key**
1   **Kitchen**
2   **Dining area**
3   **Utility**
4   **Garage**
5   **Bedroom**
6   **En-suite shower room**
7   **WC**
8   **Reception room**
9   **Sitting room**
10  **Study**
11  **Bedroom**
12  **En-suite shower room**
13  **Family bathroom**
*Images: Ashton Porter Architects*

---

**KEY FEATURES** 🔑

- Successful large two-storey addition to house in a conservation area;
- Technically-advanced structural solution which minimises the impact of the scale of the new extension;
- Modernist garden elevation which cleverly blends old and new.

**Site:** Amyand Park Road, Twickenham, Greater London
**Start on site:** March 2010
**Completion:** May 2011
**Clients:** Maddy Darrall and Simon Reay
**Contract value:** Confidential

Figure 6.15 ▶

The restrained, geometric new additions harmonise with the architecture of the rear elevation. Fully utilising the space at the side of the house meant that a rear extension was not necessary, maximising the outdoor space.
*Photo: Edmund Sumner/VIEW*

# Salcott Road, Battersea, London Borough of Wandsworth
## by Giles Pike Architects

• Victorian semi-detached house
• Conservation area

Making full use of a small side passage on a restricted corner plot, Giles Pike Architects has turned a tired Victorian semi-detached house into a smart modern residence. What was once a blank gable end has been transformed into a streamlined contemporary elevation expressing the revitalised internal spaces.

Salcott Road is one of a grid of streets between Wandsworth and Clapham Commons. The area was built up in the later 19th century with good-quality housing for the growing Victorian middle classes at a time when the growth of London was accelerating. The house, on the corner of Salcott Road and Webbs Road, with its decorative stucco window surrounds, cornicing and rusticated quoins, was built in 1895. Although it was in reasonable condition, the time had come for a major refurbishment and upgrade.

Tom Pike's clients are a professional couple, the husband a managing director of a scientific development company and his wife a corporate lawyer. During the gestation of the project, there was an addition to the family. Like many clients of the projects featured in this book, the couple has a strong appreciation of modern architecture and design. 'Their active interest in such matters was helpful to us – the husband grew up in a modernist house,' Tom explains, 'and they were always very enthusiastic when we discussed bold and imaginative design solutions with them.'

To turn the late-Victorian semi into a modern home, Giles Pike was able to maximise the potential of the plot by extending over a small strip of land between the flank wall of the existing house and the pavement of the adjoining road. This allowed the creation of a large open-plan living space on the ground floor. Bedrooms and bathroom on the first floor were remodelled, taking advantage of the additional space above the living space and the loft was converted to form a fourth bedroom. The extension also presented the opportunity of creating a new elevation to the street.

## Planning issues

Giles Pike has decades of experience of extending and remodelling houses, mainly around where the practice is based in Battersea. The firm's philosophy is set out on its website: 'We hold fast to the tenets of classical modernism and Bauhaus design principles … good design should be timeless and enduring and should not be influenced by fads and fashions.' This approach, which they describe as 'user-friendly minimalism', has resulted in a string of modern reworkings of traditional homes.

Modernist additions to traditional houses in conservation areas are easier to achieve at the rear of a property. Where they are in full view of the public, as at Salcott Road, planning officers prefer a contextual, some would say 'pastiche', approach. Giles Pike's proposals for the new elevation, as in all its projects, were uncompromisingly modern. 'Achieving planning consent for such a bold two-storey extension, plus a major alteration to the roof space was not easy,' says Tom. 'We had many lengthy discussions with the planning authority and had to make various minor tweaks to our design drawings before the planners determined to grant the scheme consent.' Although

▼ Figure 6.16

**A discreet side extension has significantly increased the existing floor area of the Victorian semi-detached house in Battersea.**
*Photo: Edmund Sumner/VIEW*

Figure 6.17 ▲

**Utilising a restricted palette of materials, the architects have created an elegant modern side elevation. The horizontal strip window lights the ground floor living room and contrasts with the vertical windows to the first-floor bedrooms. A new roof gablet terminates the composition.**
*Photo: Edmund Sumner/VIEW*

Figure 6.18 ▲▲

**The extended living area with its central wood-burning stove runs the entire length of the house. Light floods in through the high-level strip window.**
*Photo: Edmund Sumner/VIEW*

Giles Pike believes that these 'minor tweaks' compromised the original concept, the quality of the completed building was ultimately recognised by the London Borough of Wandsworth; the council commended the finished project in the Wandsworth Council 2011 Design Awards.

The use of London stock brick for the new addition ties it into the existing house and the surrounding streetscape, but the design of the side elevation is refreshingly modern; there is no attempt at 'pastiche'. Giles Pike has created a completely new façade to the gable end of the house. The composition builds up in layers to the redesigned roof.

Above a wall of London stock brick is a long strip of glazing. 'We were keen that the first-floor extension at the side of the building should appear to float above the ground floor,' says Tom. In many of the practice's rear extensions, a steel structure is inserted to liberate the space on the ground floor. At Salcott Road, the first-floor brickwork is supported by an exposed linear steel beam which runs the entire length of the flank wall and also forms the edge profile to the single-storey extension to the rear. Widely spaced stub columns which

support the linear beam are set back behind the glazing to enhance the 'floating' effect.

Hovering above the glazing is a rectangular panel of brickwork which is slashed by two symmetrically placed narrow vertical windows to the new space on the first floor. Above this, a glazed gablet terminates the hipped roof. The tall slender flue to the living room wood-burning stove adds an offset counterpoint to the composition. From the front, the new extension wall is clearly separated from the existing house by a two-storey glazed slot.

To enhance the strong architectural statement of the extension, the vocabulary of materials is limited: London stock brickwork, mild steel painted a slate grey colour, aluminium framing to the areas of glazing – also slate grey, glass and natural slate to the roof. 'The simple vocabulary of the materials helps to unify the new building elements with the host building,' says Tom. Although the project does not have the level of energy-saving features – solar panels, photovoltaic cells, heat recovery unit and so on – of some of the projects featured here, Giles Pike's extensive interventions, designed

**KEY FEATURES** 🔑

■ Blank side wall transformed into elegant contemporary elevation;
■ Large open-plan living space created out of traditional cellular layout;
■ Transformation of first- and second-floor rooms by comparatively minor addition.

**Site:** Salcott Road, London SW11
**Start on site:** December 2010
**Completion date:** July 2011
**Client:** Confidential
**Contract value:** £350,000

◄◄ Figure 6.19

**The roof of the new addition appears to float. Additional daylight enters through the frameless rooflight over the dining table.**
*Photo: Edmund Sumner/VIEW*

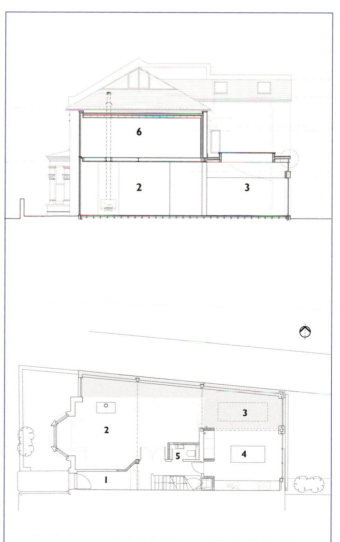

◄ Figure 6.20

**Section,** *top*
**Ground floor plan,** *bottom*

**Key**
1  **Hall**
2  **Living room**
3  **Dining area**
4  **Kitchen**
5  **WC**
6  **Master bedroom**
*Image: Giles Pike Architects*

to current Building Regulations' standards have significantly improved the energy performance of the house. 'We have taken a dilapidated Victorian house that had no insulation at all, ill-fitting single-glazed windows and was using massive amounts of fuel to heat the building, and we have totally transformed the way the building performs,' says Tom. 'It is now heavily insulated, all glazing is of the lowest possible U-value and the heating comes from a low-volume condensing boiler. The building is therefore extremely thermally efficient compared to its original state.'

As well as saving energy, the new side elevation is a positive addition to the street scene. Being close to a primary school, the house is acting as an effective advertising billboard for the Giles Pike practice, resulting in a number of new commissions.

Figure 6.21 ▶

**The client is a keen gardener and the brief was to build a new kitchen/dining room which would open out into the kitchen garden.**
*Photo: Andy Matthews*

## Buckingham Road, London Borough of Hackney

by Moxon Architects

- Victorian semi-detached villa
- Conservation area

The De Beauvoir Estate in East London was laid out in the early 19th century. The original housing was built for the prosperous Victorian middle classes but later in the 20th century the area suffered from social upheaval, bomb damage and unsympathetic redevelopment which has scarred the face of the once peaceful and leafy suburb. However, in recent decades the quality of the housing has been recognised by a new generation of appreciative residents and also by the local authority in the creation of the De Beauvoir Conservation Area.

Buckingham Road runs from east to west, intersecting with De Beauvoir Road, and contains a typical mix of housing, from the 1840s to 20th-century local authority flats. At the western end of the road is a well-preserved series of Victorian semi-detached villas with fine London stock brick walls and bold stucco window surrounds and cornicing. Some of the

villas are linked by adjoining side entrance porches, as is the house which Moxon Architects was commissioned to extend and refurbish in 2010.

The client is a well-respected product designer. He is a keen gardener, so the large space at the rear of the property and the close connection between this and a new kitchen/dining/living space were at the core of the design brief. In response, Moxon Architects has created an elegant timber-clad rear pavilion which houses the kitchen and dining area, opening on to a large paved terrace and beyond to a flourishing, productive kitchen garden.

### Planning issues

The Victorian house had fallen into disrepair and required significant structural repair and the installation of new services, so it presented a blank canvas for the architects' proposals. A cluster of ad hoc rear extensions was removed and permission was sought for a large, unifying ground floor extension with a new bathroom on the first floor. The rear garden is overlooked by adjoining houses and is in full view from the backs of the terrace on the parallel street to the south. There was also the possibility of the proposed first-floor extension being visible from the street over the single-storey side entrance porches, so there was some resistance from the planning officers.

◄ Figure 6.22

**A brightly coloured bank of kitchen units houses all the usual appliances; the rest of the kitchen is kept simple in tune with its outdoor garden context.**

*Photo: Andy Matthews*

Figure 6.23 ▼

**Huge fully-glazed doors slide back to open up the corner of the kitchen/dining space to the garden. The kitchen floor level continues over the recessed track for the sliding doors out on to the granite-paved terrace.**
*Photo: Andy Matthews*

Determined to get an acceptable scheme approved, Moxon Architects put its faith in the simplicity and elegance of the form and external detailing of the proposed new extension and, after some modifications, this approach was successful. 'The external surfaces of the additions to the house are treated as a sequence of timber panels framed by galvanised steel bands,' says Ben Addy, director of Moxon Architects. 'This strategy is also applied to the sequence of spaces within the house, where constrictions in an otherwise open plan have been controlled and manipulated to define circulation and spatial hierarchy.'

## Fully planted green roof

In the completed scheme, the bathroom is a neat timber-clad cube, perched on top of the kitchen/dining room. A small, square casement window allows a restricted view over the garden. To reduce the impact of the extension in terms of views from neighbouring properties and also its environmental impact, the roof is 'fully planted… It is not just a sedum roof,' Ben explains. 'The roof is designed as a giant "tray" with as much soil depth as required to prevent it drying out.' A deep cornice of vertical cedar boarding frames the edge of the roof. Galvanized steel trim protects the end grain and prevents staining by rainwater. Rainwater is collected and stored in an underground tank for use in the garden.

The 'tray' sits over a large kitchen/dining space. Huge fully glazed doors slide back to open up the corner of the room to the garden. Here, the steel structure is supported on a single Miesian steel I-column in its raw, red-oxide finish. The kitchen floor level continues over the recessed track for the sliding doors out on to the granite-paved terrace. Viewed from the garden, the additions form a balanced composition in complete harmony with the Victorian house. 'The rear extension replaced a hotchpotch of earlier additions with a single unifying form that is subordinate to the massing of the principal building,' says Ben. 'The traditional elements of the rear elevation sit comfortably with the proportions of the rear extension.' The limited palette of materials utilised in the new addition – cedar boarding and glass – is unmistakably modern but also harmonises well with the pale London stocks and white-painted sash windows of the existing house.

## Minimalist detailing

In the interior, the kitchen, with its understated white units and grey granite linear worktop and splashback, is minimalist, designed to merge into the background. Moxon Architects adopts a restrained approach to its domestic refurbishment work in London. White painted walls, white finishes and spare detailing are characteristics of the practice's work. 'In this case the aim was to create a multi-purpose living space, so the kitchen had to be discreet.' The client also asked for a colourful counterpoint to the otherwise muted décor. Floor to ceiling units at the rear of the kitchen/dining space which incorporate the guts of the kitchen in the form of a built-in double oven and fridge/freezer are finished in a bright orange laminate, creating a contrast to the white ceiling with its

recessed downlighters, crisp white walls and white floor of polished cementitious screed.

In this project Moxon Architects has achieved a fine balance between conservation, restoration and modernisation. Great care has been taken to restore the existing architecture and to give the historic house a new lease of life. To the rear, a contemporary extension has transformed the room layout to suit the lifestyle of a respected product designer, a resident who, like his Victorian predecessors, is contributing to the growing economy of London.

## KEY FEATURES

- Deep-planted green roof to minimise environmental impact;
- Underground rainwater storage;
- Clean, linear design of extension, which enhances character of existing house.

**Site:** Buckingham Road, London N1
**Start on site:** January 2011
**Completion:** September 2011
**Client:** Confidential
**Contract value:** Confidential

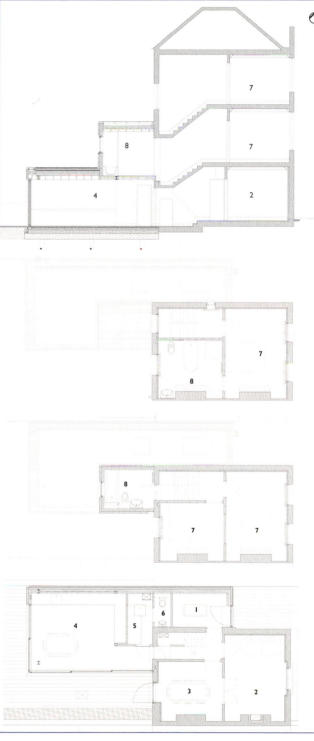

◄ Figure 6.24

*From top to bottom*
**Section**
**Second floor plan**
**First floor plan**
**Ground floor plan**

**Key:**
1  **Hall**
2  **Sitting room**
3  **Dining room**
4  **Kitchen/dining room**
5  **Utility**
6  **WC**
7  **Bedroom**
8  **Bathroom**
*Images: Moxon Architects*

◄◄ Figure 6.25

**At night the kitchen becomes an illuminated garden room with a bold punch of colour on the rear wall.**
*Photo: Andy Matthews*

# Room on the side

## Introduction

One of the most common forms of improvement to the ground floor of a terrace house is the side extension: an infill of the paved yard between the rear elevation of the main house, the side of the projecting service wing and the party wall. Enclosing this space can significantly increase the living area of the house but it can also restrict daylight to the rear reception room.

This section features four London-based versions of this type of extension and a further rear addition in the town of Arundel in West Sussex. Platform 5 Architects, like many fledgling firms before it, founded the practice on a series of small domestic refurbishment projects. The two projects – one in Camden, the other in Hackney – are both excellent examples of how to reconfigure the ground floor of a typical Victorian terrace house. Key features of the practice's work are the removal of internal partitions and the use of a limited palette of materials to enhance the feeling of space and to increase light penetration into the centre of the house. Open-plan kitchen/dining/living areas are created, closely connected to external terraces and garden – the appropriate background for 21st-century family life. Another feature of their work is the attention to detail, particularly the crafting of internal joinery – the design of elements like furniture within interconnecting spaces.

Joinery detailing is also a key element of the interiors of Joe Fraher, to the extent that he has set up his own firm of joiners which now works on projects for other architects and contractors. The Jewel Box in Camden is, as the name suggests, a jewel of a project with each element of the small ground-floor maisonette carefully crafted to achieve the perfect setting for the lawyer and jewellery maker who use it as their London base. Procter:Rihl's extension is of a similar scale. Here they have experimented with a prefabricated building system to create an unusual folded roof which floats above the linear kitchen and dining 'nook'.

In the historic town of Arundel, Waind Gohil + Potter Architects has subtly reconfigured a 200-year-old cottage, rethinking every single element of the interior to maximise the available space. At the rear the architects have rebuilt and extended the existing rear extensions, incorporating a beautifully detailed butterfly roof with a V-shaped continuous rooflight which floods the interior with light.

*Enclosing the side courtyard space can significantly increase the living area of the house but it can also restrict daylight to the rear reception room.*

◄ Figure 7.1

**The Jewel Box, London Borough of Islington by Fraher Architects**
*Photo: Andy Matthews*

Figure 7.2 ▶

**Simple planes and minimalist detailing create a modern interior in a traditional terrace house. The triple-glazed roof glazing above the dining area spans between the existing side wall of the rear wing and the party wall which has been lined with reclaimed brickwork.**

*Photo: alanwilliamsphotography.com*

Figure 7.3 ▶▶

**A huge pivoted glazed door opens the living area up to the garden. The polished concrete flooring extends on to the terrace uniting inner and outer space.**

*Photo: alanwilliamsphotography.com*

## Mapledene Road, London Borough of Hackney
### by Platform 5 Architects

- 19th century, two-storey terrace house
- Conservation area

Small house extensions and other domestic commissions are often seen as a stepping stone to larger projects. Patrick Michell and Peter Allen are the two partners at Platform 5 Architects. A series of small domestic projects supported the creation of the practice and were a test bed for the design approach of the firm. The practice is now working on larger developments, primarily in the education sector, such as Waltham Forest College in north-east London. Phase one of this development, undertaken in collaboration with Richard Hopkinson Architects, involved the refurbishment and

adaptation of an existing 1930s building. The dynamic interior with its dramatic interventions, including a suspended glazed seminar box accessed by an oak-lined staircase – both elements picked out in a vivid lime green – is a clear progression of ideas first worked out in these earlier small domestic projects.

### Cellular to open plan

Patrick founded the practice in 2006 and one of his earliest commissions was the refurbishment of a small, two-storey Victorian terraced house in Mapledene Road in the London Borough of Hackney. Situated in a conservation area, the property had been stripped of virtually all of its period features so there were few constraints when it came to the reorganisation of the interior. The traditional cellular ground floor plan was opened up and extended to the rear to create a free-flowing open-plan space which runs from the front door, around the staircase, through the kitchen and dining area and out into the garden.

▼ Figure 7.4

**Platform 5 Architects has developed a sparse and simple vocabulary for extending ground floor accommodation and adapting traditional cellular layouts to open-plan arrangements. On the left, the courtyard has been transformed into a light-filled dining area which opens into the kitchen which can be seen through the large bay window on the right.**

*Photo: alanwilliamsphotography.com*

Figure 7.5 ▶

**Typical of the high standard of detailing is the new staircase with its timber treads and risers and sheer glass balustrade.**

*Photo: alanwilliamsphotography.com*

Figure 7.6 ▶▶

**The finest quality joinery detailing is a key factor in the sleek appearance of the new interior. A previously dark room has been transformed into a minimalist, modernist, black and white kitchen.**

*Photo: alanwilliamsphotography.com*

A number of 'furniture pieces, a collection of distinct elements' punctuate and delineate the series of rooms. This approach, which has become a key principle in the practice's philosophy, is clearly shown in an exploded three-dimensional drawing of Mapledene Road. The new elements are simple forms, exquisitely detailed. Timber treads and risers fold down the staircase to meet the dark stained elm flooring. A sheer toughened-glass panel forms the balustrade. The minimalist kitchen opens into the dining area. Detailing is precise and is highlighted by the constrasting black and white finishes.

Outside and inside merge imperceptibly. The triple-glazed plane of glass which forms the roof of the side extension disappears into the exposed London stock brick party wall, a new skin of reclaimed brick built to form a cavity wall. At night, the texture of the brickwork is emphasised by wall-mounted downlights. Polished concrete flooring extends from the dining area out on to the external patio, uniting indoors with outdoors. A square bay window projects from the rear wall. The window seat is an area of repose, neither within the house or without in the garden.

Figure 7.7 ▶

**Ground floor plan**

**Key**

1    Living room
2    Study
3    Kitchen
4    Dining area
5    Terrace

*Image: Platform 5 Architects*

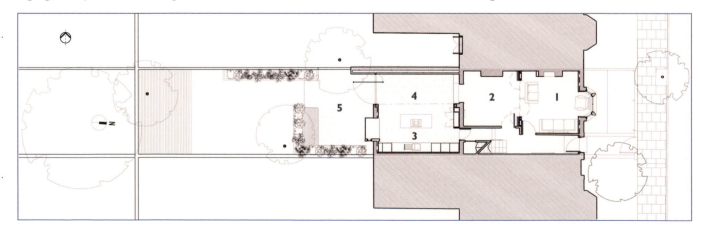

# Shirlock Road,
# London Borough of Camden
by Platform 5 Architects

- Four-storey Victorian terraced house
- Conservation area

The Mapledene Road project was well publicised, winning the Don't Move, Improve! Award in 2009 and it was shortlisted for an RIBA Award, AJ Small Projects Award and Grand Designs Award in 2009. More commissions followed and Peter Allen joined the practice that year. Themes established at Mapledene Road were developed further at Shirlock Road in Camden. The projects are in neighbouring streets; word of the success of the earlier renovation had obviously spread. Here Platform 5 reconfigured the ground and first floors of a four-storey Victorian terraced house and created a new side extension. The clients were a married couple with young twins and the house they purchased was originally divided into two flats. Whilst work was carried out on the ground and first floors, the clients remained on site, occupying the upper two floors.

## Existing constraints

Again, the cellular layout typical of this type of terraced house was swept away so that space now flows from the front door, around the staircase into the kitchen and dining area and beyond into the garden. However, there were a number of constraints. The existing rear extension with its first-floor balcony was to be retained which meant that it was not possible to raise the ceiling height in this important part of the ground floor adjoining the garden.

From the front door, the white oiled, Douglas fir timber flooring extends past the staircase and then steps down two neatly detailed steps with concealed lighting to a dark stone polished floor at the rear of the house.

As at Mapledene Road, the kitchen is white, sleek and minimalist. Adjoining it is the dining area in the new side extension formed by sitting lightweight, zinc-clad panels on top of the existing party wall. The zinc folds over to form the roof. A large rooflight floods the dining space below with

*The simplicity of the design draws attention to the restrained palette of high-quality materials.*

◄◄ Figure 7.8

**An existing ground floor extension and first-floor balcony (right) was retained and a new dining area created in the former courtyard on the left.**

*Photo: alanwilliamsphotography.com*

◄ Figure 7.9

**The party wall was raised to create a lofty, light-filled dining area. Polished stone flooring extends from the living space on to the external terrace.**

*Photo: alanwilliamsphotography.com*

Figure 7.10

**The existing rear extension has been converted into a timber-lined 'snug' where children can play close to the kitchen. Hinged seating gives access to storage for toys and games.**

*Photo: alanwilliamsphotography.com*

Figure 7.11 ▲▲

**The clean white wall and ceiling planes contrast with the dark polished flooring. A huge glazed pivoted door opens on to the terrace.**

*Photo: alanwilliamsphotography.com*

daylight. The room opens into the garden through a massive, pivoted glass door and the polished stone flooring extends out on to the patio, uniting inner and outer space.

### Timber-lined snug

Close to the kitchen is a snug created in the low-ceilinged rear extension, a seating bay which is another example of the architects' interest in spaces which bridge inside and outside. The building contractor is a joiner, introduced to the project by the clients, so the quality of the joinery and cabinetwork is of particularly high quality.

The timber-lined space, aptly named the 'snug', has seating on three sides and a long horizontal window which folds to completely open up the room to the garden. Storage is concealed behind flush timber doors and under the seats; plenty of space for toys as, here, close to the kitchen, the clients' children can play safely. To keep waste to a minimum,

the 7-m long, 400 mm-wide Douglas fir boards were carefully cut and positioned so that the grain matches across the vertical boards.

Opportunities for significant energy-use reduction were limited in both of these projects but the building fabric has been upgraded wherever possible. External walls were internally insulated and glazing upgraded to reduce energy consumption. More importantly, the ground floor of both properties has been transformed with limited interventions. The simplicity of the design draws attention to the restrained palette of high-quality materials and the high standard of finish. These spaces are now perfectly remodelled to suit today's family life; a truly sustainable approach.

Platform 5 continues to work on residential commissions alongside projects in the education, commercial and cultural sectors. In 2016, a domestic renovation and extension of a Victorian terraced house, Facet House in London, won the

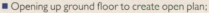

## KEY FEATURES

- Opening up ground floor to create open plan;
- 'Furniture' elements introduced to punctuate and delineate the space;
- High standard of joinery and attention to finish;
- Sensitive handling of indoor/outdoor spaces.

**Site:** Mapledene Road, Hackney, London E8
**Start on site:** November 2006
**Completion:** September 2007
**Client:** Confidential
**Contract value:** £190,000 including £90,000 for the extension

**Site:** Shirlock Road, Camden, London NW3
**Start on site:** January 2011
**Completion:** September 2011
**Client:** Confidential
**Contract value:** £225,000

won the Don't Move, Improve! Award for Best Interior Design. The firm has also completed two new-build 'eco' houses. Backwater on the Norfolk Broads takes its inspiration from the forms and materials of nearby boatsheds. Its remote, off-grid location requires on-site sewage treatment and a water borehole whilst solar panels and a wood-burning stove provide power and heating. Meadowview in rural Bedfordshire incorporates sustainable technologies such as rainwater recycling, photovoltaic array and a MVHR system.

◀◀ Figure 7.12

**The linear rooflight above the dining table also floods the kitchen with natural light.**
*Photo: alanwilliamsphotography.com*

▼ Figure 7.13

**Detail of the junction between the existing rear reception room and the new dining area. White, oiled, Douglas fir timber flooring contrasts with the dark stone polished floor. Subtle and innovative lighting is a feature of the designers' domestic interiors.**
*Photo: alanwilliamsphotography.com*

◀ Figure 7.14

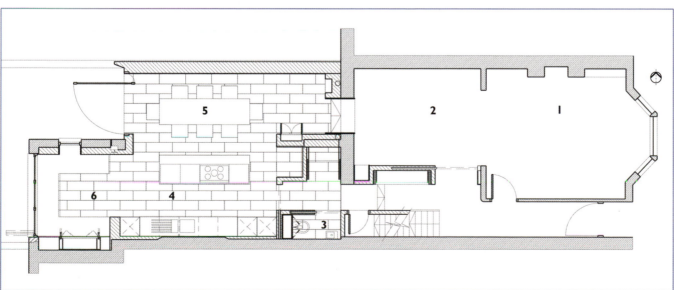

**Ground floor plan**

**Key**
1   **Sitting room**
2   **Reception room**
3   **WC**
4   **Kitchen**
5   **Dining area**
6   **Snug**
*Image: Platform 5 Architects*

Figure 7.15 ▶

**The clean geometry and use of a restricted materials palette of larch cladding and frameless glazing creates a minimalist composition which sits well with the simple classical Georgian architecture.**
*Photo: Andy Matthews*

# The Jewel Box,
# London Borough of Islington
## by Fraher Architects

- Grade II listed Georgian terrace houses
- Conservation area

Basement or 'garden' flats can be dark, damp and depressing but a skilled architect can transform such unprepossessing accommodation, once only suitable for service rooms and domestic servants, into light and airy living spaces. The aptly named 'Jewel Box' in Islington, a short walk away from the busy High Street and Camden Passage, is a fine example of what can be achieved. Attention to detail and a high standard of finish are what elevate this project into a league above more pedestrian conversions.

### London bolthole

The project was a family commission, a chance for Fraher Architects, one of a number of rising practices in north London, to demonstrate their skills. The clients, a silversmith and a QC, live in the north of England and this was to be their London base. Joe Fraher formed the practice with his partner, Lizzie, in 2009. 'Our aim is to deliver simple, accessible, environmentally aware design integrating sustainable technologies, not just as an afterthought but as a driving force that informs every aspect of a project,' says Joe.

Steps lead down from the road into the 'area' where the front door to the basement and ground floor flat opens into a small hallway. A rooflight behind the front door immediately dispels the gloom common to this type of accommodation. Any change to the front elevations of these listed houses is strongly resisted by the local planning department, so Joe Fraher considers this discreet rooflight a victory over sometimes inflexible planning criteria.

### Restricted palette of materials

Immediately off the hall, the 'vault', originally used to store coal, has been converted into valuable storage. Space in the compact basement floor has been maximised by the restricted palette of materials and the minimalist detailing of flush storage cupboards and sleek kitchen units. There are three rooms at this level. A reflective light-coloured resin floor stretches seamlessly from the front door to the garden. The living room has a window on to the small 'area'. Flush cupboard doors to the left-hand side of the fireplace open to reveal a workbench for silverwork and storage for tools, hence the name of the project.

At the centre of the plan is the kitchen. On one side are maple-veneered flush cupboards housing the oven and fridge/freezer. Recessed concealed lighting above and below this wall of units makes it appear to float. On the other side, a run of units with a monolithic cast concrete worktop incorporates the hob and sink. These units are also raised so that the floor appears to extend under them, maximising the width of the relatively narrow space. Underfloor heating dispenses with the need for radiators, further simplifying the interior.

▲ Figure 7.16

**The wildflower meadow, green roof softens the impact of the new insertion as well as providing a habitat for local wildlife.**
*Photo: Andy Matthews*

◄ Figure 7.17

**Geometric external hard landscaping – retaining walls, steps and planters – formed from in-situ concrete and the vertical larch cladding perimeter fence unify the garden and the new extension.**
*Photo: Andy Matthews*

Figure 7.18 ▶

**In the dining area, a double-canted ceiling expresses the butterfly roof construction which has been designed to maximise rainwater collection. An expressive light fitting snakes from the wall and hangs over the table.**
*Photo: Andy Matthews*

Figure 7.19 ▶▶

**Minimalist detailing of kitchen cabinets and cupboards creates a clean white interior which maximises the restricted space. Architectural interest is confined to the ceiling.**
*Photo: Andy Matthews*

### In-house joinery

'Purpose-made joinery is key to the finish of the project,' says Joe and beautifully made joinery has become one aspect which the practice is renowned for, to such an extent that a separate joinery company has been established which supplies Fraher Architects commissions but which also accepts work from other architects and contractors. 'The benefit of having our own firm of joiners is that we don't have to detail the fittings at tender stage,' he explains. Projects can proceed faster and be more accurately detailed, a prime concern on refurbishment projects where variations can cause time delays and additional costs.

The dining room extension at the rear of the house has an articulated form which disguises its small size. A double-canted ceiling follows the form of the butterfly roof, which has been designed to maximise rainwater collection. An

expressive light fitting snakes from the wall and hangs over the dining table. Every square metre of space is carefully considered. Steps lead up from the dining area to a small study overlooking the garden. With its fully glazed external walls, it sits like a pavilion in the garden, a tranquil and restful space to work away from the noise of the city.

### Green space

The south-facing courtyard garden has been designed for maximum year-round interest. There is a corner seating area, raised beds and a water feature. Rainwater collected from the extension roof fills a submerged 2,500 litre storage tank and serves a pumped irrigation system so that the garden plants

---

**KEY FEATURES** 🔑

- Carefully considered detailing in a confined space;
- Restricted palette of materials;
- Purpose-made joinery maximises space and achieves a high standard of finish;
- Rainwater harvesting to supply garden;
- Wild flower roof to extension.

**Site:** London N1
**Start on site:** April 2010
**Completion:** June 2011
**Client:** Confidential
**Contract value:** £250,000 excluding VAT

---

can thrive when the owners are away. The rear elevation expresses the elegance of the design. Sustainable Scottish larch cladding will eventually turn a soft silvery-grey colour and a series of green roofs further softens the impact of the new insertion, as well as providing a habitat for local wildlife. In the summer, the roof becomes quite shaggy before it receives its annual trim in the autumn.

Upstairs, there is a bathroom off the half-landing and two bedrooms. The high standard of joinery continues on this floor with full-height pivoting doors which fold back softly to align with the wall planes and elegant 'floating' built-in wardrobes. These minimalist additions help to highlight existing architectural features such as the decorative cornices. In an unpromising small basement apartment, Fraher Architects has created a series of carefully considered spaces accommodating a variety of different uses and has addressed a number of sustainability issues.

▼ Figure 7.20

**Ground floor plan,** *top*
**Lower ground floor plan,**
*bottom*

**Key**
| | |
|---|---|
| 1 | **Area with steps to pavement level** |
| 2 | **Storage under pavement** |
| 3 | **Hall** |
| 4 | **Sitting room** |
| 5 | **Kitchen** |
| 6 | **Dining area** |
| 7 | **Study** |
| 8 | **WC** |
| 9 | **Bathroom** |
| 10 | **Terrace** |
| 11 | **Bedroom** |

*Images: Fraher Architects*

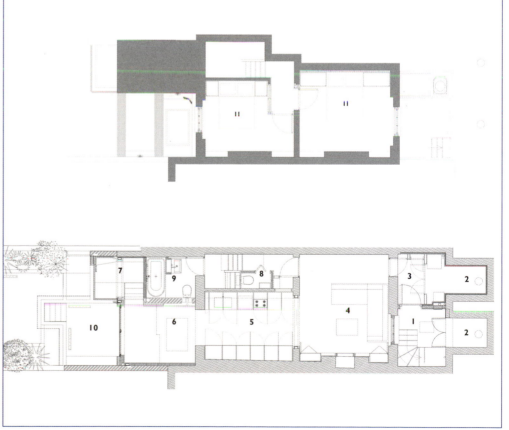

Figure 7.21 ▶

**An existing rear extension adjoining the cottage was rebuilt and extended. An additional projecting wing has been remodelled and now accommodates a shower room and utility room.**

*Photo: James Potter*

# King Street, Arundel, West Sussex
by Waind Gohil + Potter Architects

- Grade II listed cottage
- Conservation area

Viewed from the south across the River Arun, Arundel is one of the most picturesque hill towns in the UK. The skyline is punctuated on the east by the romantic battlemented outline of Arundel Castle, not the grim Norman castle it once was but a romantic Victorian fantasy of medieval England created by the Howard family, the Dukes of Norfolk. To the west rise the spires and spikes of the Roman Catholic Cathedral Church of Our Lady and St Philip Howard, a dramatic statement in stone of the resurgent Catholicism of the Howard family.

Arundel has a compact street layout with a dense mix of 18th and 19th century houses. The terraced houses on King Street tumble down the hill from the Catholic cathedral at the top. On the west side is a row of cottages, which were reputedly built by French prisoners during the Napoleonic Wars in the early 19th century. Built from rounded flint pebbles from the beach, the cottages have brick window dressings and chimneys and have served as desirable and functional homes for two centuries.

Small market towns may, on the surface, look historic and picturesque to the casual visitor but their vitality, viability and future prosperity depends on the adaptability of commercial premises and the traditional housing stock to suit new uses and more contemporary lifestyles. For the sustainability of the community, it is important to attract young families and to offer all ages a secure future. The rear view of the row of terraced houses shows the various ways that these traditional

◄ Figure 7.22

**Reputedly built by French prisoners during the Napoleonic Wars, the terraced houses on King Street tumble down the hill from Arundel's Roman Catholic Cathedral. Waind Gohil has added a gabled extension to the house on the far right.**
*Photo: James Potter*

Figure 7.23 ▶

**The main feature of the new addition is the butterfly, gull-wing profiled roof with its frameless double-glazed roof lights angled into a continuous galvanised steel V-beam incorporating a valley gutter.**
*Photo: James Potter*

Figure 7.24 ▼

**Detailing of the remodelled interior is refined and unobtrusive, particularly evident in the crisp detailing of the oak stair treads and risers**
*Photo: James Potter*

properties have been extended to house more modern kitchens and services.

## Challenging pastiche

Waind Gohil + Potter Architects was given the commission of turning one of these 200-year-old cottages into a modern home. 'We set out to create a series of contemporary spaces which would challenge the "pastiche" design guidelines which had been set by the planning officers,' says project architect John Ashton. The two-up, two-down cottages are relatively small. Each cottage has a projecting rear 'closet' wing and these gabled additions form an attractive feature of the terrace when viewed from the gardens. These rear extensions, however, tend to restrict daylight to the rear reception room. Crucial to Waind Gohil's approach was the introduction of light into the previously dark interior.

The row of houses has a series of typical rear single-storey extensions with decorative brick gables facing on to the garden. This particular cottage was unusual in having a double-banked extension projecting much further into the long garden than the additions to neighbouring properties. The outer extension was retained with a remodelled window and this now houses a downstairs shower room and utility room. An older extension, which connected this outhouse to the two-storey house, was demolished and replaced with a full-width extension with a butterfly roof.

## Butterfly glazing

The new additions are simply detailed, totally in harmony with the rustic character of the existing building. The main feature is the glazed roof which floods the interior with light. Its butterfly, gull-wing profile follows the form of the adjoining

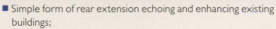

KEY FEATURES

- Simple form of rear extension echoing and enhancing existing buildings;
- Structural glass butterfly roof;
- Reconfiguration of interior to maximise available space;
- Limited palette of materials and minimalist detailing.

**Site:** King Street, Arundel, West Sussex
**Start on site:** January 2009
**Completion:** June 2009
**Client:** Confidential
**Contract value:** Confidential

◄◄ Figure 7.25

**The minimalist black and white kitchen is bathed in sunshine from the large rooflight. A splash-back formed from orange, back-painted glass panels brightens the interior.**
*Photo: James Potter*

houses but the central V-shape has been constructed as a continuous rooflight. Frameless double-glazed units joined with structural silicone span between the parallel flanged channel beams on the twin ridges to the galvanised steel V-beam which incorporates the pressed steel valley gutter. The space between the beam and the gutter is filled with spray foam insulation. The kitchen has minimalist white units with black granite worktops. To brighten the interior, the splashback is formed from orange, back-painted glass panels.

There were no original features remaining in the cottage so the ground and first floors were completely reconfigured to make the most of the available space. As the property has solid chalk walls, an internal steel skeleton was designed to transfer loads down into new foundations. The cottage has a basement which is used for storage and the attic was converted to a study. To make the most of the available space, a 'circulation core' was created with three flights of stairs stacked above each other.

## Minimalist detailing

Detailing is refined and unobtrusive, particularly evident in the clever detailing of the oak stair treads and risers and in the first-floor shower room. Materials were selected to reflect the listed building status of the property; reclaimed Welsh slates were used for the roof, reclaimed bricks match the original, and solid oak was specified rather than 'engineered' flooring, as the client wanted the floor to age naturally and to distort and wear over time. Flush skirting and architraves enhance the oak finish and the sense of space in the confined interior. A simple, practical artisan's house has been given a skilled and sensitive makeover, which should ensure its survival for at least another 200 years.

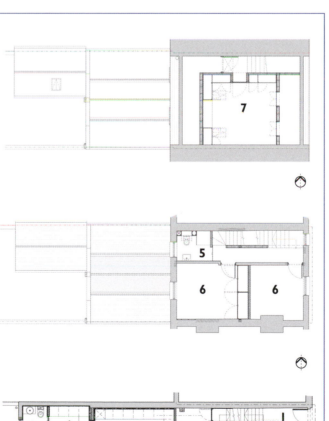

◄ Figure 7.26

*From top to bottom*
**Second floor plan**
**First floor plan**
**Ground floor plan**

**Key**
1    **Hall**
2    **Living room**
3    **Kitchen/dining**
4    **Utility**
5    **Shower room**
6    **Bedroom**
7    **Study**
*Images: Waind Gohil + Potter Architects*

Figure 7.27 ▶

**The new kitchen follows the line of the existing garden wall making the most of the space available in the restricted triangular back garden.**
*Photo: Procter:Rihl*

# Arvon Road, London Borough of Islington
## by Procter:Rihl

- Victorian end of terrace
- Few planning constraints

Proving that design innovation is possible in even the smallest project, architects Procter:Rihl have revitalised the concept of the kitchen extension with an innovative folded roof structure enveloping a new kitchen/dining room, in the process turning a gloomy lower ground floor into a contemporary light-filled space. The project is also very cost-effective as the roof is an adaptation of a building system developed for use on much larger projects.

## Space for contemplation

Everyone in London is familiar with the literal sinking feeling of taking the former servants' and tradesmen's route and negotiating the tiny external staircase in the 'area' to access the basement, lower ground floor or 'garden' flat. As unprepossessing as such properties may be, in the overheated property market of London, such flats still exchange hands for large amounts of money, particularly in favoured postcodes such as Islington.

Procter:Rihl's project has transformed the lower part of a late Victorian house close to Highbury Fields, which has been split into two maisonettes. The old kitchen at the front of the property with a window on to the entrance area has been converted into the living room, an inward-looking room for peaceful retreat and contemplation; at the rear, a new extension contains the kitchen and small dining area.

◄ Figure 7.28

**The existing garden wall was rebuilt and lined internally with insulated panels. Under the projecting folded roof, a clerestory window lights the kitchen.**
*Photo: Procter:Rihl*

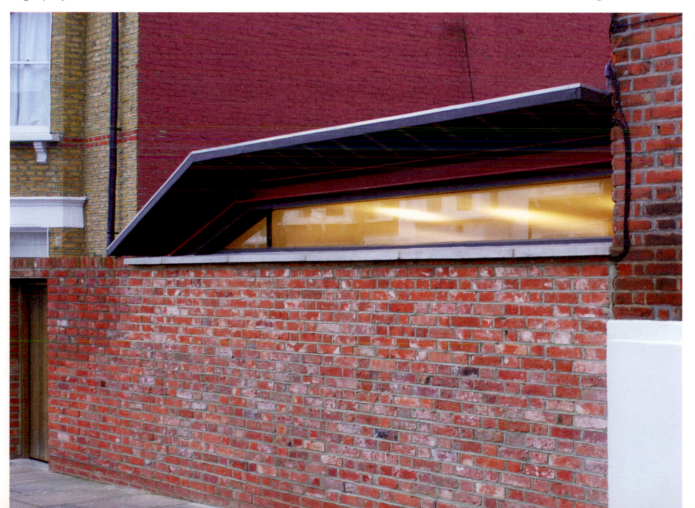

The house is not listed and is not in a conservation area so the architects had a relatively free hand. The clients – a professional couple – were looking for a distinctive modern design, not the ubiquitous glass box extension that became the norm in the later 1990s and the first decade of this century. 'We decided to make the most of the south-facing flank wall on this end-of-terrace property in the creation of a low-energy extension,' says Christopher Procter. End of terrace properties have distinct advantages in terms of extending ground-floor accommodation: benefit of natural daylight and ease of access for construction. In this case, the lower ground floor is several feet below ground level and the existing brick garden wall on to the street was 2.1 m high.

### Sustainable roofing system

Procter:Rihl decided to sit the new extension roof on top of this garden wall, bringing southern light into the interior. 'Light enters through a narrow clerestory above the kitchen cabinets, rather like a periscope,' says Christopher. The roof overhangs, allowing access to low winter sunlight but blocking sun in the height of summer. At the far end of the linear kitchen space, large double French doors swing open right out into the garden. 'The space soars above the cabinets, with the folded roof angling back down to a lower breakfast nook,' Christopher explains.

The roof is an innovative sustainable construction method designed and produced by building systems manufacturer Sips UK. The lightweight Structural Insulated Panel (SIP) units were prefabricated off site and quickly assembled in situ. Panels are a sandwich of 200 mm XPS (extruded polystyrene) and oriented strand board (OSB) sheathing. They are manufactured in hydraulic presses by pressure injecting polyurethane foam which, during the polymerisation process, adhesively bonds to the faces of the OSB. They are lightweight but strong so that they are able to span the narrow width from the brick side wall to be supported on a steel frame over the 4.8-m long clerestory window. SIPs are manufactured using between 35% and 40% less timber than would be required using traditional framing methods and the OSB sheathing is made from forest thinnings and fast growing trees

Figure 7.29 ▶

**Light enters through a narrow clerestory above the kitchen cabinets, making them appear to float.**
*Photo: Procter:Rihl*

which are grown in plantations certified by the FSC (Forest Stewardship Council).

## Honest materials

'Simple and direct building materials were used,' says Christopher. A medium lead grey colour membrane roof was laid over a ventilation cavity above the SIPs. The steel frame above the clerestory is exposed with the roof ventilation timbers forming the overhanging eaves, painted medium grey to tone in with the roof. SIPs also line the outer walls of the extension; the garden wall is finished in stucco with a ventilation cavity; the south-facing brick wall was rebuilt to look like a solid wall but it is, in fact, a single brick skin with a ventilated cavity separating it from the SIP panels.

This small extension has made a big difference to the thermal performance of the maisonette. 'We used Passivhaus principles of heavy insulation and careful window placement,' says Christopher. The roof, wall and under-slab insulation incorporates 200 mm of foam insulation. The French windows are German Solarlux which approach the Passivhaus standard.

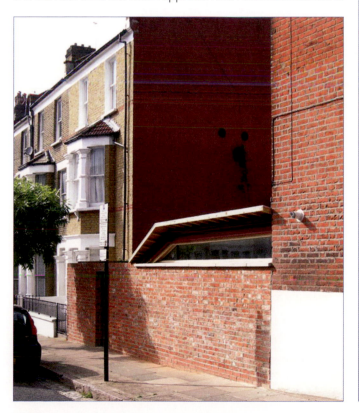

**KEY FEATURES**

- Imaginative design of ground floor extension to end of terrace;
- Innovative sustainable construction using the SIPs building system.

**Site:** Arvon Road, London N5
**Start on site:** August 2012
**Completion:** November 2012
**Client:** Confidential
**Contract value:** £100,000

◀ Figure 7.30

**Section,** *top*
**Lower ground floor plan,** *bottom*

**Key**
1   **Kitchen/dining area**
2   **Courtyard garden**
*Images: Procter:Rihl*

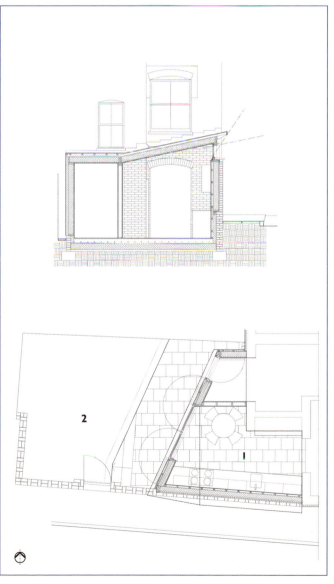

◀◀ Figure 7.31

**The folded roof of the new rear extension sits on an existing garden wall.**
*Photo: Procter:Rihl*

# Three Scottish projects

## Introduction

As many architects in Scotland will acknowledge, since the Second World War, the country has suffered from a rash of poorly designed housing, much of which takes little account of the harsher climate in the extreme north of the UK and of the country's vernacular traditions. Historically, houses in the region are more defensive – against the weather and potential invaders. Windows are smaller; walls are of thick masonry and harled to keep out the driving rain; roofs are steeply pitched. Abandoning this tradition of Scottish construction has resulted in both social problems in areas of mass housing and in building failures where poor craftsmanship and inappropriate detailing have been no match for the Scottish weather.

However, a small handful of architects in Scotland have kept faith with the country's building traditions and have developed a sensitive contemporary approach to the adaptation and extension of existing houses and to new-build housing schemes. Most notable is the work of Richard Murphy Architects (see Introduction, pages 17–9). Over the past decades, this Edinburgh-based practice has been a training ground for a new generation of architects imbued with the Scottish spirit. William Tunnell worked for Richard Murphy for several years. In 2006, he set up his own practice, focusing initially on a series of domestic extensions which explore the different means of connecting houses with their gardens. Here two of his projects are illustrated: the first a small, intricate extension to a ground floor flat in Edinburgh; the second, a project in Fife, where the remodelled interior now enjoys far-reaching views over the River Tay.

In a more exposed location in Fife, right on the edge of a rocky beach, Oliver Chapman has transformed a small fisherman's bothy, which previously turned its back on the sea and the views to the south, facing inwards to the narrow main street. The innovatively designed new extension reorientates the house, so that the rear living space now angles towards the sunlight, taking full advantage of the ever-changing and often dramatic seascape.

*Historically, houses in the region are more defensive – against the weather and potential invaders.*

◄ Figure 8.1

**Newhaven Road, Edinburgh by WT Architecture.**
*Photo: Angus Bremner*

Figure 8.2 ▶

**The angular form of the new addition to Skerrie House blends in with the busy roofscape of dormer windows and gables of the fishermen's cottages.**
*Photo: Angus Bremner*

## Skerrie House, Cellardyke, Fife, Scotland
by Oliver Chapman Architects

- 19th-century fisherman's cottage
- Conservation area

Cellardyke's harbour, one of the most picturesque sights in the Kingdom of Fife in Scotland, was first constructed in the 16th century and underwent improvements in the 19th century. Many of the cottages along the main street, which closely hugs the line of the shore, were built in the early 19th century. In the 1880s, there were more than 200 fishing boats crowding the harbour, supplying large quantities of herring to the UK. The fish curers of Cellardyke salted and smoked cod and herring, which was sent to London and even as far as the West Indies. The name Cellardyke had its origins in 'sil'erdykes' which came from the shine of the herring scales in nets hung over walls (or dykes) to dry in the sun.

### Intimate scale

The seafront houses, including Skerrie House, face away from the harsh winds which blow off the North Sea, with windows and front doors opening on to the well-protected main street. The cottages are very small. Originally, Skerrie House was a fisherman's bothy, a basic single-room shelter; it was extended in 1809 to add another room on the first floor, accessed by a 'pend' or small passageway leading to an external stone stairway at the rear, so that it could accommodate two families.

The house has been in Clare Checkland's family since 1962 and she decided it was time for a makeover. Oliver Chapman Architects was commissioned to turn the cottage into a single family home, refurbishing the bedrooms and bathrooms and extending the living space. 'We wanted to maintain the house's strong characterful relationship to the "skerrie" – rocky reef – and north shore of the Firth of Forth,' says Oliver, 'without compromising its intimate scale.'

### Contemporary approach

Cellardyke, 50 miles from Edinburgh, is a key tourist destination and the cottage is in a conservation area, but the architects did not compromise their approach to the design of a very modern extension. The planners were, at first, concerned but consent was eventually achieved. 'Typically dwellings in these fishing villages turn their back on the sea and group closely together to shelter the narrow streets from the elements,' says Oliver. 'On a modest budget, our challenge

◀ Figure 8.3

**Reclaimed timber used in the flooring, kitchen units and the timber cladding to the original stone stair harmonises with the rustic feel of the original interior.**

*Photo: Angus Bremner*

was to open up and engage the existing living area to face the sea whilst retaining the character of the existing dwelling.'

The pivot of the redesigned rear of the cottage is the original 19th-century stone staircase, which has been wrapped around by a light, glazed extension containing the new living room and kitchen. 'The folded, oxidised copper roof form and irregular plan make reference to the complex geometry of the site formed by the relationship between the row of historic cottages and the angular rock of the skerrie which they sit on,' Oliver explains.

### Shard of light

The steel-framed, single-storey, metal-clad extension is formed from a series of irregular triangles and, although uncompromisingly modern, fits in well with the jumble of ad hoc, more traditional rear additions along the long rambling row of cottages. The gull wing form of the roof, particularly

appropriate for the location, angles down to shield the extension from the often harsh offshore winds and the full-height glazing is protected by a generous overhang.

A triangular rooflight, not visible from the rear, provides a 'shard' of natural light deep into the centre of the plan, and visually separates the new extension from the house. The plan of the house has been transformed and a contrast in light and shade and scale is experienced when moving through the house from the tunnel-like street to the cosy front room to the light-filled living room/kitchen with its oblique views and unexpected glimpses of the sea.

At the top of the stone stair, worn by the feet of two centuries of occupants, a glazed door opens on to a new roof deck from which there are dramatic views across the Firth of Forth to the Isle of May. On the first floor are two bedrooms and a family bathroom; in the attic space is a master bedroom complete with freestanding bath which enjoys an amazing sea view.

Figure 8.4 ▶

**The stone stair, worn by generations of feet, was originally exposed to the elements. Now it leads to a landing with wide-ranging sea views and to two bedrooms and family bathroom on the first floor and to the master bedroom suite in the attic.**

*Photo: Angus Bremner*

Figure 8.5 ▶▶

**The hallway from the narrow main street of the village leads to the new rear extension where there is a rich mix of old and new materials. Light now floods into the whole of the ground floor through the new full-height windows.**

*Photo: Angus Bremner*

## Steel frame construction

Construction of the new extension was challenging, not just because of the changeable weather. Although there is pedestrian access to the rear of the cottage – along the shore and over the rocks – the majority of building materials had to be brought through the house, so the choice of steel frame construction was an ideal solution. The precision of the steel structure which abutted the historic staircase and bothy did cause some problems however. 'The setting out of the steel frame was tricky,' Oliver remembers. 'It was a mixture of computer modelling – and string!'

In a possible reference to the metallic sheen of the drying herring in the 19th century which was such a feature of Cellardyke, Tecu pre-patinated copper was chosen as an 'active' cladding for the new extension. The process of patination will continue, allowing the building to merge into its environment over time. The articulated form of the new metal and glass extension sits on an angular plinth of dark grey Caithness slate, which anchors the new addition to the rocky context. New walls, roof and floor are heavily insulated, 30% higher than current U-value standards.

## Sustainable interior

On the interior, the client has followed the sustainable theme in the fittings and furniture. Kitchen units and cupboards are made from salvaged French oak railway carriage panelling, which has been stained in three shades to echo the natural colours of the rocks on the shore. Cupboard handles are made of copper piping reclaimed from the old central heating system and worktops are reclaimed hardwood. Where previously, occupants would huddle inside a building, back to the wind with storms raging outside, the new extension opens itself to dramatic sea views, even from the bath!

### KEY FEATURES

- Steel frame for ease of construction on restricted site;
- Form responds to natural landscape;
- Introduction of light to dark interior;
- Sustainable and recycled materials.

**Site:** Cellardyke, Anstruther, Fife
**Start on site:** January 2011
**Completion:** June 2011
**Client:** Clare Checkland
**Contract value:** Confidential

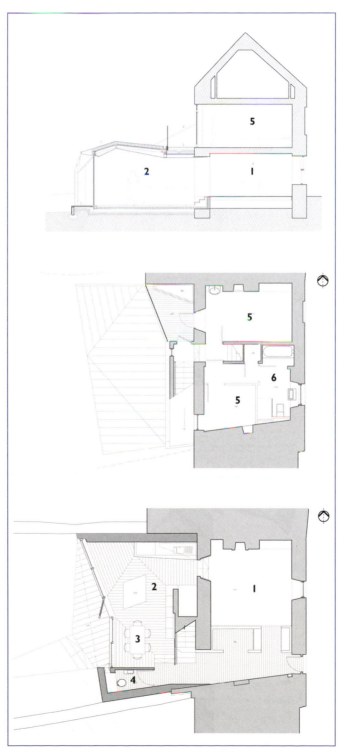

◀ Figure 8.6

*From top to bottom*
**Section**
**First floor plan**
**Ground floor plan**

**Key**
1   **Sitting room**
2   **Kitchen**
3   **Dining area**
4   **WC**
5   **Bedroom**
6   **Bathroom**
*Images: Oliver Chapman Architects*

▲ Figure 8.7

**Traditionally, the cottages turned their backs against the sometimes harsh weather. Now the fully glazed wall to the new living room has opened up long-distance views across the sea.**
*Photo: Angus Bremner*

Figure 8.8 ▶

**A crisply detailed side entrance has a curving roof to minimise its impact on the neighbouring property.**
*Photo: Andrew Lee*

# Newhaven Road, Edinburgh
## by WT Architecture

- Victorian end of terrace
- Inner-city ground floor flat

Following experience gained with leading Edinburgh architectural practices, including Richard Murphy Architects and Simpson & Brown, William Tunnell has worked on a series of domestic extensions, reconfiguring traditional houses and adding modernist extensions. He has developed what he describes as 'a simple vocabulary of clearly separate built elements – tall wrapping walls, curved roofs, sharp-edged plate roofs, unfolding planes of wall, incidental seats'.

His aim is to attempt to 'break down the barrier between inside and outside, something that modern technologies enable us to do'. William has developed this philosophy in the firm's later, larger projects, 'extending an architectural language of breaking down the defensive building envelope and connecting new structures into their landscapes'.

## Peaceful rear garden

At Newhaven Road off Ferry Road in Edinburgh, WT Architecture was commissioned to remodel and extend a ground floor flat in a subdivided Victorian end of terrace house. The two-bedroom apartment had to be extended to accommodate the clients' growing family. They also wanted to exploit fully the peaceful, west-facing garden at the rear of the property, away from the traffic noise of the busy road. One of the main requirements was the creation of an additional bedroom for the couple and their two young children. As keen gardeners, the clients also wanted a closer connection between the flat and the garden. The original kitchen was dark and they needed more light, better kitchen facilities, additional storage, and a new porch for the often-used side entrance door to the kitchen.

William's solution makes the most of the confined existing space and pushes a light and airy modern extension into the garden. Light to the rear of the house is partly restricted by a large school building at the end of the garden so the new extension has been angled towards the south to pick up as much natural light as possible at midday. An additional bonus is

▲ Figure 8.9

**A rear extension has transformed the space of this ground floor apartment on a busy road in Edinburgh.**
*Photo: Andrew Lee*

◀ Figure 8.10

**The new extension has been angled towards the south to pick up as much natural light as possible at midday.**
*Photo: Andrew Lee*

Figure 8.11 ▶

**To increase daylight to the existing rear reception room, a clerestory window with angled reveals has been tucked in above the roof of the rear extension.**

*Photo: Andrew Lee*

Figure 8.12 ▼

**To increase the sense of space and to unite the interior with the garden, the internal slate flooring continues seamlessly through the frameless glazing on to the external paving.**

*Photo: Andrew Lee*

that, in summer, the sunlight re-emerges from behind the school to bathe the extension in the late evening sunlight. To maintain privacy from the overlooking upstairs windows of the upper floor flats and to reduce solar gain in peak summer, the flat roof to the extension projects to form a shading canopy.

## Curving zinc roof

A simple zinc roof plate, supported on a portal steel frame, projects out into the garden and links the existing kitchen extension to the rest of the house. Where the roof meets the party wall of the neighbouring property it curves downwards, reducing its impact. The original house is cut into and carved out to let light deep in to the plan and to create interlocking open-plan spaces, including a dining area, additional seating and a window seat which wraps around the dining area. The space also appears larger, as it flows out into the garden through floor to ceiling glazing.

To smooth the transition, the internal slate flooring continues seamlessly through the frameless glazing on to the external paving: a particular benefit with young children. Light floods into the interior through new rooflights over the kitchen and a clerestory window with deep angled reveals above the extension roof admits light deep into the inner sitting area. A new porch has been created on the north side of the house, connecting into the kitchen. Its form echoes the garden extension and is also a source of additional natural light.

## Effective space heating

'Much of the work in this project was in opening up and enlarging openings in the original building to let light in and to let spaces flow into each other,' William explains. This has also benefited the heating requirement. The fabric of the original building has been upgraded and insulated whilst benefitting from additional solar gain from the new rooflights. The dark slate floor acts as an effective heat sink, warming up in the day and discharging its heat in the dark, with additional underfloor heating separately controlled from the heating system in the rest of the house. A small clean-burning wood stove provides additional localised heating in the sitting space for the coldest days of the year.

WT Architecture's design approach to domestic extensions and new-build houses has been developed further since this early project and the quality of the practice's work has been recognised in a series of awards. A number of schemes involve

**Opening on to the dining/living space, the kitchen is lit by a large rooflight.**
*Photo: Andrew Lee*

**Ground floor plan**

**Key:**

1    **Kitchen/dining room**
2    **Sitting room**
3    **Kitchen**
4    **Bedroom**
5    **Existing bathroom**
6    **Side entrance**
*Image: WT Architecture*

## KEY FEATURES

- Reconfiguration of small ground floor flat to maximise space for young family;
- Effective use of simple forms, limited materials and built-in seating;
- Rooflights and a clerestory window admit light into the heart of the plan.

**Site:** Newhaven Road, Edinburgh
**Start on site:** January 2009
**Completion:** April 2009
**Client:** Private
**Contract value:** £70,000

the creation of new structures within the ruinous fabric of historic buildings. Most recently, a new house in the Borders has been built inside the walls of a derelict mill. Completed in 2014, the Mill has won an RIAS Award 2015 in addition to a Saltire Housing 2015 Design Award. It was also shortlisted for a Historic Scotland Award for Conservation and Climate Change.

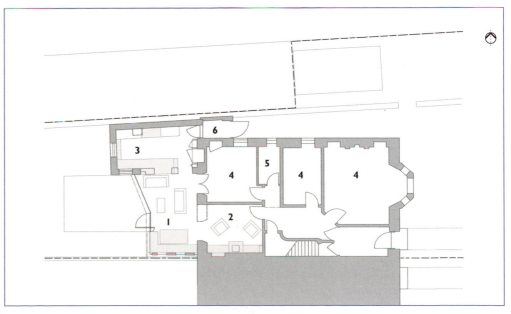

Figure 8.15 ▶

**Like many traditional seaside homes in Scotland, the house previously turned its back on the sea and the harsh weather. Now a ground-floor fully-glazed cantilevered bay window allows far-ranging coastal views and floods the interior with light.**
*Photo: Matt Laver*

# Riverside Road, Wormit, Fife
## by WT Architecture

- Victorian semi-detached house
- Riverside location

Riverside Road runs along the north coast of Fife in Scotland and the lucky residents on the north side of the road enjoy long-ranging views over the River Tay towards Dundee. Traditionally, the main rooms of these houses faced south to catch the sun and the backs housed service rooms with small windows braced against the harsh northerly winds.

WT Architecture was asked by two clients to re-orientate one of these stone-built semi-detached houses to take full advantage of the northern light and the views. They wanted a contemporary interior as a backdrop for their collection of modern furniture classics as well as room to store – and to listen to – a much-treasured collection of vinyl records.

### Cantilevered bay window

From the back of the house, the most obvious addition to the house is a cantilevered, fully glazed bay window. A large area of masonry and a small window was removed to open up the wall of this room to the view. The house is set into a slope which runs down towards the river so that it is two-storeyed

▲ Figure 8.16

**The houses along the north coast of Fife enjoy views over the River Tay towards Dundee.**
*Photo: Matt Laver*

◄ Figure 8.17

**From the bay window can be seen the Tay Bridge and the city of Dundee. A stub wall to the left of the projecting bay protects views over the neighbouring property.**
*Photo: Matt Laver*

Figure 8.18 ▶

**The basement music room can be separated acoustically from the rest of the house by a sliding screen housed in the storage wall. The door to the left leads to a guest bedroom and shower room.**

*Photo: Matt Laver*

on Riverside Road and three-storeyed at the rear. The lower floor was previously a dark basement used for storage, accessed via a steep timber staircase from the ground floor of the house.

On the ground floor, the formal sitting room at the front of the house has been retained. At the rear, the new room, containing a kitchen, dining area and seating in the bay, is flooded with light. The polished oak flooring reflects the light and a new staircase, partitioned by a full-height bookcase and storage unit, leads down to the lower ground floor. Here is the prized record collection and somewhere to sit and listen whilst enjoying the view through the large glazed square window into the garden. On this level is also a guest bedroom, shower room and utility room.

## Asymmetrical composition

The semi-detached houses are simply and plainly built, so that the pure geometry of the new bay window fits in well. Originally the clients suggested an external balcony at this

level but, taking into account the exposed site and northerly outlook, an enclosed bay was proposed. This would also increase space in the dining area by 4 sq m to compensate for the floor area lost by the incorporation of the new staircase.

In designing the form of the bay, care had to be taken with views into the adjoining neighbour's garden so the composition is asymmetrical; the base turns up to form a stub wall on the west side to avoid overlooking and to direct views towards the Tay Bridge. The roof and floor elements are kept as thin as possible, being supported on cantilevered steel frames concealed in the depth of the floor and roof which are tied back into the main cross wall in the middle of the house.

'The constraints of existing buildings put particular demands on alterations, and transforming the workings of a Victorian house requires bold but carefully controlled intervention,' says William. 'In this case the original house was not short of space, but its layout rendered much of it unusable. It was important that the bay did not appear to be stuck on to the house, but more of the inside coming out. The new overtly contemporary bay window slides out through the skin of the original building; it is more of an intervention rather than an addition.'

Built-in furniture makes the most of the available space. William was influenced by the work of the modernist architect Gerrit Rietveld: 'Fixed furnishings echo the tectonic language of the bay window. Bespoke shelving and a cantilevered desk over the staircase follow a similar sliding and geometric language and enjoy references to Rietveld in colour and composition. It is important that the stair is part of the adjacent spaces and that going up and down the stair is a pleasant journey, and the enclosing shelves and new window openings are carefully placed to enhance this experience.'

### Multi-use flexible space

The basement area is also designed to be a flexible multi-use space; with bedroom, shower room and living space, it is virtually a separate apartment with its own entrance from the garden. A sliding partition incorporated into the bookcase on the lower level can be closed to separate the room acoustically from the upper levels of the house. The interconnection between house and garden is also key to the project. Previously there was no access from the basement level; now a large glazed door opens on to the garden from the lower music room. New paving and lighting enhance the external space, extending its use into the evenings.

Although the introduction of a large area of north-facing glazing has had an effect on the thermal performance of the house, the units are double-glazed and any heat loss is compensated for by solar gain. Excessive solar gain is simply controlled by manually openable windows. The whole basement has been highly insulated and the installation of a new, more efficient heating system has reduced the energy requirements of the building.

**KEY FEATURES** 🔑

- Glazed bay window opens up living space to light and views;
- Available space maximised in reconfigured plan;
- Basement converted to create flexible, multi-use space;
- Built-in furniture makes best use of limited space.

**Site:** Riverside Road, Wormit, Fife
**Start on site:** January 2011
**Completion:** April 2011
**Client:** Confidential
**Contract value:** £100,000

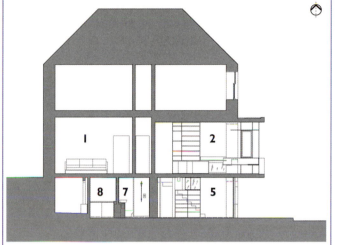

◀ Figure 8.19

*From top to bottom*
**Section**
**Ground floor plan**
**Basement plan**

**Key**
1  **Sitting room**
2  **Dining room**
3  **Kitchen**
4  **Bathroom**
5  **Living room/music room**
6  **Bedroom**
7  **Shower room**
8  **Utility**
*Images: WT Architecture*

▼ Figure 8.20

**Built-in furniture makes the most of the restricted space. A desk top is cantilevered over the stairwell and the stair divider is a bookcase on the ground floor and storage for a vinyl record collection in the basement.**
*Photo: Matt Laver*

### 1. Timber preparation

Siberian larch is primarily used. Accoya – see page 192 – is used for sash window linings and meeting rails. All timber is from FSC-certified sources. Lengths are fed into a saw machine which scans the timber, identifies defects and cuts these out to maximize the timber used. Sections are then planed ready for the next process. Waste wood is recycled.

### 3. Cassette bars and assembly

Components are assembled on clamps into a sash or frame prior to processing through a router which creates the specified profile together with any cutting required for the fixing of ironmongery and trickle vents. At this stage, 'cassette' bars, for application to double-glazed windows where 'true' bars have not been specified, are assembled.

### 5. Glazing

Single, double-, or triple-glazed units are outsourced. These are checked for quality. Toughened glass is standard and all double-glazed units carry the BSI Kitemark. Units are inserted into the frames using a simple clip system. Linseed putty requires curing time; silicone-based putty cures rapidly; or pre-finished glazing bar cassettes are applied.

### 2. Production routes

Prepared timber follows one of two production routes. The first uses the Weinig Unicontrol 10 Windowline machine to produce tenon joints and internal profiles. In the second route, a computer-controlled Profoline machine – a recent £1 million investment – uses a bank of tools to produce bespoke components and profiles at lightening speed.

### 4. Painting

Assemblies are then checked for quality and hand finished before continuing to the paint shop for hand spraying. Three coats of microporous paint in the specified colour are applied on a loop production system which avoids handling at this stage. Quality checking takes place between coats and the units are then left to dry.

### 6. Inspection and delivery

Products progress to the final stage. Quality checking has taken place at all the stages of manufacture, however, products for delivery will be once more inspected prior to wrapping. Architects are specifying the production of increasingly large glazed units. Mumford & Wood has the expertise to ensure that these are delivered safely to site.

## Mumford & Wood

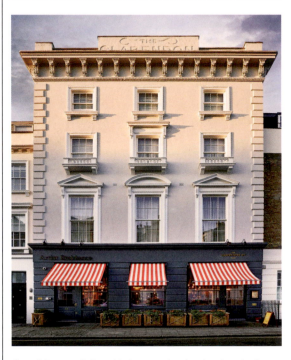

*One of the most fashionable boutique hotels in London, the Artist Residence was extensively refurbished in 2013. Conservation box sash windows were specially designed to meet the demands of the discerning customers and clients and to replicate the style of the original windows. Slender lambs'-tongue glazing bars house double-glazed units, 24 mm wide, achieving the highest level of specification for the upper-floor bedrooms where thermal and acoustic performance was paramount.*

An increasing percentage of architectural commissions for new buildings now involve some element of the restoration, conversion and reuse of existing buildings. In such projects, architects can rely on the expertise of companies such as Mumford & Wood when it comes to the replacement of historic features. Owen Dare, Technical Director of Mumford & Wood, is a joiner by trade and has more than 17 years' experience with the company. He is in charge of a team of surveyors which works closely with architects to help them to achieve the correct detailing of sash and casement windows, gain the appropriate permissions from the local authority

# Materials and technologies

*Completed in 1803, the Grade II\*-listed Duke of York Headquarters in Chelsea, London is now home to the Saatchi Gallery. Mumford & Wood supplied replica replacements of the original sash windows from the Heritage range. Existing glazing bars ranged from 15–17 mm and approval was given for a consistent and slender 17 mm bar throughout with traditional putty single glazing.*

*Rivalling the developments in nearby Bath, Portland Square in Bristol was the vision of architect Daniel Hague in the late 18th century. Replacement sash windows are from Mumford & Wood's Conservation range with slender 12 mm, double-glazed units. The sashes are counter-balanced by pre-tensioned spiral balances and supplied with three coats of factory-applied microporous paint.*

and Historic England, and to prepare detail drawings and specifications.

Owen and his team have an impressive bank of knowledge concerning the development of window design and construction in the UK over the centuries and in the potential and capabilities of the new technologies which are available to manufacture windows to a wide range of designs. The need for historical accuracy and the need to achieve energy efficiency and sustainability have to be reconciled, a compromise that today's conservation officers are increasingly likely to acknowledge.

Each development and restoration project is unique. Following an initial enquiry, Owen or a member of his team will visit the site to survey any surviving historic windows and to discuss the design brief. As Owen explains, the detailing of Georgian sash windows varies considerably throughout the country with glazing bar profiles specific to cities such as Bath, Dublin, Edinburgh, London, York and so on. The expertise of joiners during the Georgian period was concentrated in local workshops. As communications and technology improved in the 19th century and production became mechanized, window design began to be more rationalized.

An existing building may have windows of various ages as they will have been repaired and replaced over time. Mumford & Wood's surveyors will be able to identify these and to advise the architect on the best approach to window replacement and complementary windows in any new-build which forms part of the development. Local authority conservation officers and Historic England may require detailed drawings and specifications of the replacement windows before plans are approved and Listed Building Consent granted. Mumford & Wood can work in close partnership with the architect to secure these approvals.

Attention to historic detail can go as far as the selection of the appropriate style of window catch, ironmongery, design of sash pulleys and so on. Again, Mumford & Wood has the expertise to help architects make the right choices. Once all permissions are granted and the specification is finalized, the manufacture of the windows can commence at their factory in Essex. All windows are specially made to order and special tooling will be designed if necessary to suit specific glazing bar profiles and so on. Although, there has been significant investment in recent years in computer-controlled machinery to manufacture the complex timber profiles, there is still a significant amount of hand assembly and finishing, ensuring the highest standards of quality control.

The most authentic windows which Mumford & Wood manufactures are direct replacements of the historic originals complete with the correct style of ironmongery, pulleys and weights, heritage single glazing which has the look of antique glass, and traditional linseed putty. Slim double-glazed units can be incorporated in Georgian style sash windows although glazing bars will have to be a minimum of 22 mm thick and the 'putty' Mumford & Wood uses in this case is a much faster curing, hybrid silicone-based system. Heritage glass can be used for the outer face of the units to give an authentic appearance on the street façade. The most energy-efficient sash windows do not have 'true' glazing bars. Wider-spaced double-glazed units can have glazing bars to a wide range of designs applied to the front and back of the glazing. In this case the look of 'putty' is replicated using a timber bead. All windows use engineered Siberian larch which is extremely durable and stable.

Mumford & Wood organises tours of its factory in Tiptree, Essex where the potential of the skills, expertise and manufacturing capability available to architects can be appreciated fully. The tour has been assessed by the RIBA and forms part of the CPD programme for chartered architects. The RIBA also runs a CPD conservation course and Mumford & Wood offers a CPD module which examines topics such as sustainability and energy efficiency within the timber trades and the construction industry.

For further information, visit
**www.mumfordwood.com**

## Accoya wood

*Photo: Accoya® wood by Accsys Technologies*

Timber is one of the most sustainable materials used in building construction. It is naturally strong and light and can be manufactured into structural components as well as used as a decorative finish. At the end of its life it can be used to create energy in a bio-mass boiler. Effective detailing, paint and stain finishes, preservatives and other treatments can prolong its life, increasing its sustainability.

Wood is a natural material with a chemical structure which has advantages but also disadvantages. It contains a high proportion of 'free hydroxyls' which absorb and release moisture according to changes in temperature and humidity. This explains why wood swells and shrinks. It is thought that the free hydroxyls also allow the digestion of wood by enzymes, which is one of the main causes of timber decay.

The process of acetylation involves treating the wood with acetic anhydride, which comes from acetic acid (vinegar). This alters the chemical structure of softwood by changing free hydroxyls into acetyl groups. The result is that the wood is less able to absorb water; it is less digestible and, therefore, more durable; and it is also more dimensionally stable.

Although the process has been known for some time, it has only recently become commercially viable due to the shortage of sustainable tropical hardwoods and statutory limitations on treating timber with toxic chemicals. The technology has been developed and patented by Accsys Technologies, a UK-incorporated environmental science and technology company focused on 'sustainability'. The company's primary focus is on

the production and licensing of Accoya solid wood and Tricoya wood elements technology. The main processing plant is in the Netherlands and trials in the country have shown no deterioration in Accoya wood used as a canal lining over a 16-year period. Accoya can be used for most exterior applications such as doors, window frames, garden decking, cladding and sidings, boat decks and garden furniture.

Accsys manages the international rights to the process and Accoya can be sourced in the UK and Northern Ireland from a number of distributors listed on the website below.

For further information, visit
**www.accoya.com**

## Aerogel insulation

In upgrading existing houses, super-thin insulation systems are often necessary to preserve the appearance of upgraded external elevations or to save internal floor space where internal insulation is specified. One of the thinnest insulative materials, aerogel is the result of NASA's research and development in the Space Shuttle and Mars exploration programmes.

Although derived from a gel, the product is rigid. Aerogel is a synthetic, ultralight material in which the component of the gel has been replaced with a gas, resulting in a product with low density and low thermal conductivity. It appears translucent but feels like polystyrene. This has led to it being nicknamed 'frozen smoke' or 'solid air'.

The process was originally discovered by Samuel Stephens Kistler in 1931. Kistler was able to extract the liquid component of a gel by supercritical drying without causing the matrix of the gel to collapse. These early aerogels were produced from silica gels; alumina, chromia and tin oxide gels formed the basis of later aerogels and carbon aerogels were developed in the late 1980s. Early products were very fragile and it is only recently that insulative materials based on aerogels have been developed for the construction industry and that it has been possible to source the products in the UK.

Thermablok is one manufacturer which produces a range of advanced insulation products using aerogel technology, including an aerogel blanket and an insulation board. By using a special fibre to suspend a formula of aerogel, Thermablok has developed a product which can be bent or compressed while still retaining its excellent insulation properties. Aerogel has the highest insulation value of any known material with the lowest thermal conductivity of any solid – 0.013 W/mK – so an extremely thin product can produce a remarkable uplift in U-values. It is also well suited to retrofit projects, as it repels liquid but allows the passage and release of moisture vapour.

The ThermablokSP Wall and Ceiling insulation board is a laminate of rigid magnesium silicate board and aerogel insulation. It is available in three thicknesses: 9 mm board laminated to 10/20/40 mm thick aerogel, achieving U-values of 0.8, 0.51 and 0.29 W/m²K respectively. Conventional plaster systems can be applied to the board.

Similar products include Spacetherm from Proctor Group which was specified by Kit Knowles for his home in Manchester (see pages 29–35).

For further information, visit
**www.thermoblok.co.uk** and
**www.proctorgroup.com.**

### Calsitherm Climate Board

*Photo: Ecological Building Systems*

Internal insulation is, generally, the only option for upgrading solid-walled traditional houses which are either listed or in conservation areas although restrictions may be relaxed for improvements at the rear of the property. There are a number of insulation systems available which involve fixing battens to the internal walls, installing insulative material in the cavity and then lining the studwork. The drawback is that precious internal floor area is lost, which can be critical in smaller terrace houses.

Calsitherm Climate Board is an internal lining which can be fixed direct to the internal wall with a special adhesive. The board is manufactured from calcium silicate, a microporous material with good insulating properties. Calcium silicate is formed when water is mixed with sand and lime (silicon dioxide and calcium oxide). After being formed into large panels, the tiny calcium silicate crystals grow in an autoclave process while being subjected to steam and high pressure to produce a highly porous, fine structure. The high PH and molecular structure of the material mean that mould growth is inhibited.

Gypsum plaster is not compatible with the Calsitherm system. Any existing gypsum plaster must be removed prior to fixing the Climate Board. It is recommended that a lime levelling coat is applied and that the board is finished with a lime plaster and painted with a breathable 'natural' paint.

Founded in 1977, Calsitherm is a leading manufacturer of Climate Board. The company is based in Paderborn in Germany and the product has been specified in a wide range of projects over two decades. It was recently used in the refurbishment of the Rijksmuseum in Amsterdam. The sole distributor in the UK and Ireland is Ecological Building Systems, a company set up to specialise in sustainable building products. The company is also the sole agent for pro clima membranes – designed to improve the airtightness of buildings – and distributes other products for sustainable building projects including GUTEX wood fibre insulation boards and Thermo-Hemp insulation which is manufactured in Bavaria.

For further information, visit
**www.ecologicalbuildingsystems.com**

| Construction | U-value |
|---|---|
| Existing uninsulated 600 mm thick solid stone wall | 2.26 W/m²K |
| Adding 30 mm Calsitherm Climate Board including levelling coat, adhesive mortar and finishing plaster | 1.06 W/m²K |
| Adding 50 mm Calsitherm Climate Board including levelling coat, adhesive mortar and finishing plaster | 0.80 W/m²K |

## Caroma

*Photo: Maria Davies-Morgante*

The Caroma Profile 5 toilet has an integrated basin above the WC cistern so it is suitable for situations where space is limited, as in Kit Knowles' house in Manchester (see pages 29–35). The WC is also the simplest way of recycling water for flushing. When it is flushed, the cistern is filled via a tap over the basin. Hands can be washed in the cold water which then exits the basin via the waste and fills the cistern with grey water ready for the next flush. There is a 4.5/3-litre dual flush option.

Developed in Australia, the Caroma WC has been tested over a ten-year period. The product has been given the Waterwise Checkmark for water usage efficiency. It is distributed in the UK by Sanlamere, a company set up to source water-saving and energy-saving products worldwide and to make these available to the UK market. Sanlamere's website gives a list of UK retailers.

For further information, visit **www.sanlamere.co.uk** and **www.waterwise.org.uk**

## Foamglas

Foamglas insulation is manufactured from a minimum of 60%, locally sourced recycled glass, including scrap vehicle glass and off-cuts from the window industry. Raw materials are mineral based and from abundant natural resources. In 1937, Pittsburgh Corning Corporation built its first cellular glass manufacturing facility in the city after which the firm is named. The UK office opened in 1975, and is supplied with products from production plants in Europe; the newest opened in 2008 in the Czech Republic. The product range includes rigid insulation boards for most common applications including flat roofs, green roofs and car park decks, interior and exterior insulation systems as well as cavity wall insulation and under or over concrete floors.

It is the only insulation material which is totally impervious to any form of moisture, is not combustible, is dimensionally stable, has high compressive strength and is rot-, insect- and vermin-proof. It is totally inorganic and will not support the growth of mould, fungi or microorganisms, which makes it particularly suitable for insulating basements and retaining walls.

Foamglas Perinsul HL is a load-bearing insulation block which can be used in specific locations to prevent cold bridging. Pittsburgh Corning has specially developed the product for the UK market. The blocks are manufactured from high-density Foamglas and are designed to form an insulated joint between vertical wall insulation and horizontal floor or roof insulation. The thermal properties of Foamglas are combined with a high compressive strength of 2.9 N/mm$^2$.

In 2011, Foamglas cellular glass foam insulation was recognised as a 'green' building product by Natureplus, an international organisation which aims to develop a culture of sustainability within the building sector. It was originally established in 2001 by a group of specialist building product manufacturers in Germany but now has offices in Austria, Belgium, France and Switzerland, in addition to the head office in Germany. The Natureplus quality seal is only issued to building products which are comprised of a minimum of 85% of renewable raw materials or mineral-based materials which are almost unlimited in their availability. Products which carry the Natureplus label undergo a comprehensive testing process for their environmental impact and functionality. The Natureplus product database lists all the products certified by the organisation together with specification data and test/assessment results. This information is free of charge and can be accessed without registering. It can be used by planners, tradesmen and consumers to compare sustainable building products which do not pose risks to health.

For further information, visit
**www.foamglas.co.uk** and
**www.natureplus.org**

## Knauf Insulation

*Photo: Knauf Insulation*

The Thermoshell IWI System from Knauf Insulation is an internal wall insulation system designed for upgrading existing solid external walls. Thermally engineered insulated studs, EcoStuds, are fixed to the internal wall surface. Earthwool EcoBatt insulation slabs are then friction fitted between the EcoStuds and the construction is finished with a vapour control layer and plasterboard. EcoStuds are manufactured from extruded polystyrene (XPS) bonded to a layer of OSB and are available in a range of thermal performance requirements. The XPS is manufactured in the UK and has a BRE-Certified Green Guide Rating of A; the OSB is manufactured from timber supplied from Forest Stewardship Council-certified forests; and the mineral wool insulation is manufactured using up to 80% recycled glass.

A typical 225 mm-thick, solid masonry external wall with a dense plaster finish will achieve a U-value of approximately 2.10 W/m²K. The same wall insulated with the Thermoshell

IWI System using 95 mm thick EcoStuds will achieve a U-value of approximately 0.30 W/m²K, an improvement in performance of more than 80%. The Knauf Insulation Thermoshell range also includes external wall insulation systems, including similar materials such as rock mineral wool insulation. Thermoshell IWI is simple to install by a competent contractor, however it is only available to installers that have been trained and approved by Knauf Insulation.

Knauf Insulation is the only UK manufacturer of glass and rock mineral wool and extruded polystyrene insulation and the company offers a wide range of insulation solutions to meet the increasing standards of energy efficiency, fire resistance and acoustic performance in new and existing homes, non-residential buildings and industrial applications. The company has more than 30 manufacturing sites worldwide. In the UK, it employs around 500 people at its four manufacturing plants.

For further information, visit
**www.knaufinsulation.co.uk**

## MagmaTech

*Photo: Ancon Building Products*

Stainless steel wall ties in cavity wall construction are a common source of thermal bridging which can significantly compromise the external wall's thermal performance. The Teplo Tie range of masonry wall ties are manufactured by MagmaTech from a composite material based on basalt fibre. The material is corrosion- and alkali-resistant; it is stronger and lighter than stainless steel; and 20 times less thermally conductive than its stainless steel equivalent.

Teplo Ties have a thermal conductivity of just 0.7W/mK and MagmaTech claims that the product is the most thermally efficient wall tie on the market. The ties are available in various lengths to suit most typical cavity widths and the product has a BBA certificate for cavities as wide as 450 mm.

For further information, visit
**www.magmatech.co.uk**

### Passivent

A leading UK manufacturer of sustainable and energy-efficient ventilation systems, Passivent specialises in products for the removal of moisture, cooling and improving air quality, background ventilation and natural daylight. One of its latest introductions is the iMEV (intelligent Mechanical Extract Ventilation) system, which is an advance on more conventional MVHR systems. Humidity sensitive filaments determine how much extraction is needed and a choice of control levels ensures that in domestic dwellings, apartment blocks or multi-occupancy commercial buildings such as hotels, care homes and student accommodation, the system delivers the appropriate level of ventilation without excessive energy usage or the need for occupier control.

Ventilation remains constant until relative humidity increases, when it automatically boosts airflow by up to 88%. There are three different systems – iMEV, iMEV Local and iMEV TotalPassivent iMEV – each tailored to individual project requirements depending on the level of ventilation required, occupant strategy and ducting installation preferences. Passivent iMEV Local is most suitable for smaller domestic applications. When humidity increases in one 'wet' room, the system is designed to boost extraction in the critical room whilst ventilation in other rooms drops to maintain a constant 'whole house' rate, reducing unnecessary heat loss. Unnecessary extraction and the resultant heat loss is eliminated.

Other key products in Passivent's portfolio include passive stack ventilation systems and sunscoop rooflights which can channel daylight into the centre of buildings, reducing the need for artificial lighting.

For further information, visit
**www.passivent.com**

### PermaRock

PermaRock is one of the leading manufacturers and suppliers of external wall insulation systems. In 2012, the company was acquired by Sustainable Building Solutions, a division of builders' merchants Travis Perkins. SBS has been set up to provide an 'integrated approach to providing solutions' for energy-efficient building and renewable energy projects. Although the website is product oriented, SBS also offers technical advice, specifications, services and training schemes. A large section of the site is focused on refurbishment projects.

PermaRock has developed a range of six external insulation systems using a number of insulation materials, including mineral fibre, mineral fibre lamella, lightweight expanded polystyrene, expanded polystyrene and phenolic foams. Suitable for both new-build and retrofit projects, the systems can be fixed directly to almost any existing substrate – brickwork, concrete block, masonry, timber frame, lightweight metal frame or structural building systems.

External insulation systems will significantly alter the external appearance of a building and are not acceptable for application to listed buildings and to street façades in conservation areas. They can, however, improve the look of run-down housing in less sensitive areas and the company has developed an extensive range of renders and decorative finishes. These include more than 500 colours, 'metallic effect' renders and, perhaps not for the architectural purist, brick slips which can replicate traditional brickwork. It is also possible to create simulated stone coursing and shadowlines, which have some historic precedent in decorative stucco applied to Georgian and Victorian houses.

Technical developments in the systems are ongoing and PermaRock has recently introduced what it claims to be an industry first: 'self-cleaning' SiliconeUltra K&R renders based on nano-quartz technology. The renders provide enhanced repellancy against dirt and increased resistance to the growth of algae. The lightweight render also uses up to 20% less material than existing silicone- and acrylic-based through-coloured renders.

The PermaRock EPS Platinum insulated render system was specified for the Dyne Road project by Bere Architects (see pages 23–7).

For further information, visit **www.permarock.com** and **www.sustainablebuildingsolutions.co.uk**

## Unger Diffutherm

*Photo: © Unger-Diffutherm GmbH.*

The UdiIN RECO wood fibre system from Unger Diffutherm has been specially developed for the internal insulation of existing solid-walled buildings. It is particularly suitable for uneven wall surfaces as it can accommodate wide variations in the level of the existing walls of plus or minus 20 mm. This is achieved by adjustable fixings which were originally developed for the UdiIN RECO external insulation system. Wood fibre insulation board has ideal qualities for use in an existing building; it actively manages moisture, is vapour permeable and also provides good soundproofing.

Unger recommends that the boards are coated with Udi Multigrund which provides additional protection against construction damage by vapour control and forms a suitable dry, smooth, crack-free finish for paint or other internal finishes. The manufacturer also recommends natural loam plasters or mineral-based paints from its own range of products.

Unger Diffutherm was established in 1989 in Chemnitz in the Saxony region of Germany and is owned and run by the Unger family. Research scientist Bernd Unger founded the company based on his research into energy-saving building technologies in the 1970s and 1980s. In his search for eco-friendly building materials, he developed the concept of a directly renderable wood-fibre board and was eventually able to put this into production. It took more than a decade for the product to be developed and to meet the strict criteria of the German building product standards.

For further information from the UK distributors, visit **www.backtoearth.co.uk**

▶ **Hampstead Beach House, London Borough of Camden by Hayhurst and Co, detail of shutter in boarded rear extension.**
*Photo: Kilian O'Sullivan*
*www.kilianosullivan.com*

# Conclusion

## Housing for the future

The existing housing stock is one of the most important sustainable resources in the UK. As the debate continues over climate change, even sceptics have to acknowledge that the climate is changing and becoming more erratic. In certain parts of the globe, human existence is becoming less viable due to drought or, at the other extreme, flooding. A more responsible attitude to the exploitation of the planet's finite resources has to be adopted. Whilst it is essential that new homes are constructed and that the poorest quality housing which has reached the end of its useful life is demolished and replaced, the best of our housing stock should be properly maintained and adapted for today's lifestyles.

It is not just a matter of sustainability; there is a sociological and psychological perspective. The home is the essential anchor of most people's lives. It is a place to escape from the ever-harsher pressures of modern life, a place to retreat to and to recharge the brain cells for a challenging day ahead. Heritage and continuity play an important part in this cycle of human life; familiar surroundings foster security. Experiments with new types of public housing design after the Second World War destroyed communities, resulting in disadvantaged, lawless ghettoes disconnected from urban centres where social problems became so severe that whole estates had to be demolished within a generation.

This is not say that there is anything wrong with the concept of high-rise living. Properly maintained high-rise flats with adequate security have become popular with elderly residents; they proved not to be suitable for families with young children. Some former public housing estates can also be upgraded for a new generation of private tenants. The iconic Quarry Hill development designed by Alison and Peter Smithson in Sheffield, for example, is in the process of being transformed by Urban Splash from a no-go sink estate into a hip residence for city centre-based young professionals.

Such projects highlight the fact that, despite the decline in industrial and manufacturing output in the UK, the country still retains its pre-eminence in design and technological development. This is certainly the case in the architectural profession. Building conservation skills are also most highly developed in the UK. Although mistakes may have been made in the past, experimentation with housing design has been a key factor in the UK's economic success in the past two centuries.

## Patterns of urban living

To assess what is best about the historic housing stock – what to preserve and what lessons there are to be learned for the design of new housing – it is important that planners, architects and conservationists understand the factors that resulted in its design and construction. The UK was at the forefront of the development of urban living in the 18th and 19th centuries. The Industrial Revolution drove large numbers of the population from the country into towns as the economy moved from an agricultural base to an industrial one. At first the effects of overcrowding were not understood. In the country the problems of poor housing and health were often overlooked. The Victorians romanticised rural life in the late 19th century. Pastel watercolours by artists such as Helen Allingham depicting content and rosy-cheeked peasants posing outside picturesque thatched cottages with front gardens abundant with wild flowers masked the grim reality of damp and unsanitary accommodation, low wages and short lifespans.

However, as disease weakened the urban workforce, employers, industrialists and the government acted to improve housing standards, essential services and sanitation. The workforce was certainly exploited, but unhealthy employees were not sufficiently productive, so the necessary investment was grudgingly made in an attempt to raise their living standards. Medical inspections, which formed part of the conscription process for men called up for service in the First World War, revealed the terrible truth about the health of the working classes.

During the Georgian period a method of building urban houses was developed to accommodate the expanding middle classes. Agricultural estates around urban centres were gradually developed. Houses were generally leasehold and landowners were keen to maintain the value of their estates so they set standard plot sizes for a range of house types tailored to specific economic groups and introduced building standards in an attempt to ensure quality of construction. Pattern books were published illustrating different categories of classes of homes for the different strata of society.

Many of the most well constructed houses from this period still remain – and some feature in the refurbishment projects illustrated above. Over time, poorly constructed Georgian houses have disappeared; some were structurally unsound and collapsed, sometimes with loss of life resulting in the introduction of Building Regulations to ensure standards of construction and public safety. The earliest regulations were introduced in London, which has always been the UK's centre of economic development. These date back to the years immediately following the Great Fire of London in 1666 and were initially designed to prevent the spread of fire. Many other Georgian and Victorian houses were either destroyed in the Second World War or cleared away as 'unfit' in the years that followed. These clearances were often misguided and, after the mistakes of the 1960s and 1970s, it is surprising that the concept of 'slum' clearance was revived in the early 21st century.

Most Georgian houses remaining today have stood the test of time and are either listed or in conservation areas, so their future is secured. The highest-quality areas of Victorian housing are now also conservation areas and a number of local authorities have adopted the concept of 'local listing' which aims to extend the protection of statutory listing to buildings which are on the borderline of the Historic England criteria but are, nevertheless, important to a particular town's architectural heritage.

### Long life, loose fit, low energy

The quality of construction and materials of these remaining Georgian houses has helped to ensure their survival and their design has proved remarkably sustainable over three centuries. In the 1980s, the Architectural Press supported the concept of 'long life, loose fit, low energy', a concept well ahead of its time and one still not widely adopted today due to short-term economic considerations. The Georgian terrace house fulfils the first two criteria, if not the third. The simple concept of creating spacious, light-filled rooms along an economically designed urban street with a rear service wing which could be adapted and upgraded at some time in the future, has endured. Four, 21st-century adaptations of the 'closet wing' have been featured above: Henning Stummel's 'Reversible Tower' in Shouldham Street, London Borough of Westminster (pages 79–81); two adjoining projects with very different approaches in Kelly Street, Camden (pages 89–93); and 51% Studios' more extensive three-storey rear addition to a Victorian villa in Hackney (pages 83–7). The latter is also a good example of how the aspirations of a client, in this case a Norwegian artist, can be practically and emotionally satisfied. A small piece of Scandinavia has been re-created in

claustrophobic north London for an artist who takes inspiration and succour from the Nordic landscape.

### 21st-century living

The open-plan living/dining/kitchen space has become an icon for contemporary family living in 21st century society. In the Georgian and early Victorian period, the back yard and rear garden were often the domain of servants, useful for drying washing and other tasks and for their recreation, as free time outside the household was severely restricted.

Today, access to a cool green space is one of the real joys of urban living; children can play safely in a healthy environment, dining can take place al fresco, and owners can indulge in one of the most popular UK obsessions: gardening. Most of the projects featured above improve the connection between urban house and garden significantly. In several cases, space can flow uninterrupted from inside to outside. In summer the garden becomes an additional room for family recreation.

Semi-detached suburban villas provide the best opportunity for extending a house and for improving ground-floor family space. Additional space at the rear and the side of a house gives the client and architect increased opportunities for the creation of a more radical addition. Over a succession of projects, Alison Brooks has transformed a number of London houses into contemporary family homes. Her experience in working with maverick designer Ron Arad has fed through into her innovative, sculptural extensions to traditional houses. The latest technology – in CAD, in structural solutions and in the use of materials – has resulted in a series of unique London homes hidden behind unchanged, restored historic façades. But this is not façadism. Refurbishment projects work best when an extension is not merely an object stuck on to the rear of an existing house; when the spatial redesign extends into the lower ground and ground floors, the historic fabric and the new interventions can gel; traditional rooms which can accommodate more formal occasions sit comfortably alongside open-plan contemporary spaces which reflect the dynamism and interaction of today's family life.

This is demonstrated very well in Alison Brooks' Wrap House (pages 51–5) where the lower two floors have been transformed into a double-height living space with the upper, more formal sitting room becoming a mezzanine overlooking the lofty kitchen space. David Mikhail has achieved a similar effect in his Hoxton House refurbishment project (pages 129–31) where the upper ground floor sitting room looks into a double-height dining space and out through the two-storey glass bay window to the garden beyond. In Highgate, Paul Archer has created a dramatic contrast between styles and ways of living (pages 133–5). The upper ground floor sitting room, with its beautifully restored cornicing and other original features, opens into the lower living area with views through a glass balustrade to the trees of Hampstead Heath in the distance.

This type of project can be very demanding and, particularly in larger architectural practices, can become uneconomic. Alison Brooks – and other architects featured in this book – acknowledge this, but they relish the challenge of smaller projects, the closer interaction between client and designer and the opportunity they bring for design experimentation on a manageable scale. Alison, therefore, limits work on such projects to one at any time in the practice.

## Two-storey additions

Single-storey rear additions tend to be more acceptable to planning authorities – and to neighbours. A 'green' wild flower meadow roof such as those at Hairy House (pages 65–9) and the Jewel Box (pages 165–7) can do much to mitigate the impact on views from nearby properties. It is more difficult to gain approval for two-storey extensions, as they overlook neighbouring gardens and may even be visible from the street. There was a large industrial building at the bottom of the garden in Hampstead where Nick Hayhurst has created a playful 'beach house' (pages 139–41), so there were no problems from overlooking neighbours. A side extension extends the kitchen/dining/living space and the upper floor of the existing two-storey rear wing has been clad in vertical timber boarding to unify it with the new additions. As in David Mikhail's projects, care has been taken in the detailing of the garden so that it harmonises completely with the living space of the house; garden planters and seating line up with the kitchen units and flooring materials are continued on to the external terrace.

Timber has also been used by Moxon Architects to clad the new first-floor bathroom at the rear of a Victorian villa in Hackney (pages 153–5). This sits discreetly above a new kitchen/dining space created for the gardening enthusiast client. There is a precedent for such bolt-on new service

rooms. Small-scale timber additions to 18th-century houses in London were one of the inspirations for Henning Larsen's new 'closet wing' in Westminster (pages 79–81).

The two-storey extension designed by Ashton Porter Architects for a Victorian villa in leafy Twickenham (pages 143–7) addresses the street with an amusing reproduction of one of the period windows of the existing house set in a suspended white panel – like an exhibit in an art gallery. The structural gymnastics continue towards the garden where the rear elevation is deconstructed and layered. Sandwiched between an inner glazed wall to the upper ground floor living room and an outer opaque wall suspended from the steel roof structure, pierced by an unglazed window, is a cantilevered staircase to the garden. In a small-scale domestic project, design sophistication and technical brilliance can both be realised.

## Architectural start-ups

Domestic extension projects have always been seen as the starting point for architects attempting to set up practice independently. Many see them as a stepping stone to more lucrative larger projects; once the practice becomes established, this type of project is abandoned. Others, such as Paul Archer, concentrate almost entirely on domestic commissions. Specialisation can bring benefits for both architects and clients. Paul has an extensive portfolio of domestic refurbishment work, which is featured in *Old to New*, a book recently published by the practice and he has an enviable client list. Clients often approach him by recommendation as they are able to judge the quality of his previous work; he has an established track record in this particular building type, a fascination with glass technology and is able to draw on conservation skills in his confident blend of old and new.

Tom Pike is another architect who specialises in domestic refurbishment projects. He is adept at sweeping away the internal divisions of rear reception rooms and introducing a liberating, discreet steel structure to create airy, open-plan kitchen/dining/living spaces which can be opened up fully to the garden. At Salcott Road in Battersea (pages 149–51) he has extended a semi-detached house sideways, turning a blank gable wall into a sleek and carefully composed contemporary elevation which gains admiring glances from potential clients taking their children to the school close by.

▲ **The Clay Field development of 26 homes in Suffolk by Mikhail Riches with Kathy Hawley.**
**In addition to the sustainable construction of the houses, the site layout reflects ancient field patterns and there are low-maintenance communal gardens including a wild flower meadow, allotments and an orchard.**
*Photo: Tim Crocker*

The slim extension to the gable wall has, literally, given the house a new dimension.

## Housing developments

David Mikhail has a similarly impressive list of high-profile private clients. Previously, he kept his domestic commissions separate from the design of other building types, practising as David Mikhail Architects for the domestic work and as a partner in Riches Hawley Mikhail for public sector and housing association projects. Now the work of the restructured practice, Mikhail Riches, has been merged. There are crossovers between experience in the two different sectors and the quality of the firm's output is enriched resulting in a string of housing awards. The Clay Field Development of 26 sustainable homes in Suffolk, by Mikhail Riches with Kathy Hawley, won an RIBA Award and a Housing Design Award in 2009, and the Church Walk development of three houses and one apartment in Stoke Newington won an RIBA Award and the RIBA London Building of the Year Award in 2013.

Alison Brooks is also idealistic about bringing the quality and joy to be found in her one-off domestic refurbishment projects to larger new-build housing schemes. This has been a primary aim since founding her own practice. The firm's

Newhall Be development of 84 units for Linden Homes in Harlow, Essex was judged to be the Supreme Winner in the Housing Design Awards 2013. Spatial and technical concepts developed in Alison Brooks' work for private clients are refined and utilised in the larger housing scheme. The sculptural form, technical innovation and consistent detailing of materials mark out the Newhall houses as an ABA creation. Prefabricated timber cassettes avoid the need for roof trusses, so the roof space can be fully exploited. The plan form is subtly angled, creating interesting room shapes and oblique views to the landscape. There is a unity of materials and a limited palette. Horizontal, black, weather-boarded walls, inspired by traditional timber-clad Essex barns, merge into the grey roof 'slates', as the planes angle backwards creating a rhythmic streetscape.

## Construction innovation

To achieve this level of technical innovation, Alison Brooks works closely with structural engineers and specialist building product manufacturers. On smaller projects the number of available specialist manufacturers and subcontractors and suppliers will be very limited. They may feel that it is too risky and insufficiently profitable to take responsibility for often-experimental designs, so estimates for construction work can sometimes be excessive. However, as most building professionals have learned, the cheapest quotation is not always the best, a fact that clients are sometimes reluctant to accept. It is certainly advisable to use specialist contractors for challenging work. This is particularly the case for projects involving basement excavation and underpinning and for loft conversions. In London, underground extensions have become more popular as the value of property has soared. Some even extend down by two floors, incorporating swimming pools, gyms and cinema rooms – the new must-have spaces of the urban rich.

However, clients should be aware that, despite the more stringent ground condition surveys and analyses now demanded by local authorities, they will be entering into the unknown with no going back once excavation commences; construction costs can soar as the contractor battles to cope with unexpected ground water conditions and discovers the poor condition of recently exposed foundations and party walls. It is always possible that construction work may cause settlement or other structural damage to adjoining properties and some clients have ended up paying for the virtual

rebuilding of the house next door in addition to paying compensation for the noise and disruption. Fixed-price contracts are not necessarily a guarantee against rising costs; if construction costs soar due to unexpected work, there is a danger that the contractor may go bankrupt.

New materials and construction techniques can also be used in much smaller projects. Procter:Rihl has used a prefabricated building system to form a 'folded' side extension in Islington (pages 173–5), which perches on the rebuilt garden wall. Inside, they have achieved the complexity of form to be found in Alison Brooks' larger projects. The new extension to a shoreside fisherman's bothy in Fife designed by Oliver Chapman (pages 179–81) also has a folded, gull-wing form. Its metallic, angled roof sits above the steely grey rocks glistening on the shore, blending into its environment. The cottage originally faced inland, opening on to the narrow and sheltered main street of the town. Now the views at the rear have been opened up to take in the dramatic and ever-changing seascape.

## Let there be light

To bring more light into previously dark basements and lower ground floors, Phil Coffey has excavated the lower level by up to 1m in a series of renovation projects in north London, forming a concrete 'bowl' which underpins party walls and forms the new floor finish. The concrete is expressed and beautifully detailed, incorporating fireplaces, plinths and kitchen worktops. Several of the techniques were trialled in his own family home in north London (pages 119–23). His philosophy of domestic refurbishment is to create a house where occupants can arrive, personalise the space with their own furniture and artefacts, and then move on as circumstances change, leaving the house ready to accommodate a new family and a different way of life. Polished, light-reflecting concrete, exposed brickwork and simple white, minimalist kitchen units and built-in storage form a neutral, calm backdrop for the theatre of hectic urban life. Although not overtly eco-friendly, the projects encapsulate a passive approach to energy efficiency and sustainability. Opening up the ground floor space to sunlight allows solar heat to be stored in the concrete 'bowl'; open-plan staircases allow warm air to rise and exit through windows in the upper floors, encouraging ventilation which is cooling in the summer and warming in the winter and which provides a healthy clean environment for the occupants.

David Mikhail has also brought light and air into a previously dark narrow terrace house in Hackney (pages 129–31). Excavating the garden has created a closer unity between house and garden and, as with his East London House, David's refined detailing extends into the hard landscaping and furniture of the garden emphasising the connection between inner and outer space. Paul Archer has also lowered the garden in his hillside refurbishment project in Highgate (pages 133–5) and both schemes feature structural glass extensions which flood the interiors with light.

On a smaller scale, William Tunnell has added a glass bay window to the principal floor of a house on Tayside (pages 183–5), opening up wide-ranging views across the estuary and bringing light and interest into a house which previously turned its back on the elements. Roof lights and clerestory windows can also introduce light deep into the plan of terraced houses. John Christophers has taken great care with his window design at his house in Birmingham (pages 43–7), taking inspiration from Lutyens' work at Lindisfarne Castle.

◄ **At the Church Walk development of three houses and one apartment in Stoke Newington, London, David Mikhail has brought his experience and innovation in the design of houses for individual clients to a large project.**
*Photo: Tim Crocker*

## Timber-frame construction

The use of materials such as concrete and glass characterise the work of a number of designers. Other architects prefer the softer tones and sustainability of timber. One of the most sustainable and often the most practical and economic solutions for extending an existing house, timber-framed construction has a number of advantages. It is lightweight, making it possible for new structures to be built on existing foundations; timber components are small and suitable for situations where access is restricted; assembly is simple and wet trades are minimised, resulting in faster and more economic construction times.

At Goldhawk Road in west London (pages 113–5), Waind Gohil + Potter Architects has retained an existing single-storey rear extension and used this as a base for the creation of a new *piano nobile* constructed from lightweight timber with views over the garden. Here it was possible to utilise the existing foundations, although it was found that the walls of the earlier extension required stabilising and strengthening.

Under Permitted Development guidelines, however, building materials for new extensions have to follow those of the existing house. At Timber Fin House in Walthamstow (pages 103–7), Neil Dusheiko had to persuade the local planners that a timber-framed and -clad solution — a construction method favoured by his client — was suitable. He pointed out that timber was a common construction material in back gardens, used for fencing, sheds and other outdoor structures. In the large extension to a Georgian house in east London (pages 97–101), David Mikhail has designed an elegant, timber-framed structure which received a Wood Award in 2013. Its refined elegance complements the sophistication of the existing Georgian house.

In an unassuming street of 1940s houses in a suburb of Winchester which the local planners still deemed to have architectural merit, Dan Brill was unable to demolish an existing house and build the new detached home of his clients' dreams. As the existing structure had to be retained, he gutted the traditional brick structure to create a dramatic double-height living space. Existing windows remain in place like a modern art gallery installation, flooding light into the liberated volume. A vestige of the first floor remains to form a television room. Bedrooms and bathrooms are accommodated in a linear timber-framed rear extension which runs off down the garden (pages 109–11).

▲ **Church Walk, Stoke Newington, London by Mikhail Riches.**
**The houses step down to the street from a large end tower, merging the mass of the building into the differing scale of surrounding buildings and also allowing for sunlit roof terraces in the densely development urban environment.**
*Photo: Tim Crocker*

Window reveals are angled and lined with mirrors which throw light into the interior. Alison Brooks incorporates roof glazing to delineate structures and angled windows which focus on views into the garden. In William Tunnell's Newhaven House in Edinburgh (pages 183–5), the potential darkening effect of the extension which runs across the entire width of the rear of the house is mitigated by roof lights above the kitchen and a high-level clerestory window with angled reveals, reminiscent of the windows in Le Corbusier's Notre Dame du Haut chapel at Ronchamp. This has been tucked in above the roof of the new extension to enhance the natural light to the original rear reception room.

Three-storey traditional terrace houses are by their very nature dark at the centre of the plan and this can only be partially alleviated by a roof light over the staircase. Removing internal divisions to form open-plan living spaces, glazed rear extensions and additional clerestory and roof lights can transform an interior. Natural light also brings variety and interest to an interior as the light changes colour and intensity depending on the seasons and the time of day. Robert Dye has created interesting light effects at Dunollie Place, as has Neil Dusheiko at Timber Fin House.

## Eco refurbishments

Timber-framed new extensions and a wild-flower green roof cannot turn a traditional house into an energy-efficient home. Transforming an older urban house into an 'eco' home is not always practical; the process can be extremely expensive and not many clients demand it. As mentioned in the introduction, there are examples of Georgian houses in central London which have been gutted and a low-energy house has been built within its existing shell. The cost of such a project is prohibitive to the average UK family. At Culford Road in Hackney (pages 37–41), Prewett Bizley has adopted a more sensitive and achievable approach. The front façade has been strengthened and insulated internally. New steel beams have been inserted to support floor joists and rafters independently, eliminating cold bridging. At the rear it has been possible to construct a new façade to standards in excess of current regulations, replacing earlier defective structures. Such construction projects can be experimental, involving relatively new techniques and materials, and the architects of this project have been candid in their examination of areas where detailing could have been improved in an analysis of construction on the firm's website.

Other 'eco' refurbishment projects are even more experimental. Two of the projects included above are occupied by the designer and they are test beds for new design concepts, technologies and materials. Kit Knowles is a scientist who specialises in hybrid technologies and he has brought his expertise to bear on the refurbishment of an Arts and Crafts semi-detached house in Manchester (pages 29–35). Behind the apparently unchanged façade almost every element, in fact, has been upgraded; the house is a laboratory for new ideas. At the same time, it is a comfortable, healthy and energy-efficient home for his young family. His enthusiasm is boundless and he shares this in regular open days organised through the rapidly growing SuperHomes network.

Justin Bere has dedicated his professional life to the design of sustainable buildings and he is one of the UK's leading architects in this sphere. Just as in the early days of vegetarian restaurants when a visit to Cranks in Carnaby Street in the 1960s could be something of a hair-shirt experience – as the name strangely suggested, eco home designers are sometimes seen as a throwback to the time of flower power and geodesic domes. In striving to be eco friendly, design

excellence can sometimes be lost with the result that the finished concept, though worthy, is dismissed by the design press. Justin Bere has set out to change this perception, as demonstrated in his recent publication, *An Introduction to Passive House*. He has assembled a dedicated team of designers who occupied one of his recent, Passivhaus-certified, award-winning projects in east London. The house in the London Borough of Brent (pages 23–7) is an exemplar of how to adapt a traditional house following Passivhaus principles. Most importantly, Justin and other partners in his firm are influencing product manufacturers. For example, they have been working with Mumford & Wood to develop a triple-glazed, Georgian-style sash window which aims to satisfy the concerns of conservation officers; previously it was only possible to incorporate slim-line, double-glazed small panels of glass in Georgian glazed sashes.

◄ **Newhall Be, Harlow, Essex by Alison Brooks Architects.**
**Themes developed in Alison Brooks' residential extensions have been applied to a series of larger housing developments. At Newhall Be, horizontal, black, weatherboarded walls merge into the grey roof slates as the planes angle backwards, creating a rhythmic streetscape.**
*Photo: Paul Riddle/VIEW*

◄ **Newhall Be, Harlow, Essex by Alison Brooks Architects.**
**Alison Brooks believes that there is no need for housing estates to be predictable and dull, and she aims to give the owners and tenants of these homes the benefit of the same inventiveness and enjoyment of form and space as her more wealthier clients.**
*Photo: Paul Riddle/VIEW*

### Recycling and upcycling

Utilising recycled building materials in new projects is patently sustainable. In an ambitious project in London, Robert Dye has gone one step further by reusing a large proportion of the existing building materials of a previously structurally unsound house without removing them from the site (pages 71–5). Due to the building being 'at risk' and potentially a dangerous structure, the local authority accepted this approach. It was possible to retain the front façade and some of the supporting structure but much of the interior was taken down, materials stored on site and then reused in construction of a much higher standard. Transportation miles of new materials or of recycled materials sourced remotely were eliminated and the key original features of the house, such as cornicing and staircase balusters and handrail, were restored and reinstated. Recycled materials are also to be found in John Christophers' house in Manchester and in Oliver Chapman's Skerrie House.

However, Robert Dye's project is not a historic re-creation, a sham pastiche which would be unacceptable to organisations such as the SPAB; he has brought his renowned design skills to play in a simply detailed, sophisticated and elegant rear extension which liberates the house from its run-down and neglected past, combining the best of contemporary design with the peak of conservation skills. As well as successfully integrating old and new, the existing main reception rooms – previously detached from the garden due to the fall in the site – are united with the garden via a lofty, double-height kitchen/dining/living space. Long-distance views to nearby trees and local landmarks are also drawn into the design concept, anchoring the new intervention into its context.

### Side extensions

One of the simplest and most economic ways of extending a terrace house with a rear service wing is to fill in the side rear yard. However, simplicity of concept can often expose a lack of design skill and attention to detail; any blemish or unresolved junction is immediately apparent. In a series of projects, Platform 5 Architects has developed a restricted vocabulary which gives the remodelled interiors a unique identity; there is clarity of form, delightful detailing and high-quality craftsmanship (pages 159–60).

In many of the projects featured above, highly developed joinery skills play a major part in the overall standard of finish. Discreetly detailed minimalist kitchen units, wardrobes and cupboards can accommodate a great deal of clutter and possessions, freeing up interiors and increasing the sense of space. Fraher Architects has set up its own joinery firm, which now also works for other architects, in an acknowledgment of the key role carpentry and cabinet making plays in their interior design work. Some of the best site agents have a background in carpentry and joinery.

Small often is beautiful and some of the smaller projects featured above are no less impressive than the ones with seemingly unlimited budgets. Waind Gohil + Potter's extension in Arundel (pages 169–71) has a simple beauty and a perfect unity with the original cottages which tumble down the hill. The plain refurbished interior has a Shaker-like spirituality. At the rear, a cleverly detailed V-shaped rooflight unites the new side extension with the existing rear wing and floods the interior with light.

The 32 projects discussed above by 24 designers illustrate a wide range of approaches to the adaptation and extension of existing urban houses. Although many of the house types and room layouts are similar, each project is an individual creation. The combination of differing design philosophies and the needs and aspirations of specific clients have resulted in a wide variety of solutions, and it is this richness of creative endeavour which this book sets out to celebrate. Many of the construction techniques, building materials and technologies involved in the sustainable refurbishment of the traditional housing stock are still in an experimental stage. Designers and committed clients will be taking this development process forward in decades to come, adapting this very durable and valuable building stock for successive generations. Hopefully this book will have played a part in this process.

# Sources of information

## AECB sustainable building association

The Association for Environment Conscious Building (AECB) was established in 1989 to promote environmental awareness within the construction industry. It is a network of individuals and companies who are involved in sustainable building. Members of the organisation include builders, architects, designers, manufacturers, housing associations and local authorities

The AECB is run by its members and is an independent, not-for-profit organisation. Its stated aim is to 'promote excellence in design and construction, rather than gimmicks and green accounting tricks. The AECB's standards and advice are founded on a detailed and realistic understanding of the performance of buildings, constructed and refurbished in the real world, for real users.'

In 2007, the association launched its CarbonLite programme, a crash course in energy-efficient, low-carbon design and building. CarbonLite comprises a set of energy standards, a description of principles and methodologies for calculating heat loss and emissions, a training programme, and a database of buildings with measured energy results. One of the training courses can lead to accreditation by the Passivhaus Institute (see below). Participants can benefit from the expertise of some of the leading European Passivhaus professionals in a series of lectures and seminars either in an intensive course or in individual modules. Aimed at construction professionals and contractors, the course explains the principles behind the Passivhaus standard and methodologies and the use of the Passivhaus Planning Package (PHPP) for achieving low-energy performance.

The CarbonLite Passivhaus Designer Programme prepares delegates for the Passivhaus Institute's examination. On the successful completion of the exam, delegates are listed on the Passivhaus Designer database where they will be awarded either Passivhaus Designer or Passivhaus Consultant status, depending on their existing academic qualifications. The AECB has also established the Passivhaus Trust in the UK in 2010 (see below).

For further information, visit
**www.aecb.net**

## BRE

The origins of the Building Research Establishment go back to 1917 when the Department of Scientific and Industrial Research proposed the creation of an organisation to investigate and to test the performance of various building materials and construction methods suitable to use in new housing following the First World War. After the war, new methods of construction became more widely used in the UK, such as steel-reinforced concrete and, at a time when there was a huge growth in public sector building, it was important for the government to develop and monitor appropriate building standards. The British Standard for bricks was the first to be introduced.

Originally based in Acton in west London, BRE's research laboratories moved to Bucknalls, a large Victorian house surrounded by 38 acres of land near Watford in 1925. BRE occupies the same site today, although the area has been extended over the years and it now also houses the Innovation Park, where a number of low-energy projects have been constructed (see Introduction, page 11). In 1949, a separate research facility was set up in Scotland to test building materials and construction methods in the more extreme Scottish climate. Following privatisation in 1997, a registered charity was set up, now known as the BRE Trust, to 'own' BRE and to support built environment research for the public benefit.

The Trust awards scholarships and bursaries to PhD and MSc students and provides financial support for research at four University Centres of Excellence. These include: the BRE Centre for Innovative Construction Materials at the University of Bath where research areas include advanced and natural composites, low-carbon materials, timber, concrete, steel and masonry; the BRE Centre for Energy Utilisation at the University of Strathclyde where the fields of research include building controls, energy demand, carbon reduction, low-carbon offices, intelligent controls and energy reduction in homes; and the BRE Centre for Sustainable Design of the Built Environment at Cardiff University which focuses on design for sustainable refurbishment and occupancy behaviour related to energy efficiency.

For further information, visit
**www.bre.co.uk**

## Forest Stewardship Council

The vision of the Forest Stewardship Council (FSC) is that the world's forests should meet the social, ecological and economic rights and needs of the present generation without compromising those of future generations. Its mission is to promote environmentally appropriate, socially beneficial and economically viable management of forests. The Council achieves this by certifying timbers. All 10 of the FSC's principles and criteria must be satisfied before a forest management unit can receive FSC certification.

To check up-to-date certificates, specifiers should visit the Council's website **www.fsc-uk.org**

## Passivhaus

Passivhaus is the most widely recognised standard for low-energy homes in Europe. It was the brainchild of two professors, Bo Adamson of Lund University in Sweden and Wolfgang Feist of the Institut für Wohnen und Umwelt (Institute for Housing and the Environment) in Germany who began their discussions in May 1988. The first application was in a project for four terraced houses in Darmstadt, a centre for technical research since the 19th century, which was completed in 1991. The standard can also be applied to commercial, industrial and public buildings.

The Passivhaus Institute was founded in Darmstadt in September 1996 to promote and control the standards and in the 1990s a series of Passivhaus dwellings were completed in Germany. In London, the first certified Passivhaus was completed in 2011, a new timber-framed house in Camden.

Reducing the primary energy consumption and space heating demand is the main objective of the standard so that conventional heating can be minimised. A Mechanical Ventilation and Heat Recovery (MVHR) unit is generally specified to recover heat and recirculate it. Passive solar gain is also a key component with the use of natural stack and cross-ventilation through open windows to provide cooling during the summer months. Removing stale air and filtering it also improves the indoor air quality and this, in addition to water filtration and softening, is a key factor in the designs of leading Passivhaus designers such as Bere Architects.

In a Passivhaus, thermal comfort is achieved to the greatest practical extent through the use of passive measures listed below which can be applied not only to the residential sector but also to commercial, industrial and public buildings:

- superior levels of insulation with minimal thermal bridges;
- triple-glazed windows;
- passive solar gains and internal heat sources;
- excellent level of airtightness;
- good indoor air quality, provided by a whole-house mechanical ventilation system with highly efficient heat recovery;
- clean filtered water supply;
- photovoltaic cells to generate electricity;
- solar panels to supply hot water.

For further information, visit **www.passivhaus.org.net**

## Passivhaus Trust

Established by the AECB, the Passivhaus Trust is an independent, non-profit organisation that provides leadership in the UK for the adoption of the Passivhaus standard and methodology. It aims to promote the principles of Passivhaus as an effective way of reducing energy use and carbon emissions from buildings in the UK, as well as providing high standards of comfort and building health.

The Trust launched the UK Passivhaus Awards scheme in 2012 to celebrate the design and performance of Passivhaus projects in the UK. Passivhaus principles can be applied to any building type, not just houses, and a key aim of the awards is to gather data on the performance of Passivhaus buildings in the UK and to demonstrate how these buildings address occupant health and well-being, energy saving and other sustainability issues. Only certified Passivhaus projects are eligible for the awards and energy data must be available for at least one winter and one summer cycle as proof of performance is one of the main criteria.

For further information, visit **www.passivhaustrust.org.uk**

## Society for the Protection of Ancient Buildings

Set up by William Morris and other members of the Pre-Raphaelite Brotherhood at a meeting in Queens Square, Bloomsbury in London on 22 March 1877, the Society for the Protection of Ancient Buildings (SPAB) was a response to the often over-zealous restoration of old buildings by Victorian architects and amateurs in the late 19th century.

The Society developed a philosophy of sensitive repair; existing fabric was to be carefully repaired using traditional techniques and any new work was to be self-evident but complementary. In 1903, SPAB published its first technical pamphlet, 'Notes on the Repair of Ancient Buildings', which is a milestone in the UK's conservation movement.

The SPAB administers student bursaries and courses and has published a wide range of technical information aimed at both architects and the owners of historic buildings. Most recently the *Old House Eco Handbook* by Marianne Suhr and Roger Hunt has been published in association with the SPAB. A companion volume to the *Old House Handbook*, the *Eco Handbook* is a guide to a sustainable approach to retrofitting historic houses for energy efficiency. The book is primarily aimed at the owners of historic houses but will also be of use to building professionals who are less experienced in the repair and conservation of old buildings.

For further information, visit
**www.spab.org.uk**

### Solid Wall Insulation Guarantee Agency

The Solid Wall Insulation Guarantee Agency was set up in 2013 to match the safeguards offered by the Cavity Insulation Guarantee Agency, which provides a 25-year guarantee for accredited cavity wall insulation installations. Architects should be aware of the benefits the scheme brings to homeowners and to owners of domestic property portfolios.

The first guarantee was awarded in July 2013 to a refurbishment project carried out by Chesterfield Borough Council, which involved applying external wall installation in the upgrading of 79 properties in Mastin Moor, Derbyshire.

SWIGA Guarantee

Key benefits:

- 25-year term aligned to Green Deal and ECO requirements;
- vetted and accredited members with significant industry experience;
- quality framework covering survey of the property, technical detailing and installation;
- third-party surveillance covering installation and system manufacture;
- suitable for internal, external or hybrid insulation solutions under one guarantee;

- available for householders or landlords in both the private and social sectors;
- transferable guarantee with change of ownership of the property;
- not dependant on the length of the installer or system certificate holder guarantee;
- if installer ceases trading or becomes insolvent, the guarantee continues.

For further information, visit **www.swiga.co.uk**

### SuperHomes

SuperHomes is an initiative of the Sustainable Energy Academy, a charity set up to promote research into the technologies and processes which reduce the time and cost of implementing whole-house retrofits. Believing that projects on the ground are the best way of promoting low-energy sustainable retro-fits, the Academy aims to establish a network of 500 SuperHomes, so that one is accessible within 15 minutes of the majority of the population in the UK. To qualify as a SuperHome, a 60% reduction in carbon emissions must be achieved.

There are currently more than 190 SuperHomes featured on the network's website and open days are organised in March and September each year. Visitors can meet the owners and learn about the practicalities of retro-fitting an existing house and hear about other sustainable initiatives. Two projects featured above are included in the SuperHome programme: Kit Knowles' house in Manchester (pages 29–35) and John Christophers' house in Birmingham (pages 43–47).

For further information, visit
**www.superhomes.org.uk**

# Case study contacts

**Alison Brooks Architects**
Unit 610, Highgate Studios
53-79 Highgate Road
London NW5 1TL
Tel. 020 7267 9777
www.alisonbrooksarchitects.
com

**Ashton Porter Architects**
The Studio
11 Second Avenue
Bush Hill Park
Enfield
Greater London EN1 1BT
Tel. 020 8372 1619
www.ashtonporter.com

**Bere:architects**
54a Newington Green
London N16 9PX
Tel. 020 7241 1064
www.bere.co.uk

**Coffey Architects**
11-12 Great Sutton Street
London EC1V 0BX
Tel. 020 7549 2141
www.coffeyarchitects.com

**Dan Brill Architects**
34 Staple Gardens
Winchester SO23 8SR
Tel. 01962 622085
www.danbrillarchitects.com

**51% Studios**
1a Cobham Mews
London NW1 9SB
Tel. 020 3355 1205
www.51pct.com

**Fraher Architects**
The Studio
14a Gabriel Street
London SE23 1DT
Tel. 020 8291 6947
www.fraher.co.uk

**Giles Pike Architects**
537 Battersea Park Road
London SW11 3BL
Tel. 020 7924 6257
www.gilespike.com

**Hayhurst and Co**
26 Fournier Street
London E1 6QE
Tel. 020 7247 7028
www.hayhurstand.co.uk

**Henning Stummel
Architects**
Tin House
2 Smugglers Yard
London W12 8HJ
Tel. 020 8749 0794
www.henningstummel
architects.co.uk

**John Christophers
architect**
Associated Architects
1 Severn Street Place
Birmingham B1 1SE
Tel. 0121 233 6600
www.zerocarbonhouse
birmingham.org.uk

**Kit Knowles**
3 The Thorns
Chorltonville
Manchester M21 8GB
Tel. 0161 881 4173
www.ecospheric.co.uk

**Knott Architects**
98b Tollington Park
London N4 3RB
Tel. 020 7263 8844
www.knottarchitects.co.uk

**Mikhail Riches**
11 Clerkenwell Green
London EC1R 0DP
Tel. 020 7608 1505
www.mikhailriches.com

**Moxon Architects**
201 Great Western Studios
65 Alfred Road
London W2 5EU
Tel. 020 7034 0088
www.moxonarchitects.co.uk

**Neil Dusheiko Architects**
148 Curtain Road
London EC2A 3AR
Tel. 020 7729 8884
www.neildusheiko.com

**Oliver Chapman
Architects**
36 St Mary's Street
Edinburgh EH1 1SX
Tel. 0131 477 4513
www.oliverchapmanarchitects.
com

**Paul Archer Design**
103 Farringdon Road
London EC1R 3BS
Tel. 020 3668 2668
www.paularcherdesign.co.uk

**Platform 5 Architects**
Unit 102, 94 Hanbury Street
London E1 5JL
Tel. 020 7377 8885
www.platform5architects.com

**Prewett Bizley Architects**
Second Floor, 118a London Wall
London EC2Y 5JA
Tel. 020 7256 2195
www.prewettbizley.com

**Procter:Rihl**
63 Cross Street
London N1 2BB
Tel. 020 7704 6004
www.procter-rihl.com

**Robert Dye Architects**
4 Ella Mews
Cressy Road
London NW3 2NH
Tel. 020 7267 9388
www.robertdye.com

**WT Architecture**
4-6 Gote Lane
South Queensferry
Edinburgh EH30 9PS
Tel. 0131 331 2813
www.wtarchitecture.com

**Waind Gohil + Potter
Architects**
27 Bulwer Street
London W12 8AR
Tel. 020 8735 5367
www.wgpa.co.uk

# Index

# Image credits

The publishers would like to thank the following sources for permission to reproduce the images in this book